Life
with Jackie

Life
with Jackie

Irving Mansfield
with
Jean Libman Block

BANTAM BOOKS
Toronto • New York • London • Sydney

LIFE WITH JACKIE

A Bantam Book / March 1983

ISBN 0-553-05020-6
Library of Congress Catalog Card No.: 82-45943

Published simultaneously in the United States and Canada

Bantam Books are published by Bantam Books, Inc. Its trademark,
consisting of the words "Bantam Books" and the portrayal of a rooster,
is Registered in U.S. Patent and Trademark Office and in other countries.
Marca Registrada. Bantam Books, Inc., 666 Fifth Avenue, New York,
New York 10103.

PRINTED IN THE UNITED STATES OF AMERICA

0 9 8 7 6 5 4 3 2 1

To Jackie—
No day goes by that I do not think
of you—nor a night that I do not dream . . .

*My appreciation to Gloria
and Bill Adler for persuading
me to look backward over the
years with Jackie . . . and to Jean
Libman Block for accompanying me,
with patience and perception, on
my journey into the past.*

dazzling throng of actors, celebrities and book people swirls through all the downstairs rooms of the Beverly Hills Hotel on that unforgettable afternoon in June 1973. The enormous cocktail party is in honor of my wife Jacqueline Susann and her latest novel, Once Is Not Enough. *Already topping bestseller lists across the country, her new book has just catapulted Jackie into publishing history. She is the first novelist ever to write three consecutive number-one bestsellers.*

The crowd presses toward Jackie with hands outstretched to touch her, to embrace her. People have flown in from all over the United States, from London, Paris, Venice. They have all come to congratulate Jackie.

I stand off to the side, watching my wife. Perched on a stool with her friend Doris Day at her side, Jackie is as animated, enthusiastic, and glamourous as I've ever seen her. She smiles her big, wide smile. Her dark eyes glow. Everyone gets a firm handshake. She greets every guest, remembering without prompting the name of a bookshop owner from a tiny town near Tulsa. She whispers something into the ear of one of Hollywood's top leading men and they both giggle. She signs books, napkins, odd pieces of paper.

All those looking at Jackie in this moment of triumph are convinced that she owns the universe. Her childhood dream of moving intimately among the celebrated and famous has come true; she has made it come true. Her adoring friends and admirers number in the thousands. She is a STAR.

Like most men, I am not given to crying. But now I feel the start of tears. They are partly from pride in my wife and joy in her achievement.

And partly from deep, unspoken grief.

For I am the only person in that huge, festive gathering who knows that earlier in the day Jackie underwent the latest in a devastating series of chemotherapy treatments for the cancer that is spreading through her body. Under her artfully applied makeup, she is chalky white. She is running a temperature. Beneath her smartly styled black wig, her scalp is nearly bare from the vicious medication she is taking. She is sitting on a stool because she is too weak to stand alone. Doris Day is there by prearrangement to substitute as hostess if Jackie becomes faint or overcome by nausea.

Jackie and I have been living with the secret knowledge of her cancer for ten years.

Several times, as they have so many times before, her expressive dark eyes beckon me across the crowd. As always, a silent message passes between us. Barely moving my lips, I mouth the words, "It's a piece of cake." That is my loving password to buoy her spirits before she goes on TV or stands before an audience.

Now, in response, she gives a tiny wink of her left eye. I've lost track of how many times through the years she has blinked that way in front of a hundred people and only I can read the signal of love and reasurrance she is sending back to me.

"It's okay, doll," the flick of the eye says. "It's chocolate mousse."

I first met Jacqueline Susann on a summer day in 1937 when I went into Walgreen's drugstore at 44th Street and Broadway in search of a telephone. I was then a young Broadway press agent, handling singers, actresses, and band leaders and ducking every half hour into a phone booth to talk to clients and editors. I lived and worked in the Hotel Victoria at 51st Street and Broadway, a raffish establishment filled with hookers and bookmakers. Only recently escaped from under my parental roof in Brooklyn, I was in my mid-twenties and joyously realizing my fantasy of a Damon Runyon existence in the heart of the Great White Way.

The phones in Walgreen's were down a flight of stairs, and there were so many they covered an entire wall. Talking into them were some of the most beautiful girls I'd ever seen. (You must remember that in the unenlightened 1930s these young women were still known as girls.) Other beautiful girls were sitting at the soda fountain and at small tables, chattering away to each other with exaggerated animation. I made my call with my back to the wall so I could admire the perfection of the girls' makeup and the bright alertness of their glances every time they thought someone *important* had come into the drugstore. They were obviously young actresses with that special glow and sheen of small-town beauties who've come to seek fame and fortune on Broadway. They were my type of girl.

One in particular caught my eye. She had dark hair and very dark eyes, a perfect nose, and the most incredible air of freshness and innocence about her. Frank Parker, a singer I knew who had been on the Jack Benny radio show, saw me staring and made the introduction.

"Jackie Susann," he said, "this is Irving Mansfield."

"Do you come here often?" I asked her.

"Nearly every day—that's how I find out what's going on."

[3]

I glanced at the young hopefuls sipping nickel Cokes and eating tunafish sandwiches. "This looks like a hard-luck place to me," I said.

"Where do you eat?" she asked.

"Sometimes at Louis and Armand's." That was the restaurant on East 52nd Street where the CBS crowd hung out.

"Is it expensive?" she asked.

"By these standards, yes. Would you like to go there sometime?"

"Are you inviting me or feeling me out?" She was new, but quick, and the more I looked at her in her light blue summer dress, the more beautiful she was. Her huge, dark eyes were incredible.

"I'm inviting."

"How about tomorrow?" Not as shy as I'd thought.

"How do I get in touch with you?"

She was living at Kenmore Hall, a women's residence club down on 23rd Street, a popular place for newcomers to the city.

I called her there the next morning at eleven-thirty to confirm our appointment. "Did I wake you up?" I asked. Eleven-thirty was the crack of dawn for me—I was already a confirmed night person. But Jackie had been up for hours and fully made up for two hours. She took a bus uptown and met me in the restaurant. She was even more beautiful than the day before and looked younger and more innocent. I took her for about sixteen or seventeen. In spite of her careful makeup, she still had a baby look about her, and I figured she was a hick-town kid just off the bus. For the first of maybe a thousand times in our lives together, I made the mistake of underestimating Jackie Susann.

At lunch, I learned that she was from Philadelphia and had been in New York for nearly a year. She had almost had a small part in *The Women* but had lost out to Arlene Francis. Day after day, she had haunted producers' offices, reported for tryouts, gone to readings and casting calls, but never gotten beyond the universal brush-off "Don't call us, we'll call you."

We talked about how hard it was to get started on Broadway. I walked her back to Walgreen's, where she rejoined her out-of-work pals, and I went on with my day's work. I thought of Jackie from time to time, but I really had no room in my life for someone so young and vulnerable. I was way past virgins. The girls I knew were of dubious or no virtue; they were hard-working, hard-living show-business types who made their way by singing, acting, dancing, or playing the trombone. They used my apartment/office as an informal clubhouse, casually kicking off their shoes and, in the hot weather, their dresses as they entered. It was nothing for a half dozen of them to be sitting around playing gin in their slips.

Two weeks later, there was a message in my hotel box: "Call Jackie Susann." I did. "Didn't you say something about taking me to dinner at Dave's Blue Room?" she asked. "Where I come from, when a fellow and a girl have a good time together, he usually asks her out again."

"Okay," I said. "When can you make it?"

"I'm free tonight." She was too guileless to pretend she was busy. I rather liked that.

At that time, there were several midtown restaurants frequented by the Broadway crowd I was getting to know. Dave's Blue Room, next door to the Hotel Victoria, was the favorite of the music people— Russ Columbo, Bing Crosby, Lorenz Hart.

On the way to our table that night, we ran into Guy Lombardo, and I introduced Jackie to the popular band leader.

"How are you, pretty lady?" Guy asked her.

"I listen to you every New Year's Eve," Jackie told him.

At the table, she was breathless with excitement. "That's the first big shot I've ever met. Do you know everyone?"

"Not quite," I said, but I was certainly enjoying playing man of the world to this wide-eyed newcomer. I looked around for celebrities and that same night pointed out Larry Hart, Lou Holtz, Henny Youngman, and Sophie Tucker. I tell you, she was vibrating with excitement.

I let a few weeks go by, then called her again and invited her to an opening at the Rainbow Room. I was press agent for Ruby Newman's orchestra at the Rainbow Grill, so an evening there was more or less in the line of duty. She wore a beautiful black dress with pearls, and there was not a better looking young woman in that magnificent, romantic room at the top of Radio City, with its spectacular night view of the city. I enjoyed showing her off, and we both had a fine time.

A few days later, Jackie called me with wonderful news. She had gotten a part in *The Women*, and it was for real this time. Beryl Wallace, who played a minor role, was leaving to marry Earl Carroll, as famous for his Vanities as Ziegfeld was for his Follies and George White for his Scandals—all of them musical spectacles featuring lavish production numbers and incredibly beautiful showgirls. Jackie was to take Beryl's place.

Jackie opened in the matinee on June 2, 1937. Her parents came up from Philadelphia for her Broadway debut, and I went to see her the following night. She had only a small part and a few comic lines but she delivered them so well she got a big laugh. She had surprising stage presence for someone so inexperienced. Afterward, she tried to describe the thrill of hearing the first burst of laughter from her first real Broadway audience.

"That's what I've wanted ever since I was a little girl," she said, her face all aglow. "It's the most wonderful sound in the world. Let the others play Camille—I'll take laughter every time. There's nothing like it."

Jackie Susann was the most stage-struck youngster I'd ever met. Her enthusiasm delighted me. It was so fresh and naïve and contagious. I felt good when I was with her. But I was very, very careful with her—always on my best behavior. I watched my language. I didn't touch her. I didn't even make an attempt to kiss her. For me, a very free and easy bachelor who knew some of the most disreputable girls in town, that was most peculiar behavior.

One night, Jackie and I were having dinner early at Dinty Moore's—you always ate early if you were in a show—and we spotted Al Jolson sitting alone at his regular table. Jolson at that time was *the* star. When he played the Winter Garden, it just said *Jolson* on the marquee in letters about half a mile high and then below, in much smaller letters, the name of the show. Jolson was my idol.

"Mr. Jolson is sitting alone," Jackie said. "Why don't you go over and say hello?"

The problem was that I didn't know Jolson—I had just admired him from afar—but of course I couldn't let Jackie know that I wasn't an intimate pal.

"Let me see if he's in a good mood," I said.

I walked over to his table and said, "Mr. Jolson, my name is Irving Mansfield, and I'm one of your biggest fans."

"Sit down," he said. I had caught him in a good mood.

"I'm with a lady."

"Then bring her over."

I got Jackie. We sat down with him, and he told a waiter to get the food from our table. He asked Jackie what she did, and when she

[6]

said she was in *The Women*, he wanted to know if it was a leading part.

"Other people might not think so," she said, "but it's a very big part for me."

He liked that, and he told Jackie, "Stay with it—it's not easy you know. It's never easy."

Jolson insisted on paying our check along with his. He walked with us back to the theater where Jackie was appearing. I don't think either of us ever got over that magic night—we had actually had dinner with Al Jolson.

"You know," Jackie said afterward, "he's so small." She was right. Physically, Jolson was a small man, but the biggest star of them all.

We went along in this on-off way for quite some time. If I was busy with another girl, I wouldn't see her for several weeks; when I was free, I'd call her, or she'd call me.

Ben Marden's Riviera was then an important nightspot. Just across the George Washington Bridge in New Jersey, it featured major entertainers, dancing, and gambling. One night, when there was to be a big opening with comedian Joe E. Lewis, and singers Sophie Tucker and Harry Richman as headliners, I invited Jackie. Of course, she was thrilled for days in advance. On the night of the opening, I picked her up backstage at her theater after the final curtain. I had a cab waiting at the stage door. She said, "My God, how much does a taxi cost all the way to New Jersey?" It wasn't so bad because I knew Ben Marden sent you back home in a limousine. Not everyone, of course, but the friends of the house and the big gamblers.

Jackie met some of the stars and each time reacted with her wonderful explosion of excitement. I could see her eying the gaming tables, so I gave her a fifty-dollar bill and told her to have a good time. I was not a gambler. I had done some gambling when I was very young, realized I could get into big trouble with such a habit, and had given it up. Jackie, it turned out, didn't know how to play anything, but that didn't detract from her enthusiasm. She stood at the crap table, watching and trying to figure out what was going on.

Joe E. Lewis came over and said, "What are you doing, partner?"

She said, "I don't exactly know."

"How much do you have?" he asked.

"Fifty dollars."

"Okay, I'll go partners with you."

She put down her fifty, he put down fifty, and he bet it twenty-five, twenty-five, twenty-five, twenty-five, on the 4, 5, 9, and 10.

The dice came up 7, and Joe said, "We're through," and started to walk away.

Jackie ran after him, asking, "What happened? What happened?" He began to explain about the 4 and 10 and 2 and 3, but Jackie still didn't understand.

"I didn't have any fun," she said indignantly.

"All right, kid. You want your fifty back?"

No, she didn't want her money back. She just wanted to know what had happened. Joe began to explain again, but then he took a look at her face and shoved fifty dollars into her hand.

Now Jackie understood a little about roulette because she knew the ball went around and if you were lucky, it landed on the number you had picked. She sat at the roulette table next to a woman who was kind enough to explain a few of the tricks. It took Jackie a whole hour before she ran through her fifty dollars, but this time around she had a wonderful time.

The limousine took us home, driving south through Central Park and down to 23rd Street, where she lived. "That was wonderful," she said. "It's the first time I've ever been to a place like that. Can we go again tomorrow night?"

"Not tomorrow, but maybe sometime soon." I told her good night, didn't kiss her, but laughed all the way uptown at the thought of the fifty dollars she'd lost so fast at the crap table she didn't even know she'd lost it.

I was still fascinated by her innocence and her enthusiasm but didn't think of her in any way as my special girl. On that very casual basis, we continued to see each other through 1937 and 1938, the troubled years when Hitler thundered through Europe, the politicians talked about war, but most of us still pursued our dreams and spent our time digging out of the Depression, which had held on for so long.

Jackie adored being in *The Women*, but by June she and her friend Beatrice Cole felt they ought to try their wings in other roles. They left *The Women*, which was soon to close, anyway, and joined the summer-stock company at the Marshfield Hills Playhouse near Boston, Massachusetts. There they acted in *Dinner at Eight* and *Penny Wise* and in Noel Coward's *Tonight at 8:30*, *Family Album*, and *Fumed Oak*, one-acters that were great favorites of repertory groups. In *Fumed Oak*, which was billed as an unpleasant comedy, Jackie played Bea's daughter.

They also painted scenery, improvised props, and soaked themselves in "theater"—all for no money. I visited Jackie a couple of times during the summer and always took the whole troupe out to a lobster dinner. I think those may have been the only real meals the hard-working kids ate all summer.

At the end of the summer, Jackie was back in town, checking in at Walgreen's for information about casting and new shows and making the rounds of the producers. I had a date with her at least once every weekend, and sometimes we saw each other during the week. One Tuesday, she called me, and I knew right away she was very upset. "What's the matter, Jackie?" I asked.

"It's my father," she said. "He's had a heart attack. I have to rush home. I'm sorry but I have to break our date for Friday."

"That's terrible about your father," I said. "Is it serious?"

"Yes, it's very serious. We're not sure if—" She couldn't go on. I could hear her trying to swallow her tears and find her voice again. "I'm sorry, I shouldn't bother you about this, but I don't know what I'll do if anything happens to daddy. I love him so much." Her tears got the better of her.

It was the first time I'd heard Jackie cry. Her crying got to me. Suddenly I, too, was deeply distressed about her father, a man I had never met. I realized the intensity of Jackie's love and how shaken she was just at the thought she might lose him. I asked if there was anything I could do and told her to call me collect at my hotel to let me know how he was getting on. She caught a train to Philadelphia within the hour.

I didn't hear from her until Friday, and when she called, it was not collect. "Daddy's going to be all right, he's going to be all right," she sang into the phone. I could feel the happiness flooding through her. "He's got a long way to go, but he'll be all right."

"That's great, Jackie," I said. "That's very good news."

It turned out that she had tried to call me collect, but my hotel had refused to accept her call. After that, we talked on the phone every other day. A week after she had left New York, when her father was definitely on the mend, she had some surprising news. "Guess what? I've got a job here. I'm in the show at the Walton Roof. I can spend all the time I want with daddy during the day and work at night. Isn't that wonderful?"

[9]

The Walton Roof, I soon learned, was a favorite dinner and dancing spot in Philadelphia. There were about eight girls in the show, doing a not-very-complicated dance routine, which was just as well, since dancing was not Jackie's strong point. Her mother, a schoolteacher and a very proper lady, did not like Jackie's job at all. But no one could dissuade Jackie. She was going to be in show business no matter how or where.

Jackie and I continued to talk on the phone, and one day she said, "You know, I'd like you to come down and see my show. Besides, my mother and father want to meet you. I've told them a lot about you."

I was very surprised to hear that because it had never occurred to me to tell my folks anything about Jackie. "What did you tell them?" I asked.

"I told them I was going with you." This was also a surprise because it had never occurred to me that I was "going with" Jackie.

But I liked her enough to take the train to Philadelphia and catch her show at the Walton Roof. She looked very cute in her skimpy costume, and the dance routine got a big hand. But what really amazed me was the huge fuss that people were making over her. Jackie seemed to know nearly everyone in the audience, and all those handsome, expensively dressed, obviously wealthy fans of hers were saying, "Hello, Jackie," "How's your dad, Jackie?" "Great show, Jackie."

She introduced me to Ben Gimbel, Peggy Mastbaum, Rita and Ike Levy, Manny Sachs, Freddy Mann, one of the Wanamakers, and to members of the Robinson family, who had big real estate holdings, to the Annenbergs and Siegels, and to Mr. Cecil Pennyfeather, a society columnist.

I was amazed at the people Jackie knew, and for the first time I felt a twinge of jealousy. I guess I had thought of her as just another star-struck kid from a sleepy little town somewhere, not as someone from a sophisticated background who had grown up among millionaires and tycoons.

The next day, I went to see her father in the Einstein Pavilion of the University of Pennsylvania Hospital. He was sitting up in bed in a flower-filled room. I already knew that Robert Susan was a portrait painter. Now I saw that he was an amazingly good-looking man. He had the same perfect nose as Jackie and a profile that looked like Rudolf Valentino's. Even there in a hospital bed, he had a lot of presence, an air of being in charge. He made a little speech to me. He said, "I don't know if I'll ever get out of here, but I hope I will, and if you're not good to my daughter, I'm going to punch you in the nose."

How can you not like a guy who's lying in bed with a heart attack and threatening to punch you in the nose? We discovered we were both baseball fans, and that gave us something to talk about. He asked me if I hung around a lot with show-business people and looked at me rather disapprovingly when I said I did. "It's part of my business," I told him. "My job is being a press agent."

"What does a press agent do?" he asked. When I explained that my main work was to get people's names and pictures in the paper, he seemed to understand. He had less trouble with the idea than my mother, who could never figure out why a famous person needed *me* to get his name in the paper. Mr. Susan wanted to know if I made a lot of money. I said, "Not yet, but I expect to when I'm a little older, and I intend to become an important person myself."

He said, "I like your optimism and your spirit." I think he liked me right away, but Jackie's mother had serious reservations. I met her the next day at lunch. She was a very handsome woman, beautifully dressed and strictly corseted. A white streak in her very dark hair gave her an air of great distinction.

Rose Susan was not crazy about me for the reasons that any mother should be wary of a brash young Broadway press agent who might undermine the mother's plans for a glamorous and advantageous marriage for her only daughter. In Mrs. Susan's scheme of things, Jackie belonged in a grand mansion on Rittenhouse Square, safely married into a moneyed, socially elevated family and not fooling around with a nobody from Brooklyn. It didn't help, either, that I kept saying, "Yes, dear," to the very dignified Mrs. Susan.

I suppose I should have been feeling a little trapped, since I was obviously being looked over as a prospective son-in-law. But it didn't bother me that much. For years, my mother had been asking, "When are you going to find a nice girl and settle down?" so I was used to people, other people, worrying about my future. I was willing to be easygoing and just let things happen. Was I in love with Jackie? Neither of us had talked about love. We certainly hadn't been swept off our feet. But remember, these were still the Dark Ages when young people were not yet taking their emotional pulse at every turn and chattering away endlessly about their needs and their relationships.

Mr. Susan recovered. Jackie returned to New York and her job search. I still saw my other girl friends and stayed busy with my clients—Vincent Lopez, the Andrews Sisters, the Savoy Ballroom in Harlem, the radio show "Information Please," Alexander Woollcott, and columnist/commentator Dorothy Thompson.

One Friday night, toward the end of the year, when I was having dinner with my parents in Brooklyn, the phone rang. It was for me. That was surprising—I almost never got calls at their apartment. Jackie was on the line, and she was saying, "I've thought it over, Irving, and I've finally decided. Yes, I will marry you."

I guess I looked a little goofy for a minute. Then I said, "Why Jackie, that's wonderful. I better tell my mother and father."

"Haven't you told them anything about us?"

Us? I hadn't even been aware there was an "us."

"No, I haven't."

Now all of a sudden she was furious.

"What do you mean you haven't told them? I keep talking to my parents about you all the time. They're not happy about it—they think I'm making a terrible mistake. And here you haven't even said a word to your folks. That's terrible."

"It's okay, Jackie. I think it's a wonderful idea."

When I hung up the phone, my mother asked, "Who was that?"

"That was a young lady I've been seeing for the last year. Her name is Jackie Susann."

My mother asked, "What does she do?"

"She's a showgirl."

I think we had to get the smelling salts and a cold compress for my mother's head. "Do you see her all the time?" she asked.

"Yes, I do."

"And what did you say just now that you're so happy about?" I must have been grinning from ear to ear.

"We decided we're going to get married." My mother immediately grabbed a chair and fell into it.

My mother was outraged that I, her only child, had not discussed my marriage plans with her. I couldn't very well tell her that I hadn't even discussed them with myself. My mother kept saying, "How can a boy, an only child, get married and not even tell his mother?"

My father just said, "Congratulations, son. That's great. When are we going to meet the lucky girl?" My father never got excited.

"I'll bring her here for dinner next Friday," I said.

My mother was beginning to recover, and now she wanted to know about our wedding plans. I said, "Look, we've never talked about it until tonight."

"You mean tonight you first came to a decision?"

I said, "Yes, mom, that's it."

But I wasn't all that sure myself. Jackie could have been putting me on. It could have been her idea of a joke. But the more I thought about being married—married to Jackie—the more I liked it. In fact, I became so crazy about the idea that I began to be frightened that maybe she was kidding. I didn't want it to be a joke.

The next day, when I saw Jackie, I found it was no joke. She was absolutely ecstatic—as ecstatic as I was.

"But now," I told her, "you're going to have to go through inspection in Brooklyn the way I did in Philadelphia."

"That's fair," she said, "that's fair."

That Friday, we took the subway to Utica Avenue, the closest stop to where my parents lived, at 712 Crown Street, an apartment building that also housed a family named Beame. Some years later, Abe Beame became the mayor of New York City. Jackie was not then or later a subway person, but she made no comment about the ride. Now I have to tell you that I had a pair of seats that night to the heavyweight fight at Madison Square Garden. In the subway, I said to Jackie, "We have to leave by nine if we're to make the fight." It was then about a quarter to seven.

We went up to apartment F8 on the sixth floor. I walked in with Jackie, and my father said, "Oh, boy, what a lulu!" Then he said to Jackie, "Are you the one who's going to be my daughter-in-law?"

She said, "I certainly hope so."

My mother just stared. Finally, she said, "My but you're a tall girl."

Jackie wasn't all that tall. She was five feet seven, but my mother came from Vienna where I guess women are smaller. And everyone knows that all mothers are five feet two. We chatted for about ten minutes in the living room, which had been my bedroom when I had lived at home and also doubled as our dining room. A lot of apartments were set up like that in those days—with a living room, a bedroom, and a kitchen. For breakfast and ordinary family dinners, you ate in the kitchen. For important occasions, you opened up a table in the living room.

[13]

First we had some little appetizers—smoked salmon, I believe. Then we had chicken and two vegetables—always carrots and peas, as it says in the American anthem. Have you ever heard of a family of that time that did not serve carrots and peas? After dinner, my mother asked Jackie, "When did this big decision come about? When did you meet my son?"

Jackie was on her own, and I felt sorry for her because she didn't know what I had told my parents—which was nothing.

She said, "Well, it's been off and on for quite some time." She was being very careful.

My mother said, "I'm certainly surprised, but my God, you're a good-looking girl. Good-looking, what am I saying? You're beautiful."

My father said, "What are you talking about? She's gorgeous."

I think they liked her.

I looked at my watch and said, "Mom, we're leaving about nine." It was then eight.

"You mean, with a big event like this, you're not even going to talk about it?"

I said, "Mom, actually, we have another date," and off we went.

The following morning, my mother called me at my hotel bright and early, obviously to find out if Jackie was sleeping with me. Did she really expect Jackie to answer the phone? Whatever she expected, there was no problem, for Jackie had never even been up to my place. And where she lived, men were not allowed above the lobby.

The wedding was to be at the Susan's home in Philadelphia on April 2, 1939. We made several trips down there to work out plans. Jackie's mother seemed to take a deep breath and accept the inevitable. Her father made a couple of man-to-man speeches to me about doing right by his daughter. When I mentioned once that I was living in a hotel, he said, "That's not the way I want my daughter to live." Poor man, he didn't know that Jackie was *born* to live in hotels.

Jackie now moved from 23rd Street to the American Woman's Club on West 57th Street so we would not have to travel so far to see each other. We were together almost every night. We went to movies, to the theater, for long walks, and we talked about our plans and our hopes. Our dreams were remarkably similar: we both wanted to *be* someone. We wanted to stand out from the crowd, lead remarkable lives, and be surrounded by people of talent and accomplishment. I think Jackie had her dream in clearer focus than I did. Up to then, I had been willing just to drift along and see what happened next. But Jackie knew she had to *make* her future happen.

I think there was only one area in which I disappointed her. I'm afraid I was not a very demonstrative suitor. I'm not a shy person, but I was very shy about expressing my feelings to Jackie. My feelings toward her were becoming deeper and stronger all the time, but I couldn't put them into words. About three weeks before the wedding, she said, "You know something? You've never said, 'I love you.' "

I said, "I do love you. That's why we're getting married."

"I know, but you've never said it."

"Okay, Jackie. I love you."

She kissed me and said, "Just keep saying that. I hope we're going to have a long, happy life together."

I never again had to be reminded to say, "I love you." But I was never demonstrative with her in public. Oh, we kissed when we met in a restaurant, and we sometimes held hands, but we were never lovey-dovey or conspicuously affectionate. I think sometimes Jackie would have liked a greater show of feelings—she was so much more emotional than I—but I don't think she ever doubted the intensity of my love for her.

And so we were married in Robert Susan's studio at 1717 Walnut Street in Philadelphia. The Susan's apartment was downstairs, and Robert's studio, a huge room filled with racks of canvases and with easels holding partially completed portraits of judges and important public figures, was upstairs. Light was streaming in through the skylight; the room was all dressed up and filled with flowers for the occasion. It was a very romantic setting.

Jackie wore an ice-blue wedding dress of satin and lace, with a veil and a long train—the works. I wore white tie and tails. Her close friend, Hana Karol, was her maid of honor and writer Goodman Ace was my best man.

The ceremony was performed by a rabbi, and that had presented quite a problem because the Susans, not being active members of the Jewish community, did not know a rabbi. But I had to have a rabbi, not so much for my parents as for my Uncle Sam. Uncle Sam Mandelbaum, my father's brother, was a federal judge, appointed to the bench by President Franklin D. Roosevelt. He was a bachelor, very orthodox, and something of a tyrant in our family. It was unthinkable to invite him to a wedding that was not performed by a rabbi. I guess my parents expected a very big present from him. If they did, they were disappointed, for even with a rabbi, all we got was a check for one hundred dollars.

The ceremony went beautifully, although just as I was saying, "I do," Goodman Ace, who could never resist clowning, gave me a sign to speed things up so he would not miss Jack Benny on the radio. Afterward, there was a lovely reception. Everyone was wonderfully gracious to everyone else, and Robert Susan introduced my parents and me to all those fancy folk who had applauded Jackie at the Walton Roof. The only one to cry was my mother, who sobbed with joy. "I never thought I'd get such a beautiful daughter."

I looked at Jackie, so fresh and beautiful as she moved among the guests, and I felt a terrible stab of regret. Why had I wasted so much time? Why had I let more than a year go by before I discovered my love for her? Why had I left it up to her to speak the words that finally brought us together? Suppose she had been too shy to mention marriage. I might have lost her. I could feel myself go cold at the thought.

Jackie, as she would again and again in our life together, read my mind and made her way to my side. She touched my hand and seemed to drink in my face with her great, dark eyes, searching for what was troubling me.

"I have to apologize to you," I said.

"No, you don't."

"Yes, I do, for all the chances I had to say, 'I love you,' and didn't say it."

"Why didn't you?"

"I guess I thought you knew all along that I loved you."

"I didn't really. I was so afraid you couldn't tell the difference between love and friendship."

I marveled at how perceptive she was. How could someone so young and inexperienced have so much wisdom? Then, just before one of her former beaus claimed her for a dance, she took my hands in both of hers and said, "You know, you're going to be the only love of my life."

Then she whirled off onto the dance floor, and I could feel my heart thumping in my chest.

When the reception was over, I sent my parents back to New York in the limousine I had hired to bring them down, and Jackie and I drove back with my close friends Ethel and John Moses. We were so tired we hardly spoke a word in the car. We just leaned against each other in total contentment.

John let us off in front of the apartment we had rented at 433 East 51st Street at Beekman Place. We went upstairs, and Jackie disappeared into the bathroom. A few minutes later, she came out wearing the most unbelievably exquisite nightgown I had ever seen. It was a shorty gown of almost transparent midnight blue chiffon trimmed with expensive lace and hand embroidered. She must have shopped for days to find it.

She began walking toward me, but halfway across the room, she was overcome with embarrassment and modestly turned sideways. I motioned for her to come nearer. She approached, still sideways. I reached out and turned her to face me. I was stunned by the beauty of her body in the delicate blue veil.

"Isn't this what first nights are all about?" she asked tremulously.

I didn't answer but simply enfolded her in my arms.

We had no time for a honeymoon. I had to report for work the next day at Dorothy Thompson's radio show. Our wedding presents were overwhelming in numbers and lavishness. But the one that shaped our whole future life together was a portable typewriter for Jackie from Goodman Ace.

*J*ackie Susann was born on August 20, 1918, in Philadelphia, the only child of Rose and Robert Susan. The family name was Susan, with the accent on the second syllable, but while still in school, Jackie got so tired of correcting the pronunciation of her name that she added the second "n" and had no more trouble.

Her age, however, always gave her problems. She never liked the age she was. In her early teens, she added a few years, but by her later teens, she was already subtracting a few. She was eighteen when she arrived in New York in 1936 but somehow, without being very specific about it, gave the impression that she was sixteen. Later, when interviewers asked the date of her birth, she often offered ridiculous answers. A *Saturday Evening Post* profile of her in 1968 reported that she left Philadelphia to storm the New York theater in 1943 when she was sixteen. The places were right, the date and age wrong.

In every official record she could get her hands on, she managed to knock three years off her age; on most documents, her birth date is erroneously stated as August 20, 1921. The correct, year, 1918, on her passport, always drove her crazy. When she discovered that the Gabors had fanciful dates on their passports—I think sometimes they used the room number of the last hotel they had stayed in—she tried, unsuccessfully, to have the State Department provide her with a more congenial birth year. She once cornered Secretary of State Henry Kissinger at Joyce Haber's beach house to enlist his assistance in rolling back her birth year. But even the mighty Kissinger declared himself helpless in so delicate a matter. Jackie had to go on half palming her passport when she presented it and hiding it away from prying eyes between trips.

Jackie's father, Robert, was a very distinguished portrait painter. He was born in Holland of Dutch Jewish ancestry, brought to this country at a very young age, and educated in Philadelphia. His talent was recognized early and won him a full scholarship to the Philadelphia Academy of Fine Arts and two fellowships that enabled him to study and travel in Europe for several years. He quickly established a reputation as a portrait painter, charged five thousand dollars and up for his portraits, and was sought after by judges, clergymen, prizefighters, industrialists, and social leaders, including the blue bloods who lived on Philadelphia's Main Line. He was sometimes called the painter of cardinals—he painted Dennis Cardinal Dougherty of Philadelphia and the cardinal of Boston. He was also called the society painter—he painted Banning Grange, Dr. Chevalier Jackson, several members of the Wanamaker and Levy families, the Robinson family, Gov. Gifford Pinchot, George Arliss, Booth Tarkington, Supreme Court Justice James Wilson, and Dr. Draper Lewis.

To this day, you can see his portraits in Philadelphia's City Hall, in its courthouses, in many of its private clubs, in the state capital in Harrisburg, and in the U.S. Supreme Court chamber in Washington. Susan's portraits are formal, posed by their subjects, painted from life, and distinguished by a vivid aliveness, a richness of texture, and an immediacy not usually found in official portraiture of this type. His flesh tones are wonderful, his eye for detail remarkable. He also painted nudes, still lifes, and outdoor scenes.

Robert Susan was an extraordinarily handsome, vigorous man, with that Rudolf Valentino profile and a huge zest for life. He had a knack of turning his portrait subjects into his friends, expanding his social life into every level of Philadelphia society. Both Robert and Rose were in demand at parties and gatherings everywhere. The ladies loved Robert Susan—how they loved him!—and he had an appreciative eye for female company. His closest on-the-town companion was Jack Kelly, the late Grace Kelly's bon vivant father, and as I've heard it, the two of them made quite a pair. Jackie often recalled that when she was a little girl, her father sometimes sent her to a double-feature movie (to her enormous delight), then asked for a detailed synopsis of both films so that, if questioned, he could account for an afternoon of dalliance.

Jackie, naturally, worshipped her handsome, dashing father. She was daddy's little girl; they were playful and funny with each other. They had special games and secrets. He forgave her anything. The disciplining of this headstrong child fell to Rose Susan, a school-teacher to whom disciplining came as naturally as breathing.

Rose was a beautiful woman, always elegantly dressed and groomed, poised and self-possessed, and able to move easily in the world of the rich and famous. Her tastes were genteel, her concern for propriety reinforced by the willful streaks in her husband and daughter. She continued to teach at the Lea School through all the years of Jackie's growing up. The cooking, cleaning, and housekeeping were left to a succession of maids.

It should surprise no one that Jackie and her mother clashed constantly. Rose Susan considered it her duty to tame the wildness in Jackie. Jackie resisted. Her father either looked the other way or took Jackie's side. When the maids, who dealt with Jackie during the day, had to invoke higher authority, it was always "Just you wait, young lady, until your *mother* gets home." They knew it was a waste of time to threaten Jackie with her father's wrath. He would just smile and give her a hug.

But Jackie got a great deal more than indulgence from her adoring father. When she was four, he sat her on the lap of George Arliss, the famous English actor whose portrait he was painting, and she always recalled this incident as one of prophecy. She was eight when her father took her to her first matinee at a theater in Philadelphia, and from that moment on, she was hooked. "Daddy," she said, "I'm going to be an actress." She never again gave a second's thought to any other career or pursuit. The theater was the only world she wanted.

"Be a people watcher," her father told her when he was giving her drawing lessons. She had a nice talent for drawing and might have successfully developed her artistic skills if her fascination with the theater had not swept everything else aside. She did, however, take her father's advice and became an ardent and compulsive people watcher. At first, she watched to observe mannerisms and gestures, testing out her observations in front of a mirror. In this way, she taught herself to become a first-rate mimic and to do hilarious impersonations. But the watching also took root at a deeper level, and later, as a novelist, she could draw on a lifetime of people watching for a rich variety of characters, incidents, and idiosyncrasies. She was blessed with a fantastic memory—both a photographic eye and a photographic ear—and could run in her head, with sound and pictures, the tapes of any scene she had observed from childhood on.

For Jackie, the whole process of schooling was little more than a nuisance. She was bright enough to get excellent marks with a minimum of effort, but it all seemed such a terrible waste of time. Her real life took place in the summer when the family, like all good Philadelphians, went to Atlantic City. They took a house in Margate or Ventnor, just south of Atlantic City, or stayed at the Ritz Hotel or at the Villa D'Este. Aside from the ocean and the boardwalk, the big attraction for Jackie was the Steel Pier with its theater constructed out over the water. Musicals, vaudeville, dramas, summer stock, everything played at the Steel Pier, and Jackie was there. She was no more than nine when she started haunting stage doors, sometimes sneaking backstage to get autographs, at other times pretending to be writing an article for her school paper.

The all-time, pain-in-the-neck, stage-struck schoolgirl, she once slipped past a guard, got into Mae West's dressing room, and was so insistent in her demand for an interview that Mae West yelled, "Get the hell out of here," and threw her out bodily. Years later, when Jackie was a famous novelist, she recalled the incident to Miss West, who pretended to remember and was gracious enough to apologize.

Lilyan Tashman, a soignée, sophisticated, blond actress who usually played the other woman, was one of Jackie's favorites, the first of many intense crushes she developed in her lifetime. For weeks, Jackie practiced holding a twenty-inch-long cigarette holder with an unlit cigarette (her mother would have killed her if she had caught her smoking) at the devastating angle that Miss Tashman affected and nearly poked out the eyes of several friends.

In the fall of 1934, when she was sixteen and still in high school, Jackie joined the Theatre League of Philadelphia, an amateur group that was putting on plays under the direction of Jasper Deeter of the well-known Hedgerow Theatre on Sansom Street. Hana Karol, a member of the group who later became a close friend of Jackie's, recalls the first day Jackie came to rehearsal.

When Jackie was introduced to the group, Hana exclaimed, "Oh, you're the girl from the beach."

During the previous summer at Atlantic City, Hana and several other girls in their midteens, most of them gawky and still undeveloped, had eaten their hearts out watching Jackie. They had watched her walk along the sand in a breathtaking white bathing suit. They had watched her stroll on the boardwalk in an equally breathtaking white skirt and jacket and white felt hat. She was usually accompanied by one or several young men who danced attendance on her. At sixteen, Jackie already had a beautiful, full figure, a sexy walk, and an air of assurance that Hana and her friends desperately envied.

Expecting to be snubbed by such a glorious creature, Hana was surprised, and flattered, when Jackie suggested they go out for coffee after class. They looked each other over, Jackie all perfection, Hana skinny and breastless, with an oily skin.

"My goodness, don't you have an eyelash curler?" Jackie asked Hana. Jackie immediately took Hana in hand, marched her to a drugstore, bought her an eyelash curler, pancake makeup, and mascara and showed her how to do her face and stuff her bra with rolled-up silk hose. Jackie knew, even then in her midteen years, how to make the best of her own very good looks and was willing to share this knowledge with the waiflike Hana. Can you imagine how many hours Jackie must have practiced her makeup techniques in front of the bathroom mirror and how many times Rose Susan, the twenty-four-hour schoolteacher, must have ordered her errant daughter to forget the warpaint and settle down to her homework!

A high school English teacher told Jackie to concentrate on her writing—she showed real promise. But she was too zeroed in on the theater to hear. One thing she did learn to write, however, was her mother's signature, which she forged on notes excusing herself from school on afternoons when road companies of Broadway shows played Philadelphia. One such note asked for Jackie to be excused because the family's dog was sick and Jackie had to go home to feed it. The trouble was that the Susans did not have a dog, and the note somehow reached her mother's hand. There was a big blowup, and Jackie was grounded for a considerable period. Not even her father could rescue her.

In the meantime, Jackie was working on acting exercises and scenes with the Theatre League. The group put on *Cradle Song* and *Riders to the Sea* and did some of the less demanding scenes from Shakespeare. Jackie and Hana saw every play that came to Philadelphia, discussed the performances endlessly, and attempted their own interpretations. When the musical *Leave It to Me*, which launched the unforgettable "Begin the Beguine," came to town, it turned out that Robert Susan knew June Knight, the star. He took the girls backstage to Miss Knight's dressing room. This time, Jackie got her autograph.

In the spring of 1935, Earl Carroll staged a contest to choose the

[22]

"Most Beautiful Girl in Philadelphia" as part of the publicity campaign for the opening of his Earl Carroll Vanities. That was all Jackie had to hear. Rose Susan forbade her daughter to enter the competition. She thought it cheap and undignified for a girl of Jackie's age and family background to strut across the stage of the Earle Theatre in a bathing suit. Rose even enlisted Hana's help to keep Jackie from tarnishing the family's name. The concerted opposition and a conspiratorial wink from her father only sharpened Jackie's determination. Not only did she enter the contest, she won it.

I still have the cup she was awarded, a large and ornate silver loving cup proclaiming Jackie Susan as the "Most Beautiful Girl in Philadelphia." The prize also included a screen test, which Jackie took the next year when she went to New York. Alas, the test did not get her a Hollywood contract, but the act of winning the contest and the local acclaim that followed did cool her mother's displeasure. I think Jackie took careful note of the way success overcame maternal disapproval and used this knowledge years later when her mother went into shock over the sex and four-letter words in *Valley of the Dolls*.

Jackie was one of those lucky girls who never went through an ugly-duckling stage, never passed through awkward years, never felt like an outsider with her face pressed against the candy-store window. She was beautiful and sought after. She was used to attention and handled it gracefully. She basked in her father's love and devotion. While her mother's criticism often got her back up, the tension between them was out in the open and centered on decorum and appropriate teenage behavior.

The boys, of course, streamed after Jackie. The most attentive was a young man named Herman Robinson, from a wealthy and highly regarded Philadelphia family that was active in real estate, finance, and philanthropy. Rose Susan considered Herman a most suitable suitor and did what she could to encourage the match. Herman's mother was equally enthusiastic about the romance, if you could call it that, and offered a handsome inducement. Twisting on her finger a ring with a diamond as big as a postage stamp, she told Jackie, "This could be yours someday . . ."

Jackie was not overwhelmed, but she did continue to see Herman. The summer Jackie was fifteen, her parents went up to Kennebunkport, Maine, where Robert Susan had been commissioned by the local citizens to paint a portrait of native son Booth Tarkington, the celebrated author of *Penrod*. During their absence, it was arranged for Jackie to stay with a friend at a boarding house in Atlantic City. Herman was attending summer session at the Valley Forge Military Academy near Philadelphia.

At this point in her life—fifteen, mind you—Jackie had a wild crush on a wrestler named Ernie Dusek. He was one of three brothers, all wrestlers, and Jackie had first seen him when her father took her to a match. After that, Jackie tried to get to all of Ernie's matches to cheer him on to victory. Jackie *had* to see Ernie's fight that summer at the Atlantic City Convention Hall, and she explained her carefully worked out plan to Herman.

She would go to Herman's house, take the family's roadster out of the garage, drive it to the military academy, and pick up Herman, who would then drive both of them to the fight. The plan had only a few things wrong with it. The academy had a seven P.M. curfew, and Herman would be in big trouble if he overstayed it. Jackie was too young to have a driver's license. What's more, Jackie did not know how to drive a car. She had had one lesson in starting a car but none in stopping it. None of this deterred her.

Herman left his dormitory by way of a sheet tied out of the window. He made one last effort to suggest a movie instead of a wrestling match, but Jackie had made up her mind. They sat ringside, of course, and Jackie cheered her hero mightily. The wrestling matches, then as now, were a contrived show, with the good guy easily recognized by his blond hair and handsome profile and the bad guy sporting a drooping mustache and heavy eyebrows. Ernie was the good guy, but on this particular night, he was being slammed around rather fiercely by the bad guy, a wrestler called the Red Devil, who jumped on Ernie, kicked him, and seemed to be gouging out his eyes.

Jackie couldn't stand it. She started screaming, "You scoundrel, you murderer, leave him alone!" To stop the carnage, she picked up the folding chair next to her and threw it into the ring. After that, Jackie climbed into the ring herself and started to kick at the Red Devil and grab him by his hair and his red bandanna. The referee was stunned; the fans started to applaud. Herman hurled himself into the ring to get Jackie out of there. The audience screamed, and by then I guess Herman wished he was already in the stockade. A fight official finally hauled Jackie and Herman out of the ring, and the police hustled them both to the lockup. They spent four and a half hours in jail—until the attorney for the Robinson family arrived and straightened things out.

Despite such escapades, Jackie was graduated from West Philadelphia High School on January 30, 1936. Her ambition, as stated in her class yearbook, was to own a mink coat. She made this choice partly, I suppose, because she *wanted* a mink coat—it symbolized stardom. But I suspect she was also putting it to her classmates for their goody-goody yearnings (to take care of little children, to have a big family) and maybe trying to get a rise out of her mother.

Rose Susan wanted Jackie to go to Wellesley and get a proper education. Jackie, of course, wanted to go to New York and get started on Broadway. The battle raged all during her final semester in high school; in the end, Jackie and her parents arrived at a compromise. Jackie would stay home that spring and summer. In the fall, she would go to New York with the understanding that the Susans would finance her for just one year. If at the end of the year she was off and running in her career, fine. If not, she'd go to Wellesley.

That spring, Jackie attended the Bessie V. Hicks School of Drama in Philadelphia, took singing lessons, drove her family wild with her off-key rendering of "Chloe"—she simply did not have an ear for music—and gathered her wardrobe for her assault on New York. She arrived in New York in September and moved into Kenmore Hall, which was run on the strict principles of a girls' dormitory.

The job search began, and in no time at all Jackie made Walgreen's drugstore her headquarters. There she found herself in the company of other young hopefuls, among them David Wayne, June Allyson, Gene Barry, Kirk Douglas, and countless others who ate, phoned, and lingered. Word went out one day that Robert Sinclair, one of the bright young directors in the theater, was casting for a new play about bitchery and husband-snatching among the smart set called *The Women*, and written by the beautiful and gifted Clare Boothe Luce. Since Sinclair was an old pal of Robert Susan's, Jackie had no trouble getting an audition and immediately won a small role as a French maid.

On the first day of rehearsal at the National Theatre, Jackie and the other minor players stared with awe at the big-name stars—Margalo Gilmore, Ilka Chase, Audrey Christie, Phyllis Povah, Jane Seymour—and tiptoed around to get a glimpse of the chic and elegant Clare Boothe Luce. As the stage manager called, "Act one, scene one," Jackie found herself standing behind a young blonde actress with a beautiful, classic face. Jackie touched her on the arm and whispered, "Can you do a French accent?"

"Shh," the blonde whispered back.

The stage manager glared at them and said, "Quiet, please."

At a break at the end of the first act, Jackie and the blonde stepped out into the alley and introduced themselves. The blonde's name was Beatrice Cole. A little more experienced than Jackie, she asked Jackie to read the maid's part. Jackie read, "Modom 'as bean sokin' an ow-air," and looked up: "I was lousy, wasn't I?"

Bea hedged. "Everyone's nervous the first day."

The stage manager called, "Second scene. Places, please." Bea and Jackie hurried back into the theater. Jackie came in on cue and read her part. Sinclair exchanged looks with Mrs. Luce and reached for a pencil. Jackie's heart sank. She was sure she was through. The rehearsal went on until five o'clock. Just before the cast was dismissed, the stage manager read out two names and asked those actresses to remain. They were fired, and Jackie was still in.

"But I've still got to find someone to teach me a French accent," Jackie told Bea. "I've got it," she suddenly exclaimed. "Janet of France. She has a French restaurant and a marvelous French accent."

Jackie went to the restaurant that night, persuaded Janet to coach her in her lines, and at rehearsal the next day breezed through the brief part with a superb French accent. But when the rehearsal was dismissed, Jackie's was one of the names called. Jackie stayed on, and Bea waited for her outside. A few minutes later, Jackie came out, smiling bravely. She waved at some of the cast members, took Bea's arm, and they walked toward Times Square.

"They hired Arlene Francis to do my part," she said matter-of-factly. "It wasn't Mr. Sinclair's fault. Arlene Francis is famous for her accents, and she'll double as a French maid *and* a Russian princess. Mr. Sinclair was really sorry."

Jackie tried to be brave, but she couldn't help herself, couldn't hold back her tears. Then she was furious at herself. She was too proud to break down before a comparative stranger and too heartbroken to stop sobbing. Bea offered to spend the evening with her, but Jackie told her that Essie a friend at Kenmore Hall, was waiting for her and that they were going to a movie that night. Bea watched her disappear in the five o'clock crowd and worried. Jackie, under the best of circumstances, didn't look any more than sixteen, but now, with the tears rolling down her face, she could have been a little kid. But

Bea sensed a power in her and was sure she would be all right.

Jackie resumed her job hunt, and Bea stayed on in *The Women*, which opened on Christmas Eve, 1936. Jackie and Bea became close friends and remained devoted to each other all through Jackie's life. Today, Bea is my valued friend and loyal assistant.

From the very beginning of her career, Jackie was the kind of person to whom things happened. Her whole life was a drama. Almost no day was simple or uneventful. You'll see the pattern of the unexpected, the act of God, the bolt from the blue, repeated over and over. Take Essie. One day, Jackie got back to Kenmore Hall to find Essie sitting on her bed sobbing and two policemen ransacking her room. Three fur coats were lying on the bed, and a lot of expensive jewelry was piled on a dresser.

Jackie put her arms around Essie and said to the policemen, "I don't think Essie meant to do anything wrong. She really didn't know what she was doing." But the luxurious sealskin coat, the full-length mink, and the lush beaver suggested that Essie knew exactly what she was doing. One of the policemen announced that they were taking Essie to the station house.

"But you can't," Jackie protested. "She's not a criminal."

"She's got a record a mile long," the policeman said. One policeman grabbed Essie, and the other scooped up her loot.

The judge gave Essie three years, but just a couple of months later, Jackie called Bea and told her to hurry over to the Mayflower Doughnut Shop on Broadway and 45th Street. Essie was there wearing a sort of horse blanket, bedroom slippers, and no makeup. She had slipped out of the laundry room of the Women's House of Detention when no one was looking. Unmindful of the fact that they were aiding a jail breaker, Jackie and Bea got Essie some clothes, gave her three dollars, and sent her on to an aunt in New Jersey.

After the show that night, Jackie called Bea and asked, "Bea, can you use a silver fox jacket? Essie went shopping this afternoon and—"

"Shopping? With three dollars?"

"Well, this time she only took two coats."

"Two silver fox jackets?"

"But she only needs one. So I thought maybe you—She really needs the money."

Bea, who had considerably more sense than Jackie at this stage in their lives, lowered the boom on her friend. "I don't want to be a spoilsport, but I really think we should drop Essie."

"But I like her," Jackie said loyally.

Years later, Helen Gurley Brown was to say that Jackie Susann had a "mafialike" sense of loyalty to her friends—a quality, as you can see, that showed itself early and was never lost.

"I know," Bea pointed out, "but your mother's a well-known schoolteacher, and your father's a famous painter, and you have to be loyal to them. Next time, the police may pick us up, too."

Essie never popped up in their lives again. Hana Karol moved in with Jackie at Kenmore Hall. But years and years later, Jackie would stop suddenly in a conversation with Bea and say, "I keep thinking of Essie. I wish we knew she was all right."

Jackie and Bea took ballet lessons that year—all young actresses took ballet lessons. They got an odd job soaking their hands in dishwashing lotions to compare the chapping powers of various products. They were paid two dollars a day to get their hands red and wrinkled. Bea was already established as a Powers Model and ran around New York with that ultimate symbol of glamor, the black patent leather hatbox carried by models in the John Robert Powers agency. Jackie, of course, had to have one of those distinctive hatboxes. But her modeling career never got off the ground. Delicate, sunken-cheek blondes were in demand that season, not well-rounded brunettes.

Then Jackie and Bea got wind of Method acting, a new way of approaching the acting craft through improvisation. The two went to audition for the great Madame Ouspenskaya, who had studied with the legendary Stanislavsky, inventor of the Method. There were fifteen students in the huge duplex studio on West 67th Street waiting for Madame. She finally appeared, a tiny, little old woman smoking endless cigarettes in a long holder.

"We weel now have a leetle test," she announced, waving her cigarette holder. She looked at Jackie and told her to get up and describe a figure eight while reciting the alphabet backwards. Jackie hesitated and looked at Bea.

"So, the young lady eez not weeling to try. Come, your leetle friend will do eet."

Bea got up, began, "Z-Y-X. . . ," then panicked. Someone giggled, and soon the whole class was giggling.

"So you do not know zee alphabet! What a pity!"

Bea returned to her place and found Jackie gone. "Your girl friend said she'd meet you downstairs," a young man whispered.

As she left, Bea could hear Madame Ouspenskaya saying, "And now you are a leetle butterfly, and thees beeg airplane eez coming after you . . ."

"At least you tried," Jackie said apologetically. "I felt so sorry for you with all those kids giggling that I couldn't stand it. I know I should have stayed."

"Don't worry. If you did, you'd be a leetle lost butterfly."

Jackie sighed. "Maybe we're just not ready for this."

It was back to Walgreen's for Jackie, where, early that summer, we met and began seeing each other. A few weeks later, when she finally did go into *The Women*, I sent her to Murray Korman, the leading photographer of actresses and showgirls, for a set of glamorously posed photographs. With her clearly defined, perfect features, Jackie was a photographer's dream. I had no trouble placing a head shot of her in both the *News* and the *Mirror*, the city's two tabloid newspapers, with the announcement that she was entering the cast of the hit play *The Women*. That was her first publicity in New York, and she was delirious with excitement. I guess she thought I was a magician.

Jackie was paid the junior Actors' Equity minimum of twenty-five dollars a week. Her parents were sending her twenty-five dollars a week and were each slipping her an additional five dollars a week under the table for extra spending money (neither knew the other was doing it); and her grandmother was secretly chipping in another five dollars a week. So Jackie was doing just fine financially.

Jackie got a real education backstage at *The Women*, where ten young actresses shared "Dressing Room One." One of them was escorted to El Morocco nightly after the show and the next day usually displayed a new piece of jewelry or a new fur jacket to account for her night's work. Another read Shakespeare aloud with a whiskey cork in her mouth; she said all the great Shakespearean actors practiced that way to bring their voices forward. One worked to pay for her child's English nanny.

At Christmas, they were all knitting, crocheting, and stuffing sachet bags. Jackie was knitting a coat for her mother. Although she was one of the youngest, Jackie quickly became a backstage leader. She had a fierce crush on Margalo Gillmore and agonized over whether Miss Gillmore would notice her or nod to her. Miss Gillmore did notice her and eventually became a friend and mentor.

I think being in *The Women* was one of the most important things Jackie ever did. It gave her a wonderful taste of the theater. It stopped all talk about Wellesley. It introduced her to some important performers. And the fact that Clare Boothe Luce had made such a success by writing about the nasty doings of a lot of nasty people she knew in real life served Jackie, the novelist, extremely well many years later.

The Susans, of course, had had a hard time getting reconciled to me as a prospective son-in-law. With every door open to Jackie in Philadelphia, with Mrs. Robinson eager to hand over that oversized diamond ring, with a variety of handsome young men sending flowers to her dressing room at *The Women* and hanging around the stage door, Jackie still chose me, a simple press agent from Brooklyn. Why?

Part of it, I suppose, was the excitement. I represented the open-ended life she wanted to live and the people she wanted to meet—performers, stars, big names. I was well past the beginner's stage, and that was important for a girl like Jackie, so deeply involved with her father. By choosing me, she was asserting her independence from her parents and from all those home-town forces that were trying to shape her into a conventional mold. I would become *somebody*, and so would she. And I could help her live dangerously. How many girls of her age had the opportunity to chase crooks around New York in Walter Winchell's car, equipped with a police radio, sometimes arriving at the scene of the crime even before the cops?

I can't really claim that Jackie and I were propelled into each other's arms by an irresistible passion. It wasn't that kind of attraction—not at first. But I've always felt that there was a special element in our coming together, something I was not in any way responsible for. It's Jackie who deserves all the credit for her presentiment that she and I, working together as a team, would have a strength and a power far greater than the sum of our talents and abilities as separate individuals. How she knew this I can't imagine. But you know what? She was absolutely right.

$\mathcal{M}$y life story, before Jackie, is quickly told. My father was a salesman; he worked on the docks in Hoboken during World War I and later opened a hardware store in Brooklyn. My mother was a full-time mother, and I was their only child. When I was a small boy, my favorite food was huckleberries and cream. Sweet cream, they called it—God forbid I should be served just plain milk. Because the first word I learned after mommy and daddy was "huckeyberries," my parents began calling me Huckeybaby. Well into my teens I was still Huckeybaby at home. Somehow I survived.

I went to Boys' High School, where I got marks that were good but never quite good enough for my mother. My mother loved me very much, and I loved her dearly, but she believed I had to sit up all night studying and bring home perfect grades. She would say, "You're not studying like Red Denton up the block or Ted Felner down the street." I never knew who those other guys were except that they were studying harder than me, so I hated them.

Somewhere in the middle of high school, I began getting night-mares that I wouldn't pass my Regents examinations. Later in college, I had nightmares that I wouldn't graduate. Even today, I can wake up in a cold sweat of terror that I'm going to fail in some important undertaking—and then I think of my mother. I guess all mothers do that to their children.

My father was just the opposite. In his eyes, I could do no wrong. If I came home and said to my father, "I just shot ten guys in front of the poolroom," he'd say, "What did they do to you?" That's the kind of faith my father had in me. He never put a hand on me.

I once went to my father and said, "You're not going to like this, but there's something I have to tell you. Last night, while you were sleeping, I reached into your pants pocket and took out twenty dollars."

"What did you want the twenty for?"

"I was taking Linda to Loew's Metropolitan and then to a Chinese restaurant, and I wanted to take her home in a taxi."

"You wanted to take her home in a taxi?"

I nodded miserably.

"That's my son," my father said. "That's class. Forget about the twenty dollars."

We were a happy family, and I was a good son, the kind of good son who took his mother to the movies on Saturday night. We'd go to the Carroll Theatre on Utica Avenue where they were always giving away things—once she won a set of dishes. Then we'd have an eight-course, sixty-five-cent dinner in a neighborhood Chinese restaurant.

After high school, I went to New York University in Washington Square and majored in English literature. I didn't go to NYU up on the Heights, which was supposed to be better academically, because it was too long a subway ride from Brooklyn to the Bronx. Besides, Washington Square was closer to Broadway, and I was already fascinated by the people in show business. I thought they were wonderful and exciting, and best of all, they could sleep until eleven or twelve o'clock in the morning. That was my dream of heaven—to sleep until noon.

My mother's dream for me was very simple: she wanted me to be either a gym teacher or a buyer at Macy's. I don't know why she picked on gym teacher. Maybe she thought it was steady work and you got the summer off and could get a job as a counselor at a camp. Several of her friends had sons on the training squad at Macy's, and she figured they were heading for a very bright future, and she talked a lot about the big pension they'd have in about a hundred years. But I figured that to be at the store when it opened in the morning, they'd have to get up at 6:45, and that was out of the question for me.

Greenwich Village was my college campus, and I made the most of it. Joe Gould was roaming the Village then, writing a grandiose history of the world. I met Maxwell Bodenheim, a poet and eccentric. I met Elijah Siegal, another poet, and Edna St. Vincent Millay, who taught us to burn our candle at both ends. I saw Eve Le Gallienne at the Civic Rep Theatre on 14th Street, and I made pilgrimages to the houses where Mark Twain, O'Henry, and Henry James had lived.

And, of course, I took the subway uptown and caught all the Broadway shows. In those days, the cheapest seats were fifty-five cents, well within a student's budget, and half the time you could move into better seats at the first intermission.

To pay my tuition, I worked summers as a waiter, one year at Camp Copake in Crareyville, New York, where I waited on playwright Moss Hart, his brother Bernie, and the whole Hart family. Another year, I worked at a place called Log Tavern, where I served playwright Clifford Odets, who was the social director, Leonard Sillman, and Frances Gershwin, the younger sister of George Gershwin. Plunked down amid so much talent, how could I help but dream of glory?

After graduation, I heard about a job on the *New York American*. The man who was doing the hiring asked about my journalism credits. I told him I'd worked on my school paper. He wanted to know what school. For some crazy reason, I said, "Yale."

He asked, "Yale College or Yale University?"

While I was floundering for an answer, he said, "Okay, you got the job."

I worked as a copy boy for a man in the drama department named Connie Miles, running copy to the composing room. My salary was thirty dollars a week. I'd been there less than two months when a copy boy who had been hired after me was promoted to cub reporter. Not caring for that at all, I asked David Green, a press agent who often dropped in at the paper, if he'd give me a job. Green had classy clients like Edgar Bergen and one of the dinner-dance rooms at the Waldorf. He told me to write a release about band leader Xavier Cugat. Whatever purple prose I typed seemed to please him, and I had the job at forty dollars a week. Not bad.

Less than a year later, I struck out on my own and opened a small office in Radio City with Moe Gale, who owned the Savoy Ballroom in the great days of Chick Webb, Duke Ellington, Count Basie, Ella Fitzgerald, and a very funny MC named Willie Bryant. At that time, it was the big thing for the Broadway crowd and for society people, too, to pile into limousines and hit the Harlem nightspots— the Savoy, the Cotton Club, and the Apollo Theatre. I handled publicity for the Savoy.

I also worked for band leader Vincent Lopez, Leon Belasco and the Andrews Sisters, Ruby Newman, the band leader at the Rainbow Grill, Dick Himber and his orchestra, and for singer Shirley Howard.

By this time, I had moved to the Hotel Victoria, a major step, since now I was living at the hotel as well as working there and no longer accountable to my mother for my irregular hours. My mother couldn't figure out what to make of my career. The idea that I made a living, and a pretty good one, by getting people's pictures in the paper was beyond her.

"What can I tell my friends that you do?" she'd ask.

"Tell them I'm a dentist."

"I can't. You didn't go to dental school."

"Tell them anything, mom."

I don't know what she told them, but it must have worked out all right. By this time, my father was no longer working, and I was supporting my parents.

In 1936, I had the good fortune to meet Ethel and John Moses, a couple who played an important role in my life. John was the son of Broadway producer Harry Moses, who, along with Herman Shumlin, had produced a play called *Grand Hotel* that was a very big hit. John became an agent, and I eventually became the press agent for many of his clients, among them "Information Please," an extremely popular, rather high-brow radio quiz show that featured as panelists Oscar Levant, the well-known wit and pianist; John Kiernan, a sports writer and bird expert; and Franklin P. Adams, known as F.P.A., a newspaper columnist. Clifton Fadiman was the master of ceremonies. The participants on "Information Please" were so colorful and generated such good copy that I was successful in getting a lot of stories and column items about them in the newspapers. Since I already knew many people around Broadway, I was able to sign up important guests for the program, among them George M. Cohan and Burns and Allen. Word began getting around that I was a hot-shot young press agent.

Alexander Woollcott wanted the press to pay more attention to his CBS program "The Town Crier." John Moses suggested that he hire me. A meeting was arranged at "21" for five in the afternoon. Although I had never been there, I knew that "21" was the absolute top-drawer place in New York for dining and drinking. In honor of the occasion, I bought a really beautiful blue serge suit—I was sure my old suit was not good enough. I also bought a new shirt, a handsome tie, and an expensive linen handkerchief.

When I arrived at "21," the man at the door said, "Yes?" as if I'd come to apply for a job and should really be going around to the back.

I said I was meeting Mr. Woollcott. It was as if I were announcing myself at a royal palace. He told me to wait in a little sitting room at the side. A few minutes later, John Moses came in with Mr. Woollcott, his manager, and a friend. I quickly said, "Hello, John," to John Moses, and he said, "Hi, how are you?" This exchange was a big disappointment to the doorman, who was sure I was a stray cat.

We went inside, where Mr. Woollcott was treated almost reverentially, and shown to preferred seats in the front section. The captain asked for our drink orders, and the others all ordered martinis. I ordered one, too. I had never had a martini in my life, but if they were having martinis, so was I. What I didn't know was that "21" serves the biggest martinis anyone has ever seen. Fish could swim in the cocktail glasses they use.

There was talk about Woollcott's radio program and about a magazine article he was writing. He was really a difficult man; his whole world revolved around himself, and he used the word "I" about fifteen times in every sentence. I didn't know some of the people he was talking about, but I nodded gravely and tried to look knowing. Those enormous drinks came, and Mr. Woollcott said, "Here's to you, young man. I hope you have a very bright future in this business."

I said, "I think I'm having a bright future right now, and I'm delighted at the fact that you wish me to expand on my success, sir."

He said, "Don't call me sir. It bothers me."

I said, "Okay."

He talked about the kind of publicity he wanted and how we should go about promoting him. When we were halfway through our martinis, I started to perspire. Those martinis were lethal. I took out my new pocket handkerchief to wipe my brow, but the handkerchief was already wet. Woollcott then ordered another round of drinks. To get ready for the second round, I quickly gulped the third of my drink that was still left. Woollcott noticed a strange look on my face and asked, "Is something wrong, Irving?"

I said, "No, sir."

He said, "I told you not to call me sir. Are you sure you're all right?"

I said, "Yes, sir," and fell sideways off my chair.

I couldn't move—I was paralyzed—but I could still see and hear. Everyone jumped up, and someone said, "Maybe he's had a heart attack," and I wondered if maybe I was having a heart attack. Someone else said, "Nah, he probably can't handle his liquor." If I wasn't already lying on the floor, I think I'd have fainted from embarrassment. They finally carried me to the men's room, tore off my new tie, ripped open my new shirt, and put cold compresses on the back of my neck.

An hour later, when the others were ready to leave the restaurant, I was still in the men's room, gradually recovering. I managed to get up and leave with them. The doorman looked happy—his first impression was vindicated. I got back to my hotel, slid out of my shoes and clothes, and fell into bed. I slept about four hours. When I woke up, I called John Moses, and he said, "My God, you were awful."

"Did I blow it with Mr. Woollcott?"

"No, he thought it was funny. You can go talk to him tomorrow."

He hired me, and for a while I did famously. The Broadway columns and the literary columns were full of references to Mr. Woollcott. His comings and goings were reported. And what he liked best of all was that for several weeks Winchell quoted a whole series of jokes and wisecracks attributed to Woollcott but made up by me. Then I ran out of funny things for him to say. When his bons mots had been absent from Winchell's column for three weeks, Woollcott sent me a telegram: "Dear Irving, Whatever happened to my sense of humor?"

Through Moses, I also became press agent for Dorothy Thompson, a towering figure in journalism at that time, a woman who had her own syndicated newspaper column and radio program and was outspoken in her antifascist views. She was married to novelist Sinclair Lewis, who had won the Nobel Prize in literature in 1930, and for a brief time I did publicity for Mr. Lewis. I was getting myself into pretty heady company—and loving it.

It was at this point that one day, in need of a pay phone, I met a pretty young Broadway hopeful named Jackie Susann. Jackie, as I've told you, was dazzled by the people I knew and the life I led, and I was attracted to her by her innocence and freshness. She moved into my life step by step. My friends became her friends, her friends became mine, and almost unexpectedly, she became my wife.

*J*ackie and I began our married life in that Beekman Place sublet. Fortunately, it was furnished, saving us the trouble of shopping and making decisions about curtains and dishes. Domestic pursuits were not Jackie's strong point. She knew nothing about housekeeping or cooking and was in no hurry to learn. Neither her working mother nor her much-married grandmother had taught her any domestic skills.

"I really can't cook at all," she had confessed to me when we first talked about marriage.

"If I'd wanted a cook, I'd have married one," I told her.

A woman came in to cook for us three nights a week, and the rest of the time we ate out. (Later, Jackie learned to broil a mean steak, and we always kept a batch of them in the freezer for impromptu meals.) I was making about $250 a week when we married, I gave Jackie half of that, and she was very careful with our money. If we wanted to do something special, like go away for a weekend or buy a record player, she'd ask, "Do we have enough money for that?"

The first present Jackie bought me was a wrist watch that she had had inscribed: "You are forever mine." She had discovered that the watch I was wearing was a gift from Gertrude Lawrence and was engraved with an intimate message from that lady. Jackie did not want to live among souvenirs of my bachelor days.

I don't think there was ever a bride as eager to please as Jackie. Each of us wanted the other to be perfectly happy, but I believe she tried harder than I did at the beginning. I had to watch myself; if I showed the slightest preference for anything, a kind of sandwich, a type of shirt, a way of doing something, Jackie would leap to satisfy my whim. As I've told you, she had a beautifully rounded figure and wore her clothes with great style. She weighed about 130 pounds. One day, as we were walking down the street, she caught me glancing at a reed-thin girl. "Do you like the way that one looks?" she asked me.

"Sure, she has a great figure."

"She's not too skinny?"

"No, she's just right."

That very day, Jackie went on a diet and stayed on it for the rest of her life. To keep her weight down to 110—remember, she was five feet seven—she had to cut back her eating to nibbling. With iron discipline, Jackie refused gravy, potatoes, bread, cocktail tidbits, and most desserts. The one thing she could not resist was Breyer's butter almond ice cream. After an ice cream binge, she went on starvation rations for days and days.

Every morning, I went to my office, and Jackie went on her casting rounds. Show-business couples, and that's what we considered ourselves, were way ahead of the times in their attitude toward a woman's right to her own activities and her own life. It never occurred to either of us that Jackie should give up her fledgling career just because she was married. Did Lynn Fontanne quit the stage when she said, "I do," to Alfred Lunt? Of course not! It wasn't even a subject for discussion.

However, the precise goal of Jackie's ambition did vary from time to time. Eddie Cantor took us, along with his wife Ida and his daughter Marilyn, to see Gertrude Lawrence's electrifying performance in *Lady in the Dark*. Jackie was so bowled over (in spite of the tender sentiment expressed in my former watch) that she proclaimed on the way out of the theater, "You know what—I'm going to be Gertrude Lawrence."

"Not very likely, Jackie," Marilyn pointed out. "You really can't sing."

"In that event," she said without a moment's pause, "I'll be Helen Hayes."

Jackie wanted to *be* in the theater and to *succeed* in the theater in the very worst way. She tried everything, followed every lead, pursued, persisted, pestered. No stone was left unturned. But those were lean years. There were few opportunities for newcomers and few parts for young actresses. Neither off-Broadway nor off-off Broadway had been invented yet. If you couldn't get a part in a Broadway production, the only other possibility was a road show, which was a touring company of a Broadway hit, or the subway circuit—shows that played the city's boroughs and suburbs. A pair of producers named Wee and Leventhal controlled the subway circuit, and Jackie eventually made a connection with them, appearing in such plays as *Hedda Gabler* and Noel Coward's *Hay Fever*. It was rough-and-tumble and very good practice.

During that first summer of our marriage, 1939, we spent a lot of time at the World's Fair at Flushing Meadow in Queens, which was the original World of Tomorrow fair with the Trylon and Perisphere as its symbol. The cultural high points were the pavilions of the various nations of the world. It was at this fair that the United States got its first taste of the highest of high cuisine at the Pavilion Restaurant in the French government building, presided over by the legendary Henri Soule. But most of all, the public loved the Aquacade, a musical and water-ballet extravaganza mounted by showman Billy Rose, who was known as the Bantam Barnum. Billy Rose had become a friend of mine.

Many summer evenings, Jackie and I checked in at the Aquacade with Billy and then headed over to the Midway where I had as a client Dovita, a very beautiful young woman who came out on the stage covered with fluttering white doves. As Dovita danced and gyrated, one by one the doves flew off, carrying wisps of Dovita's costume in their beaks. Dovita's genteel strip act was one of the sensations of the fair.

By the end of the summer, unemployed and with no immediate prospects, Jackie was so restless that she got out the typewriter Goodman Ace had given her and in five days wrote a play entitled *Some Fine Day*. Since she couldn't find a producer who would give her a part in a play, I suppose her plan was to write one of her own. Not a bad idea. But as soon as I read *Some Fine Day*, I knew it was not going to open any doors for her.

"What's wrong with it?" she asked.

I could have said, "Everything," but I held back. I merely said, "It sounds as if you wrote it in a week." Jackie glared at me and gave me the silent treatment for a couple of days, but I guess she finally accepted my critique because *Some Fine Day* vanished.

Eddie Cantor became my client, and a great deal more than a client, for Eddie and Ida adopted Jackie and me as part of their family. Eddie sometimes referred to Jackie as "my sixth daughter." The Cantors were well known for having five daughters; the one we saw the most of was Marilyn. Jackie was thrilled to be included in the Cantors' circle, and my mother finally had something she could explain to her friends. To be Eddie Cantor's press agent was clearly superior to selling neckties at Macy's.

Eddie Cantor could have been a success at anything. Smart, alert, he was informed on a wide variety of subjects, including world affairs. He had a genius for cutting a script and getting the maximum laughter from a joke. And above all, he was a very nice man. In 1941, he came to New York to produce and star in *Banjo Eyes*, a musical based on the successful play *Three Men on a Horse*. Cantor's arrival in New York brought about several big changes for Jackie and me.

First, we moved into the Essex House on Central Park South where the Cantors were staying and where Jackie fell in love with room service. Pressing a button or picking up a house phone to order dinner, ice, or clean sheets delivered to the apartment was her idea of sheer heaven. For the first week, she ran room service absolutely ragged. Later, she tapered off only a little. During the twenty-odd years we lived in hotels and on all our travels, Jackie's greatest delight was to walk through the front door, kick off her shoes, and say, "Now for those two magic words, room service." What was cozier than dinner for two in our suite served by a room-service waiter?

Eddie Cantor did something wonderful for Jackie. He provided her with her first Broadway break since *The Women*. He found a small part for her in *Banjo Eyes*. Banjo Eyes was the name of the horse on whose winnings and losings the plot turned. The front of the horse was played by Virginia Mayo and the back by her brother-in-law. The show had a terrific cast. Jackie was thrilled with her four-line part and with all the wonderful people she was working with. When the show went to Boston to rehearse for its pre-Broadway run there, I hopped back and forth between New York, where I was handling my other clients, and Boston, where I worked on publicity for Cantor and *Banjo Eyes* and enjoyed my reunions with Jackie.

Cantor, of course, was still doing his network radio show on Wednesday nights, originating it from Boston during his tryout there. When I ran into the chance to get Errol Flynn to do a sketch with Dinah Shore on the show—a real coup for Cantor—I went to work to make sure of Flynn's appearance. He hated the idea of going to Boston, but the fee of five thousand dollars was attractive, and when I told him Boston was full of beautiful girls, he agreed to make the trip.

"Can you work it out for me to get a couple of girls?" he asked.

At that point, I was willing to say yes to anything.

I took Flynn up to Boston, and on Tuesday night we watched *Banjo Eyes* from seats in the third row. Drinking booze from a paper cup, Flynn studied the girls in the show. During intermission, he said, "You're going to get two of them for me, right?"

I wasn't prepared to go so far as to handle this matter personally, but he was such a good-looking guy and had such a legendary reputation as a lover, I figured I could take him backstage afterward and he'd have an easy time on his own. Just before the final curtain, he poked me and said, "I want a blonde and a brunette—the blonde at the end on the right and the brunette fourth from the left. That brunette has terrific knockers. Is she easy?"

I gulped and said, "She's easy for me."

"That's great. What's her name?"

I told him. "Is she single or married?" he asked.

"She's married."

"Who's she married to?"

"Me."

"Do you happen to have a revolver in your pocket?" he asked. "I think I'll shoot myself."

Flynn wound up with three girls, but I don't think there was any action. He was too drunk. The next day, when it was time for him to rehearse his part for the radio sketch, I phoned him, got no answer, went and knocked on his door, again got no answer, tried the house phone, and finally had a bell man open his door. The place was a mess—ice trays and turned-over glasses all over the floor, a girl passed out on the bed, and Errol half on the bed, half on the floor. I propelled him into the bathroom. A shower revived him, and he asked me to phone to have a barber sent up to the room. The hotel barber shop said, "We don't do room service."

I said, "It's Errol Flynn, and he wants a shave."

They said, "Yes, sir," and a barber came up right away.

In a half hour, Flynn looked great and smelled great and was a terrific heartthrob on the show. Afterward, Jackie walked up to him and said, "Mr. Flynn, I hear I lost my shot with you last night."

He said, "Oh, my God, did your husband tell you?"

She said, "Yes."

Flynn said, "You know, I'm still available."

Jackie said, "Okay, I'll keep that in mind."

At that moment, Jackie was riding high, but a few days later, it looked as if the rug might be pulled out from under her.

Banjo Eyes was running about an hour too long and had to be cut before coming into New York. Cantor cut one of the two dances by the DeMarcos and shaved a few minutes off several other numbers. Then he called and said he wanted to have dinner with Jackie and me. My antennae were up, and I said to Jackie, "That silver fox coat they borrowed for you and your four lines may be out of the show."

"Over my dead body," Jackie said.

On the way to dinner, Jackie was going over this outrage in her mind and getting madder and madder. Eddie ordered scrambled eggs and just picked at them. Jackie, who was on her perpetual diet, had three thin slices of roast beef and no gravy. She watched Eddie struggle with himself for a while, then said, "Eddie, how are the cuts coming?"

He said, "We have about seventeen or eighteen more minutes to take out."

She said, "That should be easy."

"Jackie—" he began. She stiffened. "I don't want this to affect our friendship, but one of the writers thinks we can dispense with the opening scene."

The opening scene was the one Jackie was in. There was silence for a while. I didn't know what to expect from Jackie. She just let Eddie squirm.

"You see, Jackie, we can save—"

Her hand edged toward the plate of scrambled eggs in front of Cantor. I thought for a few terrible seconds that she was going to pick it up and throw it in Eddie's face. He must have thought the same thing, for he said, "Oh, come on, Jackie, do you think I'd take away your lousy four lines?"

She smiled angelically at him, and it all ended happily.

Banjo Eyes opened on Christmas night, 1941, two and a half weeks after the Japanese attack on Pearl Harbor and our entry into World War II. It ran for 126 performances and had to close when Cantor went into the hospital for surgery. It never reopened.

My connection with Cantor led to a call by Fred Allen asking me to handle his publicity. That was another triumph for my mother— *all* her friends sat glued to their radios on Sunday nights when Allen wheezed out his jokes in that wonderful nasal voice of his and carried on with Mrs. Nusbaum and Senator Claghorn and the other colorful denizens of "Allen's Alley."

In 1942, Jackie was back on the subway circuit, and in May she was on the road with *Watch on the Rhine*, Lillian Hellman's somber, antifascist drama starring Jessie Royce Landis. Royce was a lot older than Jackie, but the two developed a wonderful friendship that lasted for many years.

I was not overjoyed when Jackie went on the road for weeks or months at a time, but we considered ourselves part of the show-must-go-on tradition, and we both knew that separations were inevitable. We tried to talk to each other every day on the phone when she was away. At the beginning, she wrote amusing notes, but these tapered off. In a way, the separations lent excitement to our marriage. I was never for a minute in all the years we were together bored with Jackie. She was too volatile and alive for that. But the rhythm of separations, reunions, being together, being apart, kept us keyed up and emotionally alert.

A few months later, Jackie was on the road again in the Theater Guild's production of *Cry Havoc*, starring stripper Margie Hart. It was playing in Chicago at New Year's, and I asked Joe E. Lewis, who was also appearing in Chicago, to take Jackie out on New Year's Eve. We all needed a little cheering up in those days. The war was going badly for the Allies both in Europe and the Pacific, and no one was feeling very hopeful or festive.

I wondered when the draft would catch up with me, and it finally did, in March 1943. I got my "greetings" then and had to report to Fort Dix in New Jersey for induction. I called Jackie in Chicago. She wanted to quit the show and come rushing back, but it didn't make sense for her to come East, give me a farewell hug, and lose her job, so I persuaded her to stay with the show and promised to come out for a weekend as soon as I could.

We decided to give up our apartment at the Essex House—not the wisest of plans. So on a wet, rainy day, I made three trips by taxi to take all of Jackie's clothes to an apartment that Bea had in the Royalton Hotel, a favorite place of theater people, on West 44th Street, across from the Algonquin.

At Fort Dix, I went through processing and a couple of weeks of training before being sent to Jackie's old stomping grounds, Atlantic City, and assigned to the Army Air Force. That was fine. I said, "At least I'll get a tan before I get shot to death." The first weekend I could get a pass, I went home to Brooklyn. My mother and father had both cried when I was inducted and said it was a terrible injustice to take an only child. But now they thought I looked great in my private's uniform and short haircut. They insisted I go out for a walk so they could show me off to all the other slackers.

That night, I reached Jackie at the backstage phone, and again she wanted to come home. But I told her to wait, I had a few plans. The next day, I went to see Fred Allen and asked him to put in a word for me with Colonel Tom Lewis, the head of special services— meaning recreation and public relations and that sort of thing. Lewis, incidentally, was married to Loretta Young. Fred called Lewis, sketched in my background, and told him I could be a real help to him in special services. Lewis took my name and serial number and said I'd hear from him in three days.

Nothing happened; six weeks went by, and I was getting leaner and tanner from training. Then the officer of the day sent for me. "You must know someone important, Mansfield," he said. "You're to report to the General Motors Building in New York."

I packed up and was there the next day. I was sent into a room with two men: playwright Moss Hart, in blue pants and a light blue shirt, and talent agent Irving Lazar, in a lieutenant's uniform. Moss, of course, I knew from my table-waiting summer at Camp Copake. Hart and Lazar had persuaded General Hap Arnold that they should produce a musical show, to be called *Winged Victory*, to do for the air force what Irving Berlin's smash hit, *This Is the Army*, had already done for the army in terms of building morale and prestige. I was to be an assistant in casting, which in this case was known as recruiting, and travel around the country with Lazar.

I don't know how much I contributed because Lazar was absolutely a wizard in lining up talent, but we put together a cast of then relatively unknowns, an astonishing number of whom later became household names.

This was our distinguished cast: Cpl. Mark Daniels, Pvt. Don Taylor, Pvt. Red Buttons, Sgt. Kevin McCarthy, Pvt. Barry Nelson, Pfc. Edmond O'Brien, Pvt. Whitner Bissell, Capt. Gary Merrill, Pfc. Edward McMahon, Sgt. Ray Middleton, Pvt. George Petrie, Pvt. Alfred Ryder, Pvt. Karl Malden, S.Sgt. Peter Lind Hayes, Pfc. Martin Ritt, Pvt. Henry Slate, Pvt. Jack Slate, Pvt. Lee J. Cobb, and a tenor named Alfredo Cocozza who turned up at M-G-M quite a few years later as Mario Lanza.

At one point, I was stationed with Lazar in Miami. He was staying at the Roney Plaza, which was off limits to me because I was not an officer. Walter Winchell's pal, Art Childers, had a cabana at the Roney which he let me use during the day, but the only way I could get into the hotel was by dressing like a civilian. At night, I had to take a bus to the air base at Hialeah Park. The first night I reported there, I was handed a rope and a net, given a lot of instructions, and assigned to a tent.

I put the net over my bed—having been told Hialeah had mosquitoes as big as bombers—undressed, and took off my shoes. But I left on my white socks because it got cold at night even though it was Florida. I couldn't remember what I was supposed to do with the rope, so I left it coiled next to my bunk and turned in. The next morning, I awoke at reveille, pulled on my clothes, put on one shoe, laced it up, then put my foot in the other and couldn't get it all the way in. Something was in there pushing back. I took out my foot and saw a snake curled in the shoe and coming up at me. I fainted.

When they revived me with cold water, the sergeant said, "Buster, why didn't you put your rope around your tent?"

So that was what the rope was for. It seems a snake will not cross a rope—at least that's what they told me. That was the closest I came to being wounded in action.

I never did get to Chicago to see Jackie in *Cry Havoc*, but she came into New York once to see me when we were rehearsing *Winged Victory*. She took a day off from her show and traveled East on one of those slow war-time trains that were always waiting on sidings for troop trains and freight trains to barrel through on the main track. We spent a wonderful night at the Essex House, or rather part of a night, because she had to run out at some awful hour to catch her train back to Chicago.

Just before the opening of *Winged Victory*, a notice was put up on the bulletin board ordering all of us to report for a physical exam. I went for mine, and two days later my name was called. I had to report to a medical officer and then to the army hospital in Brooklyn. There I was informed that I had a duodenal ulcer.

The medical people spent several weeks figuring out what to do with me and my ulcer and finally made me a proposition: stay in the army and they'd treat the ulcer, probably with surgery, or accept an honorable discharge if I signed a waiver giving up any future claim for a disability pension. I said, "Where do I sign?" and the next day I was out of the hospital, out of the army, and into a blue suit. It was November 1943. *Winged Victory* opened at the 44th Street Theatre on November 20 and ran for 212 performances. It was an enormous hit, eventually played in ten cities, and was made into a movie.

A civilian doctor later cured my ulcer with massive doses of Jell-o taken before each meal.

A few days after the war ended, Fred Allen said to me, "Guess who I heard from today?"

"Who?"

"Colonel Tom Lewis."

"What did he say?"

"He wanted your serial number."

"What did you tell him?"

"I said, 'Irving Mansfield was killed at Iwo Jima.' "

*O*nce out of the service, I returned to work for Fred Allen, picking up my other old clients and getting some new ones. Before my discharge, Jackie had returned to the city and moved in with Bea at the Royalton. Now we took a small apartment in the Essex House and happily resumed our life together. Jackie was job hunting again, and in her spare time she joined Bea and many of their friends at the Stage Door Canteen where the theater community was doing a wonderful job providing entertainment and a welcoming hand for servicemen passing through New York.

While on the road in Detroit, Jackie had met a stripper named Christine Ayres, who was probably the most beautiful girl in the world. She was sensational. Christine stood in front of a mirror and did exercises to make her bust stand out. Years later, Jackie modeled Jennifer in *Valley of the Dolls* in part on Christine.

Through Christine, Jackie met and became a friend of J. J. Shubert, the rich producer and theater owner. J. J. by then was well in his eighties. Despite his age, he loved having pretty young girls around him. He actually had a special girl of his own, Muriel Knowles, a very beautiful woman, and they were later married. Muriel didn't worry about J. J.'s "harem"; she joined in when ten or more of the young actresses came to J. J.'s penthouse in the Sardi building for dinner, bringing along their ration cards so J. J.'s cook could set a splendid table.

While I was still in the service, J. J. gave Jackie a small part as a comic maid in the fifth revival of *Blossom Time*, which had originally run in 1921. Jackie did some rewriting to update and jazz up the script. J. J. was so pleased that he put her name in lights on the marquee in letters bigger, brighter, and higher than the star's billing.

Jackie was out of her mind with joy. But knowing that such a miracle could not last long, she rushed out and got a photographer to make a permanent record of this triumph. She was right—the next night her name was off the marquee.

I was one of the very few men invited to J. J.'s soirees. I think the only other one was his elderly attorney, Bill Klein. J. J. sat there surveying his empire. Jackie and I introduced him to Lindy's and the Copacabana and other nightspots. We had many good times together.

I couldn't help liking J. J., because he thought the world of Jackie and encouraged her to write. He gave her plays to rewrite. He even encouraged her in her mistaken ambition to become a singer, and he got her a piano coach, Eddie Owens, for her practice sessions. The only song she really mastered was "Come Rain or Come Shine." Eddie selected some other songs for her that also had a very narrow range of notes, but "Come Rain or Come Shine" was her chef-d'oeuvre—after about six months of intensive practice.

One day, Jackie said to me, "You know I'm breaking in my act tonight. My singing act."

"Where is that?"

She mentioned a place on West 46th Street, a dive with a name like O'Reilly's Cafe.

I offered to come around to O'Reilly's and catch Jackie's debut, but she said, "No, you'll make me too nervous."

I couldn't figure out what she was going to sing *after* "Come Rain or Come Shine." She was very vague and a little irked when I questioned her, so I let it go. She left about nine o'clock with her makeup case and a couple of dresses on a hanger. I waited for an hour, then walked over to O'Reilly's. I stood in the back. A girl was singing, rather badly. I looked around for Jackie. She and another girl were sitting at a table with a couple of guys rough enough to be truck drivers. When the waiter took my drink order, he asked, "Do you want any company?"

"Just the drink," I said. It was that kind of place.

Another girl got up to sing. Then Jacqueline Susann was introduced. What did Jacqueline Susann sing? She sang "Come Rain or Come Shine." She was terrible.

She spotted me before she left the stage, and after the applause, she came over to me. "I can't stand back here with you because I'm supposed to mingle with the guests. But I want to know what you're doing in this place. I told you not to come to my opening."

I said, "Jackie, it's not only your opening night, it's your closing night, too. Get your clothes."

"You didn't like the song."

"It's not the song—it's this dump. Would you patronize a place like this?"

She started to cry, and then she said, "All right, but I have to get my things."

She got her stuff, and we left, and it was really very sad because that was one of Jackie's dreams—the spotlight, the orchestra, the curtain going up, and Jackie up there singing her heart out. I don't think anybody ever wanted to stop a show as badly as Jackie did—the way Ethel Merman or Edith Piaf or Liza Minnelli stopped shows. But it was not to be, and for days she hated me for taking away her dream.

Even though Jackie didn't make it big at O'Reilly's, those years after I got out of the service were great for us. We were very happy with each other, we led a wonderfully carefree life, and we saw all the shows, all the new movies, and all the night-club openings. We spent time regularly with Jackie's folks and mine, and we saw our old friends and made many new ones.

Jackie found it easy to make friends. Among her new ones was Hildegarde, a gifted singer from Milwaukee who billed herself as a French chanteuse when she played the Persian Room in the Plaza Hotel and other plush nightspots. Hildegarde flirted shamelessly with the men in the audience, tossed long-stemmed roses to her fans, and wriggled her arms in and out of her long white gloves. She was a charmer and shrewdly managed by Anna Sosenko, a bright and perceptive woman. Hildegarde and Anna were constantly in and out of the temporary apartment we took at the Essex House. We went to the Persian Room so often that we knew Hildegarde's act better than she did.

Jackie also became friendly at this time with the beautiful Joyce Matthews. It was a good thing that Joyce was blonde and Jackie brunette. If they had had the same hair color, they might have been competitive enough to act out one of those clawing and scratching scenes from *The Women*.

Jackie and her friends shopped together, went to each other's fittings for new fur coats, lunched at the Colony or "21" or Rumpelmayer's or the corner drugstore, depending on the circumstances, and kept tabs on the come-and-go romances of the single members of their circle. There was one stage when Mike Todd was hanging around with us a great deal. He was carrying a torch for Joan Blondell, whose feelings were so unreciprocal she would not see him, talk to him, or take his phone calls. Jackie kept fixing him up with her girl friends, but only Joan would do. We were getting pretty tired of Mike's wailing—until one day Jackie let out a screech as she read the morning paper. Mike Todd and Joan Blondell had eloped. It was not a happy marriage and did not last long.

Jackie persisted in her job search and picked up some guest spots on radio and minor roles in doomed plays. She appeared in *Jackpot*, a musical by Sidney Sheldon, Guy Bolton, and Ben Roberts, produced by Vinton Freedley, that managed to run for sixty-nine performances and included Nanette Fabray, Allan Jones, Jerry Lester, Betty Garrett, and Benny Baker in its cast. She appeared with Brenda Forbes in Chicago and Pittsburgh in *Let's Face It*, playing a matron on the loose. Then she got a part in a Shubert production starring Carole Landis that was originally called *The Firefly*. Jackie made revisions in the script for J. J. It played in Philadelphia (where Jackie always got good reviews) and was to open in Boston on January 1, 1945. But the night before, New Year's Eve, a devastating fire swept the Cocoanut Grove night club and killed five hundred people. All of Boston was in mourning, and no one in town would go within a mile of a play called *The Firefly*. Overnight, the show's name was changed and the billboards and marquee altered to display the new title, *The Lady Says Yes*. Jackie played a dumb doll.

That August, she was in *The Animal Kingdom* in Toronto and not long after that on the road in a horror called *Between Covers* in which she played a stripper named Fudge Farrell. I think they gave away turkeys or geese in the middle of that play. Jackie quit somewhere out in the boondocks, and when a critic suggested that she was fired, she wired him, "What do you mean fired? I was running for my life."

Years later, Jackie told interviewers that she had had a nonglorious career playing women who had been strangled, shot, or bludgeoned. But she wasn't laughing while it was happening. On a scrap of cardboard at the back of the album in which she carefully pasted all her reviews and column mentions, she jotted down her cries of pain: August '44—"Am I any nearer to success?" A few weeks later— "Slightly." Shortly after that—"Seems around the corner." Then— "Oh, yeah!" Then—"Dear God!" and—"Where do I go from here?"

In the meantime, my career was really leaping ahead. One day, I went along with Fred Allen when he was doing a guest spot on the Milton Berle radio show. During the rehearsal, I made a few suggestions I thought would be helpful. Milton Biow, the head of the sponsor's advertising agency, must have been watching me because he walked over and asked me if I had ever been a producer.

I was about to say, "No," when Fred Allen stepped in front of me and said, "Sure he has."

Biow asked me if I'd like to be the producer of the Berle show. "Depends on the money," I said.

"It's six hundred dollars a week."

"I'll take it." When they asked me when I could start, I said, "Yesterday." I was plenty nervy to take on such a job; I didn't even know how to handle a stopwatch. But I knew an opportunity when I saw one.

Fred Allen always said it was one of the worst things that ever happened to him—two of us came over to the Berle show, and only one of us left. I think he always felt a sense of rejection, although the next year I became producer of Fred's show, and along with Nat Hiken, the head writer, we all worked beautifully together.

The day the deal was made with Biow I went home and said to Jackie, "Your high school wish just came true."

"I've got high school wishes coming out of my ears. Which one?"

"The big one. You're getting your mink coat." I told her about my new job and my new pay. She was ecstatic and even offered to chip in some of her savings of $1,000. That's when I said to her, "Absolutely not. A lady only gets a mink coat from a lover or a husband, and since I consider that I am both to you, I am going to buy you your mink coat." And I did.

She had a fitting the next day. The coat cost $3,200, I paid $1,500 down and gave the furrier $150 a week. Jackie loved that coat so much that a few months later I had a hard time persuading her to send it off to summer storage.

About this time, I ran into Murray Korman, the photographer, and found him in the blackest of moods. His wife had called him the night before from California; she had gone off to take a screen test. Win or lose the test, she loved the palm trees and was going to stay in California. It was the end of his marriage, and his biggest problem was the lease he had just signed on a beautiful apartment in the Hotel Navarro on Central Park South at a rental of $650 a month.

"Maybe you should run after your wife," I suggested.

"But what about the apartment?"

"You're going to find someone to sublease it—like me."

Jackie and I moved in and stayed for twenty-six years. For all that time, Jackie had her beloved room service.

We were still going to those dinner parties at J. J. Shubert's, where he used to complain a lot about my hero Jolson, claiming Jolson was always running out of a show and going to Florida to renew his tan. Thinking about the wonderful way Jolson lit up the whole vast Winter Garden when he played there, it occurred to me that the story of the Winter Garden and all its hits would make a terrific movie. J. J. liked my idea and suggested I get permission from his brother and partner, Lee Shubert. J. J. could not get this permission because he and Lee had not spoken to each other for years. I don't know whether anybody knew what the feud was about, but everyone knew it existed.

Mr. Lee liked the idea. Jolson liked it too. What he liked most about the idea was that he could make a comeback as a picture star.

Jolson and J. J. maintained a strictly quarrelsome relationship. Once, when Jackie, J. J., and I ran into Jolson at Lindy's, Jolson said, "Hello, J. J."

J. J. said, "Don't say hello to me. The Jolson I knew died a long time ago." Jolson shook his head and walked away.

Jackie was furious at J. J. "That was a terrible thing to do," she scolded. "You're going to lose every friend we have."

Despite all the bickering, I went out to California, to firm up the picture end of the deal not knowing too many people at this stage, and finally got to Johnny Hyde, who was head of the William Morris office. We spoke for an hour about the Shuberts, about Jolson, and about the legendary Winter Garden. He liked what he heard and took me to Harry Cohn, head of Columbia pictures and a very powerful man. It looked as if it was set.

However, once I got back to New York, there was trouble. J. J. balked at the idea of paying a commission to Johnny Hyde and a finder's fee to me. We argued about that for a couple of weeks—until the newspapers announced that Al Jolson had signed on his own with Columbia Pictures for a film to be called *The Jolson Story*. The rest of us were out of the deal.

The Shuberts sued Columbia Pictures for invasion of privacy because they were using scenes of the Winter Garden, which was

Shubert property. They lost. *The Jolson Story* was a smash. I got no money for my idea and my efforts, but looked on the whole experience as my initiation into the wheeling and dealing, cutthroat ways of the big, bad guys. And Jackie, I'm sure, tucked all this away into that computer in her head and dug it out decades later for some of the dog-eat-dog episodes in *The Love Machine*.

Somewhere in the middle of 1945, Jackie got out that portable typewriter Goodman Ace had given her, and she asked him to give Bea a typewriter, too. He did. Jackie and Bea started calling each other George and Moss after George S. Kaufman and Moss Hart, and one day Jackie brought Bea home and said to me, "Honey, this is Moss, and we're going to write a play."

Day after day, they met, sometimes at our apartment, sometimes at Bea's. I thought the whim would pass after a few weeks, but it didn't. Good weather, bad weather, they were at that typewriter, except for the stretches when Jackie got a spot in a play and took off. What they were writing was not one of those five-day quickies like the play Jackie had zipped off right after our marriage. Bea and Jackie really slaved away, wrote and rewrote, argued, tussled, and called each other up in the middle of the night when inspiration struck.

Their play, originally called *The Temporary Mrs. Smith*, was loosely based on the escapades of a beautiful Russian woman who lived near us and centered on her efforts to snare a wealthy husband who would bail her out of her financial embarrassments. Frantic complications were provided by the woman's ex-husbands, who kept coming home to roost in her one-room apartment—all this handled in the wildest of farce fashion. When Jackie and Bea finished the play, Vinton Freedley took an option to produce it, hired Francine Larrimore to star in it, and tried it out in Wilmington, Washington, D.C., and Baltimore. It was not exactly a smash. The authors did some more work on the script, changed the name to *Lovely Me*, and got a different producer, David Lowe, who recast it with Luba Malina and Mischa Auer.

In the meantime, to our intense delight, Jackie had become pregnant. Ever since my return from the service, we had been wanting a baby, and like millions of wives of former GIs, Jackie found herself pregnant in the spring of 1946, the first year of the postwar baby boom. Jackie was happy, I was happy, and the grandparents-to-be were out of their minds. When you are both only children, as Jackie and I were, you hold the sole responsibility for carrying on the family line, and your parents eye you with certain expectations. Ours were too well trained to say anything, but they had been eying us, all right. Now everyone was delighted.

Jackie felt fine, her doctor was pleased with her, she exercised regularly, took her vitamins, and the only thing odd about her pregnancy was that she suffered from evening sickness instead of morning sickness. I remember one night in her eighth month she nearly fainted while we were having dinner at Toots Shor. She spent a few minutes in the ladies' room, came out, stabilized herself with a little ice cream, of all things, and we walked home.

Jackie, being Jackie, was not going to let a little thing like a pregnancy keep her from going about her work, which, at this point, was to get *Lovely Me* restaged and churning out royalties.

And so it happened that December 1946 was an extraordinary month for us. Guy Hildy Mansfield was born on December 6, and *Lovely Me* opened at the Adelphi Theatre on December 25.

*J*ackie and Bea went to Philadelphia in late November 1946 to work on last-minute revisions for the opening of *Lovely Me.* Jackie was in her eighth month and figured the baby would arrive at the end of December. I had tried to make her stay home, but it was impossible to make Jackie do anything. As long as it was Philadelphia, I didn't mind too much. She was close to New York, her parents were there, and I knew she and Bea were comfortable at the Ritz Hotel.

She looked so glowing at this time that her father painted her portrait. It still hangs in our living room, a poignant reminder of that happy time. Jackie is wearing a black evening gown, her dark hair is parted in the middle and swept back, she is glancing over a bare shoulder, her skin is an iridescent pearly pink, and she is absolutely gorgeous.

In the very early morning hours of December 5, Jackie woke up knowing something was wrong. She was wet and felt strange. Bea got up, and they phoned a doctor Jackie knew, but instead of sending her to a hospital, he told her to get back to New York and her own doctor. "First babies always take their time," he said reassuringly.

They ran out of the Ritz with one of those fluffy Ritz towels between Jackie's legs and another over Bea's arm. They caught the early-morning train to New York. A porter put them into a drawing room and rushed off, saying, "I'll get the vinegar." They never did find out what the vinegar was for. Jackie stretched out and made it to New York, where I was waiting on the train platform at Penn Station with a wheel chair. Luckily, she was going to French Hospital, which was just a couple of blocks from the station. In the lobby of the hospital, they started peppering Jackie with questions about insurance and next of kin and what her greatgrandmother died of.

"Let her go upstairs and I'll answer your questions," I said in a voice that told them I was prepared to punch someone in the nose. They took Jackie up to the labor room where her doctor was waiting for her, and I went into the lounge where fathers waited and worried.

I must have smoked a hundred packs of cigarettes and chewed ten packs of gum. Other fathers came and went. Nurses brought me coffee. A whole day went by and part of a night. Finally, someone said to me, "Congratulations, Mr. Mansfield. You have a son."

Jackie had been in labor for seventeen hours. Guy Hildy Mansfield arrived at four A.M. on December 6, weighing six pounds, seven ounces. As a result of what was called a "mid-B forceps" delivery, the baby had slight bruising on his forehead. The forceps apparently were necessary because it was a "dry" birth—Jackie had lost her water back in Philadelphia.

I didn't know all this. Groggy from waiting and worrying, I asked to see the baby and was taken to a window that gave a view of the newborn nursery. Another father at the window grabbed my arm and said, "Do you want to see a great-looking kid? That one there. It's my third."

I said, "Congratulations. I just had my first." I pointed to the tiny dark face of the infant in the bassinet marked Mansfield.

The other father said, "Oh, that's very nice." I was disappointed. He wasn't as enthusiastic about my baby as he was about his.

Jackie looked tired but radiant. We were both thrilled to be parents, and we sat in her hospital room holding hands and thinking how lucky we were to have everything—the whole world, everything we wanted. It was a very joyous time.

When we brought Guy home from the hospital on a very cold December day, I carried my son in my arms in a blanket into the hotel lobby. The manager of the Navarro said, "Everyone out of the elevator—we have a brand-new baby coming in." Jackie pulled back the blanket so she could have a look, and the manager pronounced Guy the most beautiful baby ever.

We had already fixed up the room that had been Jackie's den as a nursery with adorable furniture and stuffed animals, but the hundreds of gifts that had poured in from friends and family spilled out of the nursery and were scattered all over the apartment. We could have opened a baby clothing store, a baby toy store, and a silver spoon shop. Later, Jackie bought a woolly jacket for herself and two bathing suits with the credit slips from Guy's duplicate gifts.

From the start, we had a baby nurse who did all the drudgery and daily work connected with a tiny child. She slept in the room with Guy, took care of his laundry, prepared his formula and later his food, fed him, and wheeled him to the park in his handsome perambulator. Jackie and I had all the fun. We played with Guy in the morning, often bringing him into our bed to kiss and tickle and do patty-cake, and we played with him again at the end of the day. Jackie took complete charge of him on the nurse's midweek day off, and we both wheeled him to the park on Sunday. Both sets of grandparents came frequently, bringing gifts and exclamations of "My, how he's grown!" My mother wanted to sleep over on the nurse's night out, but Jackie explained that she really wanted to take care of her son herself on those nights, but grandma could visit whenever she wanted to.

I have always looked back on those first years of Guy's life as a time completely bathed in sunshine. As Huckeybaby, I had been kissed from morning to night, and I simply could not stop kissing my son. Guy had fine blond hair, blue-gray eyes like mine, silky skin, and a quick laugh. I couldn't keep my hands off him. I'd rush home from my office, eager to kiss him, play with him, see what he'd learned since I'd left him in the morning. He was an affectionate, responsive baby, always ready to play.

When he was a toddler, I loved to watch him pedal around the apartment on his little tricycle. In Central Park, I sat on one end of the seesaw, and Jackie held Guy on the other end, and he shrieked with joy as he rose into the air. When he was a little older, he proudly handled his end of the seesaw all by himself. He enjoyed the merry-go-round in the park and pony rides. But the best times of all were in the bathtub. Jackie, Guy, and I, all three, piled into the tub together along with a whole school of plastic fish and a fleet of little boats. We splashed and giggled and tickled, and in the end there was often more water on the floor than in the tub. Guy loved it, and so did we.

The first summer, we took a house near Atlantic Beach, New York, to get away from the hot city—this was in the pre-air conditioning era. The next summer, we rented a house just a block from the beach at Margate near Atlantic City, and the summer after that we vacationed at Ventnor. The nurse came with us, and one summer my parents stayed, and another summer, Jackie's parents. Jackie remained at the shore the whole summer; I flew down every Friday night. Those summers, too, I recall as a magical, golden time.

What I recall is the truth—but not the whole truth.

The whole truth, as I piece it together now by forcing myself to think of the bad times as well as the good, was a lot less rosy. First, there was the feeding problem. Guy was a very finicky eater. Jackie and the nurse were constantly trying to get him to finish his bottle, his cereal, his strained fruit. For months at a time, he ate so little that he gained almost no weight at all. Weighing a baby back in the 1940s was an important weekly ceremony, and I remember how upset Jackie became as Wednesday—weighing day—approached. If Guy picked up an ounce or two, we celebrated. If he lost weight, and some weeks he did, we made frantic calls to the pediatrician, who usually told us that babies made progress in their own sweet time.

Through his whole first summer, June, July, August, Guy gained only twelve ounces. By then, the doctor, too, was worried, and he decided to test Guy for TB—maybe that was why he was not gaining. Jackie and I went through agonies while we waited for the results. They were negative. We breathed easily again; Guy was all right. In October, the doctor discontinued his cod liver oil, and he suddenly spurted ahead. Then there were more setbacks, and in November it was discovered that the poor little fellow had a hernia and needed a truss.

His eating improved temporarily, but just before Christmas, he was not eating again, and Jackie had two things to worry about: Guy's weight and her father, who had suffered another heart episode and was in the hospital. It was not a very happy Christmas or New Year's for any of us.

Jackie's father recovered, and early in 1948 we took Guy to Philadelphia where he underwent surgery for his hernia. Later that year, he had his tonsils out. Jackie and I were worried sick about both operations, but Guy took them in stride.

During Guy's second year, eating continued to be a problem, and he often slept badly—his nanny was frequently cranky during the day because he kept her awake most of the night. He said daddee and mommee but did not do much other talking. I found it so miraculous that he could shriek, "Daddee," and fly into my arms when I came home that it didn't occur to me to worry. But Jackie saw him with other children more often than I did in the park or on visits to friends with babies, and she couldn't help making comparisons. When she saw children, often many months younger than Guy, talking away and using whole sentences, she became very distressed.

[58]

Guy, at some point when he was about two and a half, stopped going near other children in the park and lost interest in playing with his toys. There was a period when he refused to go into the living room. He was not toilet trained. (At that time babies were toilet trained very early.) He wouldn't give up the bottle. He began having temper tantrums. Jackie was upset about him but hated herself for being depressed.

She asked the pediatrician if she should take Guy to a child psychologist. He told her just to leave the boy alone and let him eat off the window sill if he wanted to. He assured her that Guy would work his way out of this difficult stage. She read in Dr. Spock about the "terrible twos" and tried to cheer up but had a hard time. I remember that I had tickets for the opening of the baseball season that spring, but Jackie was too upset about Guy to go to the game with me. She sent me off with some of my friends.

Looking back to the way my mother had worried and fussed over me when I was little, I felt that Jackie was just doing the kind of worrying that all mothers do. Mostly to put her mind at rest, I went with her in June when she insisted on taking Guy to a psychologist. Guy behaved so well during the evaluation that I was sure nothing could possibly be wrong. But two days later the psychologist called us in and gave us news that terrified us.

She told us that Guy seemed to be withdrawing into himself and that psychologically this was a very dangerous development. How dangerous? What did she mean? She wasn't sure. She said it would take time to see how things worked out. She wanted to see us again in a few months.

That night, Jackie and I were both physically sick with worry and fear. This was far worse than the TB scare.

We got through the night and called the pediatrician in the morning. He was much more encouraging than the psychologist and told us to be patient. That summer at Atlantic City, there were good days and bad days, depending on Guy's moods and actions. On balance, as I recall, it was a pretty good summer, and by early fall I had convinced myself that Guy was going to be fine. What Jackie wanted most was for Guy to talk. She'd hold his wriggly, active little body close in her arms, and looking deep into his eyes, she'd say, "Please, Guy, start talking. Tell mommy, tell daddy, how you feel, what you want. Tell us your name, Guy. Say, 'Guy.' Please, Guy, say it."

But Guy only kissed her and wriggled away.

The roof fell in during the summer of 1950 when Guy was three and a half. One day, the nurse brought him home from the park in his stroller, and he was screaming, screaming, red in the face from screaming. His nanny said that for no reason at all Guy had suddenly started screaming. She couldn't get him to stop. It was a different scream from his temper tantrums. No, nothing had happened in the park—no fall, no blow, no incident of any kind. Just screams.

Jackie tried to quiet him but couldn't. She phoned me and phoned the pediatrician. I hurried home; the doctor was not immediately available. A doctor in the neighborhood came up and gave him half an aspirin. That calmed him a little. But later he started again and was up the whole night—screaming. None of us slept. Eventually, he stopped from sheer exhaustion, but as soon as he rested a little, he began again.

The next day, I went to the park and questioned everyone in the area where Guy and his nanny had been sitting. Had he fallen, hit his head, been struck? No, nobody had seen anything. Later, I hired a detective agency to go over the area inch by inch and talk to everybody. Nothing—the investigator didn't turn up a thing.

The pediatrician gave us something to keep Guy calmed down, and now began a terrible period as Jackie and I searched for answers and explanations. At this time, also, the rocking began. In his carriage, in his crib, on a chair, Guy rocked, rocked, rocked, from side to side to some rhythm deep inside himself.

We called and consulted everybody, doctors, psychiatrists, psychologists, any expert we heard about. For months, we took Guy daily to a child psychiatrist. The screaming had stopped, but Guy was withdrawn and turned in on himself. There were no more happy times or fun on the swings or splashing in the tub. Jackie and I were heartbroken. Our parents were beside themselves; we had to put on a brave front to keep them from falling apart. I was staying home more. We were both canceling appointments right and left, making odd excuses for not going to all those dinners and openings and parties that usually filled our evenings.

Guy was not making any progress with the psychiatrist. We took him to a woman doctor who was the head of the whole children's psychiatric division of a major hospital. We had to leave him overnight, and the next day we went to the hospital with a new toy for him, and there was Guy sitting with four or five other children but looking so lonely and lost we could cry. The famous woman doctor suggested shock treatment.

We were aghast and checked with the psychiatrist, whom we knew well by now and trusted. He said, "She's the best child psychiatrist in the United States, and if she says shock will help, try it."

We took Guy to the hospital; he stayed there a week for a series of shock treatments, and I think they destroyed him. He came home numb, with no expression, almost lifeless. He didn't seem to hear us when we spoke to him. Grasping at straws, we decided that maybe he had a hearing problem. We got the name of the best hearing specialist in New York and took him for tests. His hearing was fine.

By then, I was producing "Talent Scouts" with Arthur Godfrey. One day, Jackie and Guy stopped by at a rehearsal on their way to or from one of the doctors. Guy showed interest in the drummer. It was the first time in weeks he had shown interest in anything. After that, we took Guy regularly to rehearsals. He loved Specs Powell, the drummer, loved to watch him use his sticks. Guy sat as close to the drummer as he could get, and holding onto his chair so he wouldn't fall off, rocked and rocked to the drummer's beat.

Finally, there came the black day when we took Guy to still another specialist, a woman doctor who was reputed to be the best at treating children like Guy. She talked to Guy, tested him, studied his medical records—how could such a little fellow have piled up such a stack of documents?—and finally said to us, "Do you want the truth, or do you want a nice fairy tale?"

Jackie said, "The truth, please tell us the truth."

"All right," she said. "If I were you, I would put this child away, forget about him, and have another child."

We couldn't believe our ears. How could anyone say such a terrible thing? How could anyone be so cruelly blunt? We ran out of there, and I remember we walked along the street holding hands, and I was crying. Jackie was not crying, but I was unashamedly walking down the street and crying. Now Jackie had two patients—Guy and me. I just couldn't stop crying. "We'll take him somewhere else. We'll get the right opinion," I said. "There has to be an answer. We just haven't found it yet."

What was wrong with Guy? I'm not sure we'll ever know. Some of the doctors talked about brain damage. Others used the word autistic. That word was not well defined at that time, but we gathered it meant a withdrawal from emotional contact with people and usually a failure to communicate and learn. In the 1940s, there was not much research into autism and no known treatments. Today, a little more is known, and there are accounts of children who have been heroically rescued from their emotional isolation.

In a recent pamphlet from the Development Center for Autistic Children in Philadelphia, this is the description of an autistic three to four-year-old: . . . behaves strangely . . . keeps to himself . . . shuts the world out . . . rocks, spins . . . bangs head . . . grimaces . . . moves head and fingers oddly . . . walks on toes . . . echoes others' speech . . . babbles, grunts or talks strangely . . . appears to be seeing things. It doesn't all apply to Guy, but it is painfully close.

And so began our search for a place for Guy—a search that still continues thirty years later.

*T*he time came when we had no more choices. We had to accept the grim conclusion that it would be best for Guy and best for everyone to send him to a school that was equipped to deal with his special disabilities. We could no longer handle him at home. The nurses wouldn't stay. Jackie was a wreck—I was afraid she'd break down completely. I was holding on only by digging my fingernails into my palms at least a hundred times a day. I was rushing home early to be with Jackie and neglecting my work. Neither of us could sleep, and it was at this point that we both began using sleeping pills.

We went back to the psychiatrists and other experts for their recommendations of schools and treatment centers. We considered dozens, visited several, and finally chose one in New England that was highly praised and fairly close to New York. Accessibility was important because we wanted to visit Guy as often as possible. The place had a long driveway through green lawns to a cluster of red-brick buildings. The staff seemed to be kind and understanding. Yes, they thought they could help Guy; he would have individual treatment and instruction, a carefully worked out medical program, sports, play, and leisure activities.

On a beautiful, sunny Saturday we drove Guy there. He was quiet and listless in the car, and after we kissed him good-by and promised to be back the following week, he walked off with the nurse without a murmur. Jackie and I cried the whole way home. I don't know how she saw to drive. (I don't drive. I have a problem in color vision that prevents me from getting a license.) That first night at home, with the empty crib, the toys, the little suits and shirts all around us, was the most awful time we ever lived through. I remember that Jackie and I got into an argument about whether to keep

Guy's bed and toys. I said we should keep them; he might need them again sooner than we expected. Jackie said no, we could always buy him a new bed, new clothes if—or rather, when—he came home. In the end, we disposed of everything.

One thing we agreed on from the beginning: we would not tell anyone, except the few intimates who already knew, what had happened to Guy and where he was. People then were not as open as they are now about mental and emotional illness, and I think that general attitude influenced us. But we still had hope. Perhaps the school in New England would help him and he would make enough progress to come home. Maybe a new drug, a new brain operation, who knows what medical advance, would get to the root of the boy's trouble, and he would be, miraculously, whole again. If that happened, wouldn't it be better if he could pick up his life without the stigma of mental illness?

We heard of someone whose child had gone out to a famous hospital in Denver to be treated for asthma, and we used that as our story. We simply spread the word that Guy was in Arizona for a year where the wonderful doctors would cure the asthma that had been troubling him. Each year, we stretched out the treatment for another year, and gradually people stopped asking us about our son. I'm sure there was plenty of talk behind our backs, and I suspect some pretty awful things were said—that we were neglectful parents, that we just didn't want to bother having a child around, that we put our careers ahead of our son. We ignored it all. Among our friends, only Bea and Hildegarde and Anna Sosenko knew, and perhaps a few others.

As for the grandparents, what can I tell you? At first, it was as if their world had come to an end. They had such love for this child and such hopes pinned on him. How could it be? Maybe their grief helped to keep Jackie and me from falling apart—we had to comfort them. I think Robert Susan was the most inconsolable. Here was a famous man without a son to carry on his name but a beloved, adored daughter who gave him a grandson. He had written in Guy's baby book when he was born, "Grandson Guy—Only God could love you more than I. I have waited for you a long time, and when you arrived, you filled all my expectations to their entirety. Great goings to a swell little fella! All my love, Grandpa Susan."

Jackie was in terror that the news about Guy would bring on another of her father's heart attacks. But there was no way she could protect him or her mother or my parents. They had to work their own way out of their grief as best they could.

Every weekend, Jackie and I went to visit Guy. He usually seemed glad to see us. He kissed us and held our hands and looked well fed and cared for. But he was not making any progress and not talking at all, just mommee and daddee and a few babbling sounds. The not talking was the most frustrating part of his illness because he couldn't tell us how he felt or what was happening to him. Guy stayed in the place in New England for several years, and in all that time I don't think we missed more than half a dozen weekend visits. We invented all kinds of stories for people who wondered about our weekly disappearances. Basically, we didn't care what they thought.

Disappointed, eventually, at his lack of progress, we searched for a more promising place for Guy. We heard that a center run by New York State was well in advance of many private institutions in its program for autistic children. With high hopes we transferred Guy there. It was closer to the city and near Jones Beach, so all one summer we took bathing suits and beach toys with us on Saturdays and drove Guy to the seashore. He seemed to love those excursions. We stopped for hotdogs and ice cream on the way. Hotdogs were his favorite food, and he drowned them in ketchup. When he played and splashed at the water's edge, it almost seemed like the old, happy days.

Once when we were driving him to the beach, Jackie turned to Guy and said, "Guy, when are you going to talk?"

"When I'm ready," he said.

Jackie nearly swerved the car into a tree. "Did you hear him?" she said to me. "Did you hear him? Guy, what did you say? Say it again."

Yes, I heard him. Guy did speak, but there was no way we could get him to speak again or say anything else. He fell back into silence. Of course, we reported this development with jubilation to his doctors. They tried in every way they knew, but Guy did not talk again.

Guy's stay at the state-run place came to an abrupt end when we read in the newspaper that prisoners from overflowing jails were being sent there. That's all we had to hear. We found a place down South where, again, we were promised the world. Then he was in a school in Pennsylvania. From time to time, we tried bringing him home for a weekend or a longer stay, but these visits were always a disaster. Any change in routine, strange faces, a new place, upset him enormously.

Someone had to be with him every minute. The school always reported severe behavior problems after his return. After a while, we had to give up on the home visits.

When he became a teenager, we sent Guy to a school in Texas because once again the staff and the program gave us hope of improvement. By then Jackie and I were making frequent trips back and forth to the coast, sometimes for my TV programs, much later for her book tours and for the filming of her books.

I can't tell you on how many of these trips we stopped to see Guy either on the way out to the coast or on the way back. The stopovers were always exhausting; we had to change to a small local airline, stay in a motel, rent a car to drive to the school, and fly back to the main airport to get our plane to New York or Los Angeles. The visits were emotionally exhausting, too, because as Guy grew into manhood and became a handsome, well-built adult with dark hair and a sweet smile, we became more and more conscious of the tragic waste of a human life. It just shattered us every time. Jackie cried after each visit and said things like "Why did I do this to you? Why did I let it happen?"

Jackie carried an enormous burden of guilt over Guy. She felt that his problems were somehow her fault. She shouldn't have gone to Philadelphia just before he was born. Once there, she should have stayed and not tried to come back to New York. She shouldn't have let nurses spend so much time with him. She should have been with him herself every moment. Maybe a nurse or a sitter had dropped him on his head or let him fall. She tortured herself with these thoughts, and when she slipped into a mood of self-blame, I could find no way to comfort her.

To add to our misery, there was the awful fact that we did not know back then—and still do not know—what really happened to our son. Autism is the diagnosis most often given, but not all the doctors agree. Was he damaged before birth, during birth, afterward? Was he a perfectly normal baby during his first years, as he seemed to us and to the doctors who took care of him? Or was it hopeless from the beginning? I suppose we'll never know; it will be a mystery forever.

Guy is now thirty-six, a tall, well-built, good-looking fellow who appears younger than he is. As I began writing this book, he was in a school not too far from New York, where for quite a number of years he was happy and well treated. But recently there were violent episodes; Guy thrust his arm through a window and needed several stitches. There were complaints from the school that he had attacked another patient. Guy had always before been gentle and docile. I couldn't tell whether this was a new stage in his illness or the result of changed medication. Since I couldn't get the answers I wanted from the medical staff, I had to go through the whole process of finding a new place for him.

Early last year, he was moved to a school much closer to New York where I am now able to visit him as often as I like—at least once a week, sometimes several times a week. Guy loves his TV set and knows, without being told, when "M.A.S.H." goes on. He can put together a jigsaw puzzle of a hundred pieces in no time flat. But he still does not talk or read or communicate in any way. When I arrive to see him, he is always happy to see me, and we slap ourselves and slap hands together and say, "Hi five," the way basketball players greet each other.

Long before her last illness, Jackie used to say, "Promise me one thing, doll. Please don't die before me. Don't leave me alone. I won't be able to take care of Guy without you." She worried constantly about what would happen to Guy after we were both gone.

Then, as the bills for Guy's care began coming in—it takes many, many thousands of dollars each month for his room, board, medical attention—Jackie's attitude toward money changed. She had never in her life really had a money problem; she had wanted to earn money more as a symbol of her success than as an objective in itself. But after Guy left home money became very important to Jackie. She felt an urgency to earn money, lots of money, to assure his continuing care. I was doing very well financially, but even "very well" does not give you a sense of security when you are meeting those overwhelming current bills and trying to save vast amounts of money to guarantee your son's care long after your own death.

So now, added to Jackie's innate drive to succeed, to reach some pinnacle of achievement, was this new sense of desperate need to earn money, big, big money, for Guy's sake and security.

$\mathscr{I}$n late December 1946, three weeks after our son's birth, Jackie and Bea's play, *Lovely Me,* opened at the Adelphi Theatre in New York with Luba Malina, Mischa Auer, and Millard Mitchell in the leading roles. It was a wonderfully happy occasion. We were there, of course, all dressed up, with friends, family—everyone we knew—all tense with excitement. Jackie, the radiant new mother, was still being congratulated on the birth of her baby. Jackie and Bea, the hard-working Moss and George, were treated like stars—the stars they were both so desperate to become. Except for one small, and perhaps prophetic, thing there were no biographical notes about them in the *Playbill.*

The lights went down, the curtain went up, the actors spoke their lines and Jackie clutched my right hand with both of hers. Not until the audience laughed and applauded did she relax her grip. After the last curtain call, I had my arm around Jackie as we walked up the aisle. I couldn't help marveling at the miracle that Jackie and her friend had pulled off. These two very minor-role actresses, both still in their twenties, had actually written a play that was produced in a real Broadway theater with real Broadway stars and had just been cheered by a real opening-night audience. I thought I had to be the luckiest man in the world to have such a talented and brilliant wife.

Afterward, we all went to Sardi's to wait nervously for the reviews in the morning papers. Critics are notoriously less kind than opening-night audiences, and the reviews were pretty bad. But not all *that* bad for a pair of neophyte playwrights and for a play that had had a rocky time on the road. To make things harder for Jackie and Bea, the Adelphi was a musical-comedy house, big enough for *The Passion Play* and all wrong for a one-set comedy. Also, there were two other plays opening that night, so several papers had sent second- or third-string critics to *Lovely Me*.

The *New York Times* and the *Tribune* panned it. The next afternoon, the *World Telegram* described it as "a rowdy, bawdy farce. It stops at nothing for a laugh." Walter Winchell was uncomplimentary enough to dub it a "feeble farce," and Douglas Watt in the *News* was murderous. Jackie took particular umbrage at Watt's review; she said she was mad enough to slap him in the face.

The good news was that the public liked the play a lot more than the critics did. The bad news was that a theater shortage forced its premature demise. *Lovely Me* had to leave the Adelphi early in January because *Street Scene* was coming in. It moved to the Coronet where Arthur Miller's *All My Sons* was booked for the end of the month. We tried desperately to find another theater, and Jackie and Bea hoped against hope up to the very last minute. But there was no reprieve even though more than two dozen standees crowded the back of the house for the last two performances.

During the play's run, Jackie and Bea each drew three hundred dollars a week in self-reduced royalties. But after all their hard work, they were done out of a long run by the lack of a theater! At any other time, I think Jackie might have been murderous in her rage over the closing of the play. But luckily she was so absorbed in being a new mother that she stayed calm about the closing.

During the first years of Guy's life, Jackie made no effort to get back into the theater as an actress. In fact, she turned down several offers to go on the road. Home was where she wanted to be, and she spent far more time at home than ever before. But it was not in Jackie's nature to be without a project. So Moss and George dusted off their typewriters and once more began to write—a novel this time. It was called *Underneath the Pancake*, meaning the pancake makeup used on stage; quite naturally, it dealt with show business.

The two friends worked diligently for several hours every day, usually while Guy was napping or being taken to the park, and by the end of the year, their manuscript was ready to be shown to an agent. They selected Helen Strauss, who handled literary properties at the William Morris office. For weeks, Jackie swooped down on the mail and leaped at every phone call in her eagerness to hear the agent's opinion. The agent requested some changes, so it was back to the salt mines.

I think it was at this time that Jackie began to make her bargains with God. If only the book got a publisher, she promised God, she'd give up smoking or curb her quick temper or stop eating a food she loved. I used to tease her and tell her that she was treating God like the William Morris office, making deals with him. Sometimes she did her wishing in Central Park on a hill right outside our window where she often wheeled Guy in his carriage. It got so we called it the Wishing Hill. She spent a lot of time there during the dark days in her life. You can find the Wishing Hill in *Once Is Not Enough*, and it was there that the last photograph of Jackie was taken in the summer of 1974.

Despite whatever bargain she made, the novel did not pay off. The agent decided that the story did not work in novel form but might have a chance if changed into a play. Too discouraged to face that heavy revision, Jackie and Bea put the book aside and tried their hand at a radio situation comedy called "There's Always Albert," which was produced on CBS in 1948. Albert was a composer unable to find a job, a failure that prevented his brother and his girl friend from getting married. It starred Jan Murray, Pert Kelton, and George Matthews. *Variety* said of it, "Savvy when it comes to fast Broadway dialog." It ran long enough to console the writers a little for their defeat over the novel.

Since Jackie had been particularly incensed by Douglas Watt's review of *Lovely Me*, she had vowed to get even with him. She was probably taking out on Doug Watt, whom she didn't even know, all her frustration over the early closing of the play. I knew Watt and saw him regularly at Toots Shor and other spots around town. He never said a word about his review, and, I never said anything about Jackie's threat to retaliate. Several times when he stopped by our table at Sardi's, I simply did not introduce him to Jackie, or else I muttered some other name. She just might have been serious about her threat.

Then one night a year after the opening, I saw Doug Watt and his wife across the room at Sardi's. When he got up to go to the men's room, he paused at our table and said, "Hello, Irving, how are you?"

I figured enough time had passed and it was safe for me to say, "Hello, Doug. I'm fine," and he continued on his way.

Jackie put down her fork and said, "Was that Doug Watt?"

I said, "Yes, but Jackie—" I was too late. She got up, followed Watt, and then I heard something like a slot. A few minutes later, Watt appeared holding his cheek.

"You know your wife just slapped me," he said.

"It was inevitable, wasn't it?" I said to him.

He returned to his table. Jackie came back to our table and was very cool about the whole business. Only now she was mad at me. "You fooled me long enough," she said. "You always said, 'Hello, Sam,' or, 'Hello, George,' when you knew it was Doug. Why didn't you tell me who he was?"

"Because I knew you were going to slap him in the face."

"Oh, boy, did I give him a shot!" she said.

Watt and I continued to be friendly, and the incident was never mentioned.

In December 1948, Jackie did a sketch on the Milton Berle TV show with Red Buttons. Walter Winchell made a nice comment about her. By then, she had a time-to-time part on a soap opera called "Hearts in Harmony," and she also played Lola, the cigarette girl, on "The Morey Amsterdam Show." Her earnings at the end of the year added up to less than $4,000—far from a fortune but enough to make her feel that she still had a toe in show business.

Then, after Guy left home in 1950 and after six months of what can only be described as a period of deep mourning, Jackie absolutely threw herself into radio and TV. She was everywhere, doing anything she could find. She was on a disc jockey show with Ed Weiner from the Hickory House, a jazz joint on Broadway. She did an interview show three times a week on ABC-TV. She and Joyce Matthews did commercials on the "Somerset Maugham Theatre" on TV. She also had a local program on WABD-TV called "Open Door," which aimed to find jobs for people, patch up personal problems, and rehabilitate the handicapped. Critic Harriet Van Horne praised Jackie's "breezy, likable personality."

On Mondays, she was hostess on the "Jackie Susann Show" on Dumont TV which combined interviews, fashions, controversial guests, and a phone-in advice service for viewers with offbeat problems that were never really solved but provided entertaining moments for other viewers. Jackie used a seven-second delay button on the call-in lines so she could punch her advice clients off the air if their confessions were likely to endanger the station's license.

In 1951, she was a guest on quiz shows, variety shows, and game shoes. She appeared on "Danger," "Suspense," on telethons, and on soaps. She also did a local show on WABC-TV that combined interviews with celebrities who were opening in plays, musicals, night clubs, or on other TV shows with five-minute news breaks by an announcer. This format was a forerunner of the live-at-five shows that are today so successful and popular.

To look at her scrapbook from those years, you'd think from the hundreds of clippings of interviews, head shots, and column mentions that Jackie *really* was queen of TV. But, of course, she was no such thing. She was a small fish in a very big pond, and even her photograph in full, glamorous color on the cover of the *Daily Mirror* Sunday Magazine in 1953 did not fool her. She was nowhere in terms of the stardom, the acclaim, the sense of making it big, Big, *BIG*, that she had sought since childhood.

While Jackie's career marked time, mine zoomed. I was already producing the "Milton Berle" radio show, and the following season I went on to produce the "Fred Allen Show," which became a runaway hit.

In 1946, I joined CBS in the program department. Two other bright young men, Cy Howard and Ernie Martin, started at the same time. It was our job to come up with ideas for new shows. I was very ambitious and at the beginning submitted almost an idea a day to Davidson Taylor, the vice president in charge of programs. He always said, "I don't like it. I don't think it's very good." One of the ideas he rejected was for a talent-scout program—professional performers who had not yet made it would do their stuff on the air to find out how the audience responded.

Taylor said, "No, it's terrible."

After three months of rejections, I asked to see William S. Paley, the head of CBS, who had hired me. Taylor came along with me. I said, "Mr. Paley, there's a good show called 'Major Bowes Amateur Hour' which people like, but it's for amateurs. There are a lot of fine professional people around, singers, comics, actors, who never get on a network. I want to give them a chance on the air. They should be introduced by someone who knows them—a cousin, an uncle, a neighbor. A strong MC should hold the show together. I think it's a good idea and will get a big audience."

Paley said, "Let's do it." It was a quick, instinctive go-ahead decision.

My first choice for an MC was Eddie Cantor, but that didn't work out. Mr. Paley suggested an announcer named Arthur Godfrey who had been fired from the Fred Allen show because his leisurely speech pattern was too much like Allen's. He was doing a daytime show for CBS, mostly unsponsored, plus an early-morning disc-jockey show from WTOP in Washington. I went over to the Lexington Hotel where Godfrey lived and explained the show to him. He was receptive and said he'd be delighted to try again on a prime-time network show.

"Talent Scouts" got under way the first Friday night in July 1946 with good notices and terrible ratings. It went a full season without a sponsor, and the only reason it wasn't canceled was because the press supported it. CBS bit the bullet, hoping for a breakthrough. During the summer of 1947, Joan Davis, a comedienne with high ratings, had a falling out with her sponsor, and we got her time slot—Monday night at 8:30 E.S.T. Within eight weeks, "Talent Scouts" was in the top ten.

By the end of the year, we were number one most weeks. In those days, our lives and our blood pressure were regulated by the Trendex ratings. For the next two years, we almost never were beaten by any other show, and CBS was in constant ecstasy. A partial list of performers who made their debut on "Talent Scouts" includes Tony Bennett, Rosemary Clooney, Eddie Fisher, Gene Barry, Bobby Vinton, the McGuire Sisters, Pat Boone, Dick Shawn, Jonathan Winters, and Edie Adams.

When you are number one, the time period behind you becomes a treasure, and CBS made one of the smartest moves in history by putting there the incomparable Lucille Ball in a show called, "I Love Lucy." At first, CBS was not joyful about using her husband, Desi Arnaz, because his English was not too good. Lucille was adamant, and she was right. Before the first season was over, "I Love Lucy" was number one, and "Talent Scouts" was in second place. In 1949, "Talent Scouts" became a simulcast (radio and TV at the same time); the following year, the radio version was dropped.

In 1948, Milton Berle did eight television shows for NBC on Tuesday night, and his ratings went through the roof. As a result, he got the longest contract in history and probably sold more sets than any single force in the infant industry. He did for TV what Al Jolson and The Jazz Singer had done for talking pictures many years before.

In 1949, I proposed an idea to CBS called "This Is Show Business," that would let newcomers perform on the air before a panel of seasoned pros. When CBS gave me the go-ahead, I called Clifton Fadiman and explained the show to him. He asked who else would be on. Since I didn't know, I said I'd get back to him. I called Helen Hayes, who didn't know me from a hole in the wall but

[73]

graciously invited me up to her home in Nyack to present my idea. When she asked who else would be on, I told her Clifton Fadiman and George S. Kaufman. Problem: I didn't know Kaufman and had never even spoken to him. He was riding high at that point as a brilliant wit and playwright.

When I got home and told Jackie I hadn't the remotest idea who represented George S., she immediately went to work. She called her buddy Joan Castle, a stunning stage ingenue who said she was seeing good old George that very night. Jackie delegated Joan to get George's number. Joan came through with flying colors, and the next morning George called me. When we met and went over the idea, his expression never changed. All he said was, "How much money am I to receive for this?"

I told him, "Seven hundred and fifty dollars."

Again, without betraying by a single facial gesture whether he liked the idea or not, he surprised me by saying, "And where do I show up for all this happiness?"

My next call was to Abe Burrows in Hollywood to ask him if he could get away from his piano and his Girl with the Three Blue Eyes and come to New York. Within two weeks, Abe was in New York, and we were on the air (radio, then television) from July 1949 to September 1956. In 1953, Jack Benny replaced us every fourth week for a season until he went on regularly in his own time the following year.

Just before Christmas 1952, Kaufman created a tempest by remarking during the show, "Let's make this one program on which no one sings 'Silent Night.' " From the way the network switchboard lit up, you might have thought that George had repealed Christmas altogether. All he wanted to do was call attention to the overcommercialization of this beloved Christmas carol. But viewers were incensed.

Within a week, at least a thousand letters of protest poured in, and there were daily threats by the sponsor to cancel if Mr. Kaufman was not removed from the program. To the everlasting credit of CBS, the network held fast, Kaufman stayed on, and we got a new sponsor. It didn't hurt that Bishop Fulton Sheen backed George in a telegram to CBS.

Some of the performers who made their debut on "Show Business" were Joey Bishop, Charles Trenet, Jack E. Leonard, Carol Lawrence, Robert Clary, Paul Lynde, Sir John Gielgud (his American debut), Lenny Bruce, Pearl Bailey, Gary Morton, Sam Levenson, and Nat King Cole—and we almost had Edith Piaf.

Jackie was a big fan of "The Little Sparrow," and we went regularly to the Versailles, a night club where she was starring with Les Compagnons de la Chanson. One night, Piaf said to Jackie, "You come here every night. How can you afford it?"

Jackie said, "My husband is a television producer, and he would like to have you on his program." Piaf said she would watch the show the following Sunday. Two days later, Piaf agreed to go on, provided she could have her backup group with her. It was an expensive combination, but it didn't matter because I, too, was hooked on her. We arranged to meet at her apartment on the following Tuesday— this was in October 1949—to make arrangements for her to sing "*La Vie en Rose*" and "*Je ne Regrette Rien.*"

Unfortunately when I arrived at her apartment, I heard crying and moaning. That very morning, her lover, Marcel Cerdan, the fighter, had been killed in an airplane crash in the Azores. The mourners around her were the most agonized group I had ever seen. She never made my show, and Jackie and I were surprised to learn later that she did her own show at the Versailles the night of her loss.

Everyone in the world wanted to be on "Show Business." Agents and performers ambushed me in corridors and elevators. Jackie even got a call from her father. His old pal, Jack Kelly, had asked, "Hey, can you get my daughter Grace on your son-in-law's TV show?" Getting Grace Kelly on was no problem at all. She was a beautiful, articulate actress and a real catch for the program. I booked her immediately.

A comic named Sam Levenson, who had played some of the mountain resorts, made a big hit on "This Is Show Business." The warmth of his humor was so attractive that I was soon producing "The Sam Levenson Show." Sam became not only a star but my closest friend. When Abe Burrows left "Show Business" to write Guys and Dolls, Sam replaced him and worked beautifully with Clifton Fadiman. Often, "Talent Scouts" and "Show Business" were both in the top ten ratings, which gave me a one-two punch on Sunday and Monday nights.

Godfrey by then had a Wednesday night show called "Arthur Godfrey and his Friends," and his afternoon show had expanded from a half hour to an hour and then to ninety minutes. But Godfrey's attitude toward me and my friends was becoming unbearable, and I knew our relationship would soon end. But I didn't let it bother me; I had more serious problems. Our son was getting worse and would soon have to go away to a special school. That was my main concern, along with Jackie's growing panic over Guy.

When I finally left "Talent Scouts," my agent worked out a deal for a royalty payment and for a solo credit at the end of the show, both on the screen and spoken by the announcer. But Godfrey always tried to make the show run a little overtime so my name would neither be seen nor heard.

Ah, well, fame is a fleeting thing in television. One night about this time, I was at the bar at Toots Shor with Billy Rose and Mike Todd when I was approached by someone who looked vaguely familiar.

"Hey, Mandy," he said to me, "how are you?"

Mandy was my nickname at college, so I figured this guy must have been at NYU with me. "This is my wife Selma," he said. Then he said to me, "Hey, Mandy, isn't that Billy Rose and Mike Todd you're with? How come you know such big shots?"

"I'm in TV," I said.

"You are! Gee, wholesale or retail?"

Early in 1950, my good friend Eddie Weiner and I ran into Sherman Billingsley, who owned the Stork Club. Through the war years and the 1950s, the place was the delight of the debutantes. Rarely did a day pass without a picture in the papers of a young celebrity or a movie star visiting the famous Cub Room and Table Fifty, where Walter Winchell and Morton Downey entertained their friends. If you sat at Table Fifty, you had real clout.

Eddie and I were invited in for a drink, and as I watched the parade of celebrities, I had an idea. Why not do a televised talk show from the Cub Room at dinner time? Billingsley said it couldn't be done at dinner time because it would ruin his dinner business. But he owned the building, and upstairs there was a dentist's office and another huge room where Billingsley either made or packaged a perfume called Sortilege.

I suggested to Hubbell Robinson, vice president in charge of programs at CBS, that we do a talk show from the Stork Club with Peter Lind Hayes and Mary Healey as hosts.

I explained that the engineers and designers could reproduce the Cub Room upstairs for $150,000. He called the sales department and asked if there was a market for such a talk show. In forty minutes we got the answer. Liggett and Meyers would buy it out Monday through Friday.

During the next week I met with Billingsley's attorneys and with Steve Hannagan, his press adviser who wanted to know if there would be any trouble with the Federal Communications Commission.

"Why would we have trouble with them?"

"Didn't you know? Sherman was once in the slammer on a bootlegging charge."

I said, "It doesn't bother me a bit, but if he was in the slammer, how did he get a liquor license for this place?"

Hannagan told me the club was in somebody else's name. I said, "Steve, please don't tell me who owns it. I don't want to know."

We made a trial tape with the room jammed with celebrities. Even though we had to do the opening six times because Sherman never quite mastered his cue to say, "Welcome to the Stork Club." Peter and Mary were wonderful, and the show had a sparkling look.

When Jackie and I went to New England to see our son, I thought I'd left a happy group. But while I was gone—only three days—Sherman asked CBS to get rid of Peter and Mary, Yul Brynner, our director, and most of all, me.

CBS, of course, refused.

The show went on, but almost daily Sherman wanted to know why we needed Peter and Mary. After the show, Yul, his then wife, Virginia Gilmore, and Jackie and I usually had dinner together at the Stork Club. One night, Sherman asked to see me privately. I walked into the other room with him.

It's unbelievable, but here is what he said all in one sentence: "I just found out that Yul Brynner is a chink how did Jackie Gleason get in here with that loud necktie I wish you'd tell your friend Milton Berle to stay out of here he's making everybody around him laugh too loud for this room."

I finally screamed, "Oh, shut up! I'm running a TV show, not a restaurant. Besides, Sherman, I wish you'd get rid of that ridiculous toupee. You're getting more laughs than Berle. Don't you know it's about six sizes too big for you."

He said, "No kidding. This is the third one I got from Eddie Senz."

For the next few weeks, Sherman ordered more wigs than the Carnegie Delicatessen has matzoh balls. He also charged them to CBS.

[77]

Several months after the show started, we were driving home on a Sunday night, and we heard Winchell announce that Jackie and I were breaking up. We drove straight to the Stork Club to tell Winchell we had spent Sunday at Billingsley's home in Westchester with Mary and Peter. How could he do such a thing without checking with us first? Winchell said casually, "I guess you can blame it on Sherman, your new false friend."

I knew the jig was up. Yul was leaving to co-star with Gertrude Lawrence as the king in *The King and I*. Peter and Mary were annoyed that Sherman was doing interviews that didn't make sense. And Jackie said "Show Business" and the "Sam Levenson Show" were plenty to keep me busy—I should give up "The Stork Club."

Abe Burrows became the new producer and I was barred from the Stork Club.

On midnight, Saturday, October 7, 1950, Jackie and I came home from the movies to find in our mail box several urgent messages to call Harry Ommerle and Hubbell Robinson immediately. When I did, I found they were both sitting at the Barberry Room of the Berkshire Hotel.

"Did you see the Frank Sinatra show tonight?" Hubbell asked.

"No, we went to the movies. How was it?"

"Terrible. It was a disaster. Irving, can we have a meeting?"

"When?"

"Now."

I said, "Look, fellows, I only met Sinatra once in my life when I produced the Milton Berle radio show. I thought he was wonderful. Besides, how does the Sinatra show concern me?"

"We want you to take over the show and meet Frank."

"I'd like you to know, in case it slipped your mind, that tomorrow I'm producing 'This is Show Business' for CBS. How can I do two major shows? Besides, what makes you think Frank would want me? This whole conversation is crazy. Talk to Frank and call me at the Hammerstein Theatre tomorrow."

That Monday, I tried to convince CBS that I was too busy to be involved with the Sinatra show, and if Frank was so eager to have me do it, why wasn't he there? They talked about team spirit and my ability to organize things properly. (This came as a surprise to me.)

Hugh Wedlock, Howard Snyder, and Harry Crane, the writers on the show, were talented and couldn't write a bad show. Axel

Stordahl was the music director. I admired him. The regulars on the show were Ben Blue and Sid Fields, both talented, and the Moon Mists singing group, whom I didn't know.

Finally, Robinson and Ommerle asked everyone to leave the room, and they put it to me bluntly. "Do it for us and the next show you create goes on automatically. Now what salary do you want for this?"

If my agents from MCA had been there, there would have been a fist fight when they heard my answer. "I'll do it for one dollar a week." They stared at me. "I want one dollar a week and the right to quit on one week's notice."

For the next eight weeks, I produced the Sinatra show but I didn't know what was going on. I asked Frank if he would stay after the show so we could talk about future guest stars. But he was into his limo and on the way to L.A. before the applause was over. My only communication was through the writers, who knew what I was going through. Sinatra kept complaining about the stagehands being slow. But most of the time, *he* was two hours late, and that meant we had to throw out a sketch because it hadn't been rehearsed.

When we threw out a sketch, he filled in with songs from his repertoire. I will admit that he sang like a doll. Sometimes he did a bit with tea and a cup and saucer and got laughs like a professional comic—thanks to his talented writers.

One night, he invited me to dinner with the writers, and we sat upstairs at Toots Shor. I thought we were going to talk about future guests, but it never came up. I finally decided the hell with it and left the table.

The following Saturday night, he showed up late again, but it didn't bother me a bit. I had quit that morning.

During the rehearsal, I pressed the talk-back and said, "Frank, I think we better go over that bit again. The dynabeams were off, the curtain was too slow, the—"

He said, "I can't see in there. Who said that?"

I said, "Irving Mansfield."

He said, "Come on out here."

I walked out of the control booth, and he said, "Listen, pal, I don't have time today to do it again, and I don't care what you like or don't like. You don't like me, either, do you?"

I looked him squarely in the eye, and behind him I noticed the tension among his pals standing in the wings. Frank Sinatra is surrounded by a dedicated group of people who speak only in hushed, worshipful whispers. The die was cast.

"Frank, as an artist, you are incomparable. Nobody can touch you. But where you're a failure is as a human being!"

It was about eight o'clock in the evening, but as far as the stage was concerned, it was freezing at "High Noon."

*W*hat was life with Jackie like? It was a roller coaster. It was a merry-go-round with plunging horses at full gallop and the riders' arms outstretched for the brass ring—no, the gold ring, the solid gold ring.

In other words, there was never a dull moment.

The one thing that was steady was our love. We always loved each other, through joys and sorrows, through disasters and triumphs. The love was rock solid. Sometimes we expressed it through joking and bantering. At other times, we prayed together. We were always honest with each other. Many times I was protective of Jackie, but never at the expense of honesty. I was faithful to her through the thirty-five years of our marriage, and I believe she was faithful to me.

I decided early in our marriage that I would never win small arguments. I never tried to and never did. After we had been married about fifteen years, Jackie once said, "How is it that every time I want to go somewhere or do something, you say it's okay?"

"What's wrong with that?" I asked. "Isn't that an ideal situation?" I suppose I could really have been sore at her question after all the rotten movies and lousy restaurants she had dragged me to.

"No, it isn't. It shows a lack of spirit on your part."

I just looked at her and then said, "Jackie, do you want me to argue about everything?"

She said, "Yes, I'd like to see a little spirit."

Take my word, there was plenty of spirit in our marriage. But if Jackie wanted some action, I was agreeable enough to give it to her. So a little later I said to her, "You know, maybe you're right about lack of spirit. I think from now on I'm going to be a free soul."

"What do you mean, a free soul?"

"I'm going to find myself a young, beautiful, attractive woman, and I'm going to have an affair with her."

"You're kidding."

"No, I want to show you some independence on my part."

She said, "Listen, if I hear one word, one nuance from anybody that you're fooling around, I won't have to hear from anybody, I'll *know*! I tell you there won't be one stick of furniture left in this goddamned apartment."

I thought that was the end of it and that it had been a pretty good joke. But for several weeks Jackie was very suspicious of me. She didn't ask any questions—we never asked each other what we did or where we went—but I could see she was taking what I had said seriously. I finally said, "You know, I was only kidding."

But I think she was mad—not that I'd had or not had an affair—but that I'd even *thought* of the idea. She didn't want me to be that much of a free spirit.

A woman I don't like at all once called up Jackie and told her I was involved with a young girl at a night club. Jackie told the woman to mind her own damned business and didn't say a word about it to me for six months. Then, when we were having an argument about something altogether different, she said, "And what about your little romance with that girl at the club?"

There had been no romance. I would never do that to Jackie. I wouldn't do it for a lot of reasons, and one of the most important was that it would show a lack of respect for Jackie. A husband can often get away with a small frolic and pay for it with only a bit of gossip, a few winks, some leers. But his wife is humiliated, and how can you humiliate someone you love? I couldn't.

Jackie had her crushes. One of her wildest was on Yul Brynner. She was completely captivated by his mysterious blue-green eyes and gave them to several of her fictional characters, particularly to Yargo, the hero of her science-fiction novel. Another crush was on Ian McKellan, the fantastic English actor whom we saw in London alternating Shakespeare and Marlowe. She was so in love with him that she named our second dog, Josephine's successor, Joseph Ian in his honor and sent him a telegram: "Today a poodle, tomorrow the world."

Jackie sometimes got annoyed that I took her crushes so calmly. "Why is it you don't object when I go crazy about someone? I think you wouldn't even care if I ran off with Clark Gable."

"You can't do that," I told her. "Clark Gable's dead."

When Rex Reed was interviewing her, he once said, "Jackie, I know your marriage is like a rock, but suppose, just suppose you were to have a fling with someone. Who would it be?"

Quick as a flash, she said, "It would be between George C. Scott and Mick Jagger."

Rex was astonished by her answer, and every time he saw her, he asked, "Which one did you get?"

If Jackie had one great fault, it was that her tongue was sometimes quicker than her discretion. She shot from the lip and was often sorry afterward. Even as the barbed quip or the sharp word came out, Jackie often knew she was saying something wrong, but she couldn't help herself. In England once, everyone was applauding the announcement that Sir Lew Grade had been given the rights to weekend television as an alternative to the BBC. Jackie said, "That's great. Now you'll have two kinds of TV—high grade and lew grade." That was unkind and unnecessary, and she knew it.

But at other times her cracks were well earned. *Portnoy's Complaint*, which examined masturbation, was the book that *Love Machine* had to beat for the number-one spot on the bestseller list. When Oscar Dystel, president of Bantam Books, once asked Jackie what she thought of Philip Roth, the author of *Portnoy*, she said, "He's a fine writer, but I wouldn't want to shake hands with him." That line swept New York like a prairie fire, and people still quote it.

When *Valley of the Dolls* was about to be published in England, Jackie received a cable from the publisher that read: "I WOULD LIKE YOUR CONSENT TO CUT OUT F--K THROUGHOUT BOOK STOP IF YOU CAN AGREE WILL GREATLY INCREASE SUCCESS EMPIRE MARKET STOP." Jackie cabled back: "F--K YOU. LOVE JACKIE SUSANN." The publisher ignored her instructions.

Sometimes she was funny without knowing it. As an inveterate people watcher and a people listener from her earliest days, she listened everywhere, especially to the gossip around the pool at the Beverly Hills Hotel, the richest and purest source of big-name gossip in the world. Jackie even listened in at restaurants. Once we were sitting at the table next to Winston Churchill's son Randolph and his then wife, who were engaged in a knock-down, drag-out argument. Jackie was so closely tuned in to the battle that when I handed her a menu and said, "What do you want to eat?" she gave me a shove with her elbow and hissed, "Ssshhh, don't interrupt me."

When a young woman who wanted to get on "Talent Scouts" sent in a suggestive photo of herself and wrote, "I'll do anything to get on your show—and when I say anything, I mean anything," Jackie intercepted the note and wrote back, "I am Mrs. Mansfield, and I do everything for my husband—and when I say everything, *I mean everything.*"

No question, Jackie was volatile. She exploded easily. She went wild when I was late and kept her waiting. One night, I sent her ahead to an important Broadway opening. I had an emergency to straighten out at one of my shows. I told her I'd be there in about fifteen minutes. But the play was into the third act before I got there. When I reached the theater, she gave me the cold treatment, and later in the restaurant, where we joined friends for supper, she was still chilly. Jackie and her friends were doing quite a bit of drinking, so at two A.M., I went home and asked them to drop her off:

At home, I figured I hadn't made such a smart move. I called the restaurant, but Jackie had gone. I waited a half hour, got frantic, and started calling her friends. She was at Anna Sosenko's and wouldn't talk to me. In the morning, our dog Josephine jumped off the bed with a wild whooosh, so I knew Jackie was coming in the door. Without speaking to me, she got out her suitcase and started packing. I tried to apologize for being late at the theater and leaving the restaurant, but she was neither listening nor talking.

Jackie said good-by to Josephine, not to me, and was out the door, with Josie howling to follow her. I talked to Anna, who told me that Jackie was really livid. I figured she had gone to her mother's and called her there that night. No answer. Then I tried the Ritz in Atlantic City. Her mother got on the phone and said, "Irving, Jackie does not want to talk to you."

I said, "Well, do you want to talk to me?"

She said, "Sure, how are you? But if Jackie's going to be mad at you, then I'm mad at you."

I said, "Okay, please tell her I love her."

I went to the movies, called when I got home, but got no answer. They were probably at a bingo parlor. The following day, I sent about fifty dollars' worth of flowers and a note: "What happened to our promise that we would never go to bed without speaking to each other? Whatever happened was my fault. I'm sorry and I love you."

No word, nothing. She still wouldn't speak to me when I called that night. Okay, it was time to be inventive. I sent her a telegram to be delivered immediately: "You know how much I love you. Life is not the same without you. Love, Irving. P.S. Guess who moved in next door?"

I went to the movies again, took Josephine for a walk, and went to bed. About twelve o'clock, Josephine jumped off the bed with a blood-curdling scream. I heard Jackie's footsteps in the hall, and I heard her giving the bellboy a tip for bringing in her things. She marched in and said to me, "Okay, you bastard, who moved in next door?"

I said, "Some very nice people."

She said, "You knew that would get me. I'm going back to Atlantic City."

I said, "Wait a little bit and I'll go with you."

She started to laugh and said, "Isn't it terrible—I went for it."

You know something—everything was fine.

Jackie had been frustrated when she lost her fifty dollars in a single roll at the crap table with Joe E. Lewis. Someone else might have sworn off gambling at that point. But not Jackie. She became hooked. She would bet on anything. Every Sunday, we called a bookmaker and bet on the big football games. We went to the first Muhammad Ali fight with Joe Frazier at Madison Square Garden. Jackie knew I had bet on Frazier. She started screaming for Muhammad Ali. If it had been the other way around, if I had screamed for the fighter she had bet against, I'd have heard about it for the next thirty years. But Jackie felt it was okay to root for Muhammad Ali—he lived in our building, and she had once helped him pick out a necktie.

Jackie thought she was a great twenty-one player, but she was really terrible at it. Even if she had seventeen, she'd say, "Hit me." She just couldn't bear to let a hand pass her by. She hated to fold. At roulette, she liked to play twenty because she was born on August 20 and twenty-three because July 23 was my birthday. She had mysterious little combinations that rarely made sense, and she played certain corners that appealed to her. But it didn't matter because she was having a good time.

She adored poker. Her interest in that game started with something that happened to me on her first trip to California. When we arrived that night, we had drinks at Chasen's, and Ernie Kovacs, whose show I was producing, dropped Jackie off at the Beverly Hills Hotel. I went along with him to his home at Beaumont Drive for about an hour of poker with two of his friends. But the next thing I knew, I looked up and saw daylight. I said, "Oh, my God, I've got to go home." They kept me for another round.

When I got back to the hotel, it was six o'clock. Jackie turned over and said, "How did you do?"

I said, "I think I lost sixteen hundred dollars." She didn't say anything. We slept until about ten, woke up, and ordered breakfast with that wonderful, fresh-squeezed California orange juice and a single rose on the tray. Jackie said, "You know, it's funny, but I have this wild idea that you told me you lost sixteen hundred dollars."

I said, "That's right."

She said, "How could you lose sixteen hundred dollars?"

"I lost it."

"That's terrible. Are you going to get it back?"

I said, "Yes."

"How?"

I picked up my glass of orange juice. I said, "See this juice. It costs a dollar eighty." It did then. "If we live here three years and I never order orange juice again, we'll be even." We didn't know then that the hotel would be our second home for the next fifteen years.

Then Jackie started playing poker seriously. In New York, she got into a regular Monday night poker game with Dave Garroway and Lee J. Cobb. I think she was the only woman in the game. One night, she lost $3,600. By the time it hit the newspapers, her loss was up to $36,000 or $400,000 or something ridiculous. The real $3,600 was bad enough. I heard later that she conferred with six of her girl friends before she got the courage to break the news to me.

She always remembered one hand in which she and Lee J. Cobb stayed to the end and then lost to the third player. Lee said to her, "Why is it, Jackie, that nice people like you and me are always the losers?"

Jackie said, "I don't think you're a loser. I think you're a winner."

He said, "I'm talking about cards."

She said, "Never mind about cards. Cards are not important. You're a winner in life. That's what's important."

Lee never forgot.

Jackie's worst gambling adventure occurred when Flo, a friend of hers, started taking her to a semiprofessional poker game on nights when I was busy with a show. The game went on every night in an apartment building on the West Side. At one table, they played for one or two dollars; at another for five and ten, and at a third for table stakes.

"Do the police know about this place?" Jackie asked the first time she went there.

"I think they do," Flo said, "but they get paid off."

The other players recognized Jackie, but they called her Miss S. Everyone was known only by an initial. At first, Jackie played at the one- and two-dollar table. She had $90 with her, bought $85 worth of chips and kept $5 for the taxi home. The $85 was gone in no time. She signed a marker for $200 in chips, lost the $200, and decided she wanted to get into the five and ten game. She signed another marker for $500, and that was gone in a flash.

The trouble was that Jackie couldn't let a pot go by. She'd bet on anything—even a two and a five. When she got home that night and told me she had lost $900, I said, "You know, there's a rule in poker that you have to have a hole card that is as high or higher than almost any upturned card on the table."

She said, "No kidding." Then she bought a book on poker and soon was playing three nights a week. I don't think she ever came home a winner.

One night, someone walked into that semipro game and said, "This place is under arrest."

Jackie said, "Hold it. I have kings back to back."

The officer said, "Okay, Miss Susann." He recognized her right away. But, of course, everybody else dropped out, so all she got was the original round of bets. Then all the players were hauled off to the local precinct house and signed in as Mr. X or Miss X. It was a token arrest, like a scene out of *Guys and Dolls*.

After that, I called her "jailbird."

Gambling had such a strong hold on her that years later when our dear friends Frenchy and Marty Allen took us to the Riviera in Las Vegas to see Shecky Green's act because he was going to play the important role of the comic in *The Love Machine*, Jackie wandered off with $200 in silver dollars in the direction of the dollar slot machines. She found a way of putting five single dollars in at one time. Shecky was really brilliant that night, but Jackie didn't hear a word. She was married to that machine. When we pried her away at four in the morning, she had managed to lose $700 in a dollar machine, and her arm was stiff for a week.

Later, when Shecky knocked the picture, I couldn't exactly blame him. That was not one of Jackie's shining moments.

Her friend Anna Sosenko taught her to play backgammon, and by the second lesson, she wanted to play for money. Anna, of course, kept winning. After a while, Anna was so embarrassed by her winnings that she asked me to help figure out a way to give the money back. "Can't you let her win once in a while?" I asked.

"I've been trying," Anna said.

Eventually, Jackie started winning from time to time. Then she read of a backgammon competition at the Hotel Plaza. She wanted to enter. I tried to tell her that this was out of her league, but it was hopeless. I was too embarrassed to go with her, but Anna went along. She played in the medium-level group—not the top players and not the worst—and would you believe it? She won.

She loved to win.

One of the few things Jackie was frugal about was typing paper. She always swiped paper from offices. She didn't care whether it was first sheets, second sheets, or onionskin, she'd filch what she could. She loved to pocket paper clips. She'd drop her treasure trove on her desk and exclaim, "Hey, look what I got." She did it even in the years when she could have bought the paper-clip company along with the clips she needed.

Another thing that brought out her chintzy impulse was the room rate at the Beverly Hills Hotel. Every time we stepped into our regular suite there, she'd quickly drop her bag on the bed and open the closet door where the price of the room was posted. At each check-in, the rate was usually eight to ten dollars a day higher than the last time, and Jackie would exclaim, "Hey, doll, it's up to one hundred and seventy-five dollars." Then a month or so later, "Guess what, it's one hundred and eighty-five dollars."

We made our last trip to the hotel in the spring of 1974 when they were filming *Once Is Not Enough*. Jackie was in terrible shape—she had just a few months to live—and we had most of our meals in the room. But one night she said, "How about getting all dressed up tonight and going to the dining room for dinner."

I was so delighted she was feeling well enough that I agreed immediately. We got dressed, and as we headed for the door, she

Jackie's father, Robert Susan, a noted Philadelphia portrait painter.

Rose Susan, Jackie's mother, in a portrait painted by her husband.

LEFT:
At the tender age of seven months, Jackie being kissed by her adoring father.

BELOW:
The two of us at eight months. That's Jackie on the right and me on the left.

Jackie, age four, and her mother enjoying the Boardwalk at Atlantic City.

Posing on the Atlantic City beach is a fourteen-year-old Jackie.

Her first break, being chosen "most beautiful girl in Philadelphia" by famed showman Earl Carroll (left of Jackie), and Sam Saxe (on her right). (1935)

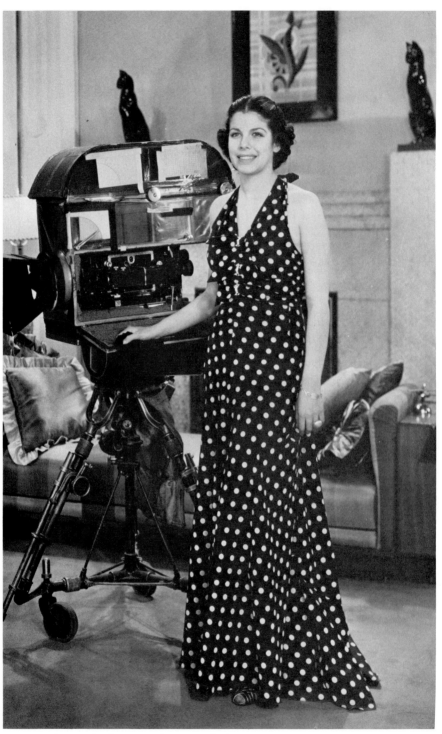

As a result of winning the contest, Jackie gets a screen test at Warner Bros.

Bea Cole and Jackie, the budding playwrighting team, at the typewriter given to Jackie by Goodman Ace.

Jackie, a young Guy Mansfield, and myself having fun on the Jersey shore.

A later picture of Guy, giving us his beautiful wide-open smile.

ABOVE:
Robert Susan squiring his daughter to a nightclub in 1949.

RIGHT:
A loving wife, Jackie giving me a goodbye kiss before I head to work on Talent Scouts.

One of my first clients, famed correspondent Dorothy Thompson, and myself at a Nazi Bund rally in 1937.

Another client, the inimitable Fred Allen, and I having a skull session for his radio show.

BELOW:
With Arthur Godfrey, going through a rehearsal for Talent Scouts.

ABOVE:

Bea Lillie, a guest on my controversial Stork Club *show.*

LEFT:

Jackie, along with other stars in Clare Booth Luce's hit play "The Women." That's Margalo Gillmore (left) and Jean Cooley (center). (1937)

Jackie's first professional photograph, taken in 1937, when she was only nineteen.

ABOVE:

Jackie on stage with friend Eddie Cantor in the Broadway hit "Banjo Eyes."

RIGHT:

Off-stage and on the golf course at the Roney Plaza with Walter Winchell.

BELOW:

Before the television cameras, Jackie doing one of her Schiffli embroidery commercials.

Jackie makes an appearance on This is Show Business *with regulars (l-r) Sam Levenson, Clifton Fadiman, and George S. Kaufman. (1952)*

At Sardi's after an opening, Jackie has dinner with our dearest friends Joyce and Billy Rose. (1957)

The celebrated poodle, Josephine, tries to upstage her chronicler.

turned back and said, "You go down first, and then when you get back, I'll go have dinner."

"But wasn't the whole idea for us to eat together?" I asked.

"I know, but how can we both go? The management will see us leave together, and someone will sneak in here and raise the room rate."

Although we kidded about the rates, we were enormously fond of Muriel and Burt Slatkin, who owned the hotel. Muriel was the daughter of Ben Silberstein, a big real estate operator from Detroit who had taken his family out West in 1953 and stayed at the Beverly Hills Hotel. Muriel fell in love with the place and said, "Daddy, if you really want me to take an interest in real estate, just buy me this hotel."

He did, and Muriel and her husband eventually went to live there. Jackie and I became intimate friends of the Slatkins, and Muriel and Jackie went shopping together, exchanged confidences, and were close "girl friends."

Jackie, as a person, went through a number of stages. In the beginning, she was all innocence and vulnerability; it was that wide-eyed quality that first attracted me to her. I suppose time robs everyone of innocence, but Jackie lost her early-morning freshness in a hurry during the terrible years when we struggled with our son Guy's problems. She developed a protective shell to fortify herself against wave after wave of bad news. Or maybe you could say a kind of steel entered her character.

Later, she needed that steel to carry on, as she did after her mastectomy. Later still, she needed it to stay self-chained to her typewriter month after month when she was writing *Valley of the Dolls*, especially after the failure of all her previous writing efforts. And in the end she needed it to go out with her head high and colors flying.

Jackie was always kind and generous to her mother; she bought her beautiful jewelry and furs. Every year she gave a birthday party for her mother to which she invited all her mother's friends and supplied them with all the Dom Perignon champagne and caviar they could eat. The women looked forward all year to that party. Jackie basically loved her mother and loved her very deeply, but she often showed it in an exasperated sort of way because Rose Susan was sometimes hard to take.

We made countless trips to Philadelphia through the years to

[89]

visit her or met her in Atlantic City where she and Jackie were instantly off to the nearest bingo parlor. Mrs. Susan was the last to survive of our parents, and after Jackie died, she became my responsibility. I saw to it that she had nurses and the best medical care following her stroke in 1968 and that she was properly looked after in her last years when she was in a wheelchair. She outlived Jackie by nearly seven years and died in January 1981.

Jackie was always good to my mother and father. Many women consider their mother-in-law a pain, but Jackie treated my mother like her own and got from her the warm, enveloping kind of mothering she had never known before. Jackie called my mother Annie, phoned her every day when I was away, and loved to give her presents.

After my father died, we sent my mother to the Concord Hotel every summer and to Florida in winter. On her first trip, my mother was worried that she didn't have the right clothes, so Jackie took her to Florence Lustig, from whom she bought a lot of her own lovely outfits, and bought my mother several dresses that cost about $135 each. But knowing that my mother was not used to such expensive clothes (this was nearly thirty years ago) and would probably refuse such an extravagant gift, she told her that the dresses cost thirty-five dollars each. In a week, my mother was on the phone, saying, "Mrs. Braff loved the dresses you gave me, and when I told her they only cost thirty-five dollars, she asked if you would pick up a couple for her, size fourteen. And could you get two for Mrs. Rosen, size twelve? Is that too much to ask?"

Gently, Jackie had to tell my mother that it was too much.

The years she was in the public eye, Jackie adored buying exquisitely made designer clothes. For travel, she thought that Emilio Pucci's printed silk jerseys were unbeatable. She could roll them up in a bag, then unroll them without a wrinkle. Their bold patterns photographed very distinctively, although Rex Reed once wrote disparagingly of her "banana print" dresses. (He was right.) For evening, she had wonderful gowns designed by Stavropoulous and by Donald Brooks, and hand beaded and sequinned outfits by Swee Lo.

When we were in Paris in 1960, through CBS we were invited to the couture showing at the House of Chanel. The room was crowded; there was only one seat up front alongside Audrey Hepburn and Sophie Litvak, the wife of the producer Anatole Litvak. Jackie signed the guest book as we went in and took the seat. I stood in the back. The clothes were magnificent, and one suit, in particular, made

Jackie gasp with pleasure. Later that day, there was a knock on our door at the Ritz, and a messenger delivered a package from the House of Chanel. Jackie opened it—it was the suit she had admired. A little note on Ritz stationery tucked into the pocket said, "In appreciation for the light in your eyes, Coco Chanel."

Knowing that Mlle. Chanel had an apartment at the Ritz, Jackie struggled with the house phone until she reached the couturière, said she loved the suit, then murmured something about buying it, since we didn't know whether it was a gift or a mistake or what. We did know it had to cost thousands of dollars.

"Oh, it's my gift to you," Chanel told Jackie.

Jackie said, "I'm overwhelmed—I don't know if I can accept."

"It is an insult to give it back, a big insult. Will you come some weekend as my guest to my place in the country?"

Jackie said, "I'd love to. I'm here with my husband—"

" 'usband? 'usband?" There was a click on the phone, and that was the end of that. Jackie kept the suit.

Jackie discovered pants sometime after Marlene Dietrich and before the rest of the female population. She always wore pants for sports and leisure, and Georgio on Rodeo Drive ran up a handsome midnight blue tuxedo for her for evening. She was a great collector of beautifully tailored silk shirts. But her all-time favorite outfit, I think, was what I called her Marlon Brando get-up: black slacks, a black leather jacket, like a bombardier's jacket, and a little black Dutch wool cap. Rudolf Nureyev, our neighbor at the Navarro, had a cap exactly like hers, and they always tipped their caps to each other when they passed in the neighborhood. Jackie wore this outfit when she walked Josephine and later Joseph Ian in the park.

Although Jackie was famous for her great mane of black hair, she really had very little hair. It was thin, baby fine, and hard to manage. Also, it went gray very early. There were already a few silvery flickers when we first met. "If I ever come back here, I'd like to have hair, lots of hair," she used to say. She skillfully created the illusion of luxuriant hair with falls and hairpieces. She pinned these on, tucked them in and among her own hair, brushed and teased her hair over the inserts, and lo! the great head of tresses. She had falls and wigs of various lengths and often traveled with half a dozen different hair-pieces. With the help of her hairdresser, she kept her own hair a shimmering blue black.

Because her front teeth were a tiny bit irregular, she had them capped back when our son was a baby and had the capping redone several times through the years. In Paris, in the summer of 1960, someone mentioned that she looked a little tired. That's all she had to hear. She made a series of inquiries, got the name and address of a world-famous plastic surgeon, and had the area under her eyes tucked up a little bit.

Jackie was a great reader, reading two or three books a week. She read all the current books and gradually caught up with the classics and the important ones she had missed by not going to college. Early in our marriage, she asked Clifton Fadiman to give her a reading list. He drew up one that included *Moby Dick, U.S.A.*, by Dos Passos, *Washington Square, Anna Karenina, The Magic Mountain*, books by Faulkner, Thurber, Virginia Woolf, Dostoevski, George Santayana, the short stories of Katherine Anne Porter, and he told her to get a copy of *Fowler's English Usage*.

Jackie read right through his list, but her attention span for heavy books was not always unlimited. On a plane once, she was working her way through *The Gulag Archipelago*. After an hour of dogged concentration, she glanced over to my seat and asked, "How soon will you be through with that *Playboy?*"

The older she got, the more she regretted having only a high school education. She loved to talk to students, tell them to stay with their studies, learn their trades, prepare themselves the best way they could for the world. Once when she was telling the members of a college writing club never to give up, to ignore the rejections and keep going, a young girl raised her hand and said, "Miss Susann, may I ask you a personal question?"

"Sure."

"I notice that a lot of authors don't have their name in front of the title of their books. It's *Gone with the Wind* by Margaret Mitchell or *The Source* by James Michener. Why are yours always Jacqueline Susann *The Love Machine*—with your name first?"

I was sitting up front, and I began to worry for Jackie. How was she going to answer this one? But Jackie was unflappable. She said, "I'd like to ask the audience a question. How many of you know who wrote *The Wizard of Oz?*" Four people raised their hands.

"Okay. How many know who wrote *Ben Hur?*" Nobody put up a hand.

Then she asked, "How many know who wrote *Valley of the Dolls?*" Every hand went up. "Does that answer your question?"

Then, a few minutes later, as we were getting into the car, Jackie said to me, "Who wrote *Ben Hur?*"

Much earlier, when Jackie was still trying to beat her way into the theater, a casting agent named Myra Streger went up to her and said, "I'm casting for a George S. Kaufman play, and I think you're perfect for a part." She told Jackie where to go for an audition. Jackie did not tell the woman that she knew Kaufman through "This Is Show Business," which I was producing. But she went to try out. Jackie always went.

When she got up on stage in the darkened theater, Miss Streger said to Kaufman and Max Gordon, who were sitting in the audience, "Isn't she perfect for the part?"

Kaufman took one look at Jackie, said, "I think not," and he and Gordon got up and walked out without another word.

Jackie was crushed and upset for days. Then, about six months later, Jackie was booked as a guest on "This Is Show Business." When the panelists began talking about cruelty in show business, Jackie said—on the air, mind you—"Something very cruel happened to me," and proceeded to tell the story about Kaufman, who was sitting there right next to her.

When she finished, Fadiman said, "George, were you guilty of such terrible conduct?"

George Kaufman said, "Don't believe a word of it. The whole thing is apocryphal."

Poor Jackie. That was the only time in my life I saw her floored. Her problem was that she did not know the word apocryphal and had no way of guessing that Mr. Kaufman had humiliated her a second time by accusing her of making up the whole thing. Needless to say, George S. Kaufman was not one of the people Jackie admired most.

One of my all-time favorite Jackie incidents occurred when we were living at the Navarro Hotel. Our neighbors across the hall were Lynn and Frank Loesser, the song writer. They were lovely neighbors, and we were very friendly with them. About that time, I had brought Abe Burrows, the gifted comedy writer, to New York to appear on "This Is Show Business." Late one afternoon during the Christmas season, Lynn Loesser rang our doorbell and said, "Jackie, we're having quite a few people up tonight. Do you have any extra ice cubes?"

Jackie gave Lynn all the ice trays we had in our freezer.

A little later, our bell rang. It was Abe Burrows and his wife Carin. They just wanted to say hello to us; they were on their way to the party across the hall. In a few minutes, the bell rang again. It was Ernie Martin and Cy Feuer looking for the Loessers' apartment. We thought that rather odd—that the Loessers had invited so many of our friends to their party, had even borrowed our ice cubes, but hadn't invited us. We had no explanation, so we had a quiet evening and went to bed. From the sounds in the hall, the party broke up about twelve-thirty. We were still awake, and Jackie began to do a real burn. She got madder and madder, and finally, at three o'clock, she got up, put on her bathrobe, and rang the Loessers' doorbell.

Through their front door, we could hear Frank say to Lynn, "I wonder who the hell that is at this hour?" then Frank called out, "Who is it?"

Jackie said, "It's Jackie."

Lynn asked, "Jackie, do you know what time it is?"

"Sure, it's three o'clock."

Lynn asked, "What do you want?"

Jackie said, "Please open the door."

They opened the door, and Jackie said, "I'd like to have my ice trays back."

That was life with Jackie Susann.

he decade of the 1950s, a great time professionally for me, was, for the most part, a down time for Jackie. Nothing seemed to work for her. The writing projects with Bea, for which she had had such high hopes, dribbled away to nothing.

Then one day I came home and found her at the typewriter.

"Another play?" I asked.

"No, a book about way out there." She pointed skyward with her finger.

Long before the general public took off on space odysseys, Jackie had been a fan of science fiction. She devoured all the books on the subject and demanded new ones at the bookstores. Now she was busy writing a science-fiction novel. The hero of Jackie's fable was Yargo, a gorgeous creature from another planet with a shaved head and eyes that "were large, emerald green in color, almond in shape and so beautiful that they appeared almost unnatural." I hardly have to tell you that that was our old friend Yul Brynner, on whom Jackie had such a terrific crush.

The heroine was Janet Cooper, a small-town girl with a no-nonsense mother who had once won a beauty contest at a summer resort and was now about to marry a very proper young man. Recognize her? Of course, our old friend Jackie Susann. Janet /Jackie was snatched away aboard a UFO and fell in love out there in the galaxies with Yargo of the emerald-green eyes. It was a sweet, romantic tale, rather slight but charming.

In the summer of 1956, when we were sailing home from Europe on the *Liberté*, we ran into George Chasin, an important agent. Jackie just happened to have the manuscript with her and gave it to George. George promised to read it and get in touch with us. He submitted the script to a number of movie companies but was not able to stir up any interest. Once more, Jackie was terribly discouraged.

"It's always that quart of vinegar with the glass of wine," she said, and put *Yargo* out of her mind. Four years after Jackie's death, a copy of the forgotten book surfaced. It was published by the *Ladies' Home Journal*, which pointed out that "it reflects the idealism and imagination of the young Susann." Bantam Books published it in paperback. It was selected by the Doubleday Book Club and became Jackie's fifth consecutive novel to appear on the bestseller list. But it brought no comfort to Jackie when she needed it.

I don't think there was ever a particular morning when Jackie woke up and said to herself, "Face it, doll, you're not going to make it on Broadway." She never really admitted defeat on the stage. In fact, she made a last, valiant try many years later in *The Madwoman of Chaillot*, after she had had two novels hit number one on the bestseller lists.

But simple reality—and Jackie never turned her back on reality— told her that she was not going to be Gertrude Lawrence, or even Helen Hayes. All right, she decided, then maybe she could be *someone* on television. That medium had certainly been kind to me. Maybe it would catapult her to stardom. She tried every approach that she or anyone else could imagine: actress, hostess, interviewer, commentator, advice giver, voice-over. I suspect she would have learned to juggle if a producer had promised her a prime-time spot. I was about to say she would have done a dog act—but just wait. In a sense, that's exactly what she did.

In the meantime, even if success still eluded her, Jackie led an extraordinarily rich life with her friends. Someone once said to me that only-children are especially good at making friends. That was certainly true of Jackie. She had a way of getting close to someone very quickly. I guess it was her warmth and the genuineness of her interest. She really listened when a stranger or a friend shared a confidence. She remembered and took the trouble to follow up.

Jackie always listened eagerly to my stories of what went on in the office and the studio. She enjoyed my success as much as I did. I loved her for her enthusiasm. Every day when I got home, we had a drink, and I had to give her a full accounting of my day's events. She demanded every last tidbit of gossip I had collected. She was the best audience in the world. And she often came up with marvelous ideas.

At the time when I was racking my brains for bigger and newer celebrities to guest on "Show Business," Jackie said, "If you want someone hard to get, why don't you get Garbo?"

I looked at her in amazement. Of course! It was a perfect idea. Do you realize what a triumph that would have been? Garbo was already, back then, a famous recluse. Still a relatively young woman, she lived a hermit's existence on the East Side of Manhattan, accepted no invitations, went to no public events, but was often spotted striding around in a heavy coat, a pulled-down hat, and flat-heeled brogues.

I got in touch with George Schlee, a businessman who was one of Garbo's few friends. He arranged for me to meet him on a Friday afternoon at the Ritz Tower Hotel, where Garbo lived under the name of Harriet Brown. I explained that Garbo could be a panelist and sit between Abe Burrows and George S. Kaufman, or if she preferred, she could be a guest and do a four- or five-minute spot on the show, perhaps a recitation from one of her films.

Schlee wanted to know if the show had a studio audience. When I told him it did, he said that would be an obstacle. Miss Garbo would never appear before an audience. This was before tape, so there was no way to tape her alone and then insert the tape into the show, but I said perhaps we could do a remote—meaning we would photograph her live from her home or any place she chose.

When it came to talk of money, I heard myself offering Mr. Schlee $25,000 for the five-minute appearance of Greta Garbo. That was an unheard-of fee for a guest appearance at that time. But I think the money may have been tempting because Schlee said he would let me know. As I left, I heard a mouselike sound behind a partially closed door and knew Garbo had been listening all along.

The story reached the newspapers, and there were headlines all over: "Garbo Offered 25G for Five Minutes on TV." It was great publicity for my show and for me. But Schlee called me a day or two later to report, "Miss Garbo says she skipped radio and now she's going to skip TV, too. But thank you for asking her."

I said, "Thank you for considering it."

We got another big round of publicity on the turndown. Then Hubbell Robinson said to me, "Irving, how were you planning to get that twenty-five thousand dollars to pay Garbo? You know that's way over your budget."

"I tell you what," I said, looking him in the eye. "You could have taken it out of my salary at a dollar a week."

Jackie was disappointed that the Garbo caper never came off and even more disgruntled by the Walter Winchell venture, since she had a hand in it. One day, while I was still doing the Stork Club show, Jackie came home and said, "A funny thing happened to me today. I was sitting at the counter at Rumpelmayer's and guess who sat down next to me—Walter Winchell."

I knew there had to be more, so I waited.

"He said, 'Hey, Jackie, how come I never hear from your husband anymore since he's become such a hot-shot producer?' "

We both knew this was an odd statement by Winchell since I'd never been in the habit of calling him or going to see him. Like everybody else around Broadway, we ran into him at openings or at Lindy's or at the Stork Club and sometimes on the putting green at the Roney Plaza in Florida. But we were not phone pals.

"What do you suppose he wants?" Jackie asked.

"Let's find out."

I typed him a little note, saying, "I'm always available to you. Where and when and who's mad at whom?" and signed it, The Hot-shot Producer.

Shortly after that, we arranged a meeting in the lobby of my hotel. Winchell was not a man to make small talk unless the subject was himself. He said right off, "If you could get a schmuck like Billingsley on the air, maybe you could get me over to CBS. Remember, Paley gave me my first job at CBS in 1938."

This was a sensational request. Winchell was one of the hottest properties on the air and the crown jewel at ABC. If I could capture him for CBS, the CBS brass would have to give me my own parade up Madison Avenue.

The next morning, I flew into the office of Bill Gittinger, executive vice president of business affairs for CBS radio, and said, "How would you like to have Walter Winchell on CBS every Sunday night at nine?"

He instantly started arranging meetings, and I left a message at the St. Moritz for Winchell to call me when he got up. It was five in the afternoon when he called back and asked, "Well, am I CBS's new star?"

We set an appointment for two days later at Sherman Billingsley's office at the Stork Club. When I went to pick up Gittinger for the meeting, I gulped to see that CBS chairman and chief executive officer Bill Paley and CBS president Dr. Frank Stanton were joining us. CBS had called out its biggest guns.

At the Stork Club, Winchell opened the conversation with a fifteen-minute harangue about his ratings, his syndication, the lack of appreciation from Jergens, his sponsor, the lack of promotion from his network, and the inadequacy of his pay for the huge ratings he was delivering. I think he was getting $5,000 a week and wanted twice that.

Mr. Paley indicated that CBS was definitely interested if Winchell was free to make the switch and if the CBS legal department could go over his contract. The meeting lasted about twenty minutes, and as it broke up, Winchell asked Gittinger for a letter spelling out the deal. With that, everyone smiled at everyone and shook hands.

As we walked back to CBS, I told Gittinger he ought to get a letter from Winchell saying Winchell had agreed to the deal. I guess Gittinger had more faith in Winchell than I had because in the morning Winchell got his letter from CBS, but CBS never asked for a letter in return.

The next Saturday, Mr. Paley called me at home and asked what had happened with Winchell. I said I'd find out. Winchell didn't answer his phone, so I sent him a telegram from the lobby of his hotel telling him I'd be waiting at home to hear from him.

Jackie went off to play golf without me—she wasn't going to waste a beautiful Saturday on the off chance Winchell would call back.

He phoned after five and with false innocence asked, "Irving, what's that telegram about?"

I virtually screamed at him. "Don't you know that CBS has been waiting to hear from you and your lawyer. They have a sponsor all lined up and want to complete the deal."

"Oh, tell those guys, 'Thanks for the trouble,' but I signed a new deal with Jergens and ABC at more than twice the fee."

Late that night, a blue necktie from Sulka's arrived with a "Guess who?" note. The following morning, I received a telegram: "Dear Irving, Thanks for getting me a raise, but what have you done for me lately?"

"Too bad, doll," Jackie said, "but I had a great day on the golf course."

*I*n June 1951, something astonishing happened. Jackie's very close friend, Joyce Matthews, locked herself in the bathroom of the apartment of my friend Billy Rose atop the Ziegfeld Theatre and started to scream. What was so astonishing was that neither of us knew that Joyce and Billy knew each other, much less that they were sufficiently involved for Joyce to try to nick her wrists.

Joyce recovered. Billy never discussed the matter with me. Joyce and Jackie had endless heart-to-heart talks, and the relationship between Joyce and Billy continued, intense and stormy. They were married in 1956. (I was supposed to be best man but was pushed aside at the last minute in favor of Abe Burrows.) We spent many weekends with the Roses, first in a beautiful house at Mt. Kisco in Westchester County, later on Tavern Island in Long Island Sound, where Billy bought a lavish house. The Roses were divorced a few years later, remarried in 1961 (this time I made it as best man), separated again, and were on the verge of getting back together when Billy died in 1966.

In the fall of 1951, CBS gave me an interesting special assignment—to produce a one-hour radio show on November 8, the night before the Friars were to give Jack Benny a testimonial dinner. Ronald and Benita Colman, Milton Berle, Ethel Merman, William S. Paley, Don Wilson, and of course, Jack and Mary Benny starred in the show.

The black-tie affair at the Waldorf the following night could be called "Almost the Making of a President."

Jesse Block, chairman of the Friars' dinner and probably Jack Benny's closest friend, arranged a brilliant dais but had a tough fight with the committee to permit the governor of Illinois to appear and speak. They said, "Who ever heard of Adlai Stevenson?"

But Jesse Block prevailed, and the governor of the state in which Jack Benny had been born was allowed to sit in the front row of the dais. Before he was introduced, everybody wondered who he was. Afterward, they knew.

That night, Fred Allen made the most brilliant and wittiest speech in the history of the Friars. When Fred finished his comedy blockbuster, the audience gave him a standing ovation. It took George Jessel, the toastmaster, more than three minutes to get the audience to sit down. Then he gave the impossible next speaking opportunity to Governor Adlai Stevenson of Illinois.

Stevenson calmly approached the podium and, smiling, said, "Ladies and gentlemen, when I came here tonight, I met Fred Allen in the lobby, and he told me he did not have a speech prepared and did not know what to say. So I gave him a copy of my remarks. I would like to thank all of you for the wonderful way you received my speech."

Again, there was a brilliant ovation for a witty man who knew that nobody could possibly follow Fred Allen. George Jessel then said, "Astute showman that I am, I shall now recite Lincoln's Gettysburg Address."

It was a historic night.

In the fall of 1952, I produced "The U.S.A. Canteen" with Jane Froman. Jane had been in a terrible plane crash in Lisbon while on a USO trip to entertain GIs during World War II. She had undergone twenty-eight operations and skin grafts and always wore a brace on her right leg and full-length gloves to hide the scars on her arms. Her face luckily had not been damaged. Jane had stammered as a child, and the operations did not help. Amazingly, the stammer never occurred while she was singing, only while she was talking. She was completely unable to use the phone; someone had to relay messages for her. This was a big problem for TV.

The director on the show was Byron Paul, the writer Howard Teichman, the song writers Ervin Drake, Jimmy Shirl, Irvin Graham, and Al Stillman. I don't know how we came up with new ideas and fresh songs and dialogue every week, especially after we went to twice a week. It was sheer frenzy. The late Charles Revson personally came to supervise his Revlon commercials, and his search for perfection ate up our rehearsal time until I persuaded CBS to give him another studio for his endless rehearsals.

For years, Jane had been identified with her theme "With a

Song in My Heart." But during 1953, I asked if she'd like to try something new. She became indignant.

"Would Bing Crosby give up 'Where the Blue of the Night Meets the Gold of the Day?' " she demanded. "Would Judy Garland give up 'Over the Rainbow?' "

For a while, she was chilly toward me. If I wanted a change, I knew I would have to offer her an alternative song. I explained my problem to Drake, a wonderful composer and lyricist. A few weeks later, he sat down at the piano and played and sang one of the most beautiful and feeling songs I had ever heard. It was called, "I Believe."

You could tell it would be a hit before he finished sixteen bars. Drake sang it for Jane the next day. Jane was very touched by it and agreed to sing it. But not as a theme—as a closing song for the Thanksgiving show.

Jane got an ovation when she sang the song. Immediately, she wanted to record it. Mitch Miller wanted to record it with Frankie Lane. The whole world wanted to record it. "I Believe" became an instant smash. In four weeks, it was number one on the *Variety* and *Billboard* charts. Jane wanted to sing it again at Christmas. "Why don't we open and close the show with it?" she asked.

I smiled innocently and said, "Why Jane, that's a wonderful idea."

That's how "I Believe" became the first theme that was developed directly on television and did not come from a Broadway musical or a motion picture.

After the show was finally disbanded, Howard Teichman went on to write *The Solid Gold Cadillac* with George S. Kaufman and, later, bestselling biographies of Kaufman, Alexander Woollcott, and Henry Fonda. Ervin Drake wrote many big hits, including, "It Was a Very Good Year" and the words and music for the Broadway hit *What Makes Sammy Run*.

Then, in the fall of 1953, CBS invited me to produce a show in Washington for the black-tie dinner at the Mayflower Hotel of the radio and TV correspondents. President Eisenhower and members of the Supreme Court, the Cabinet, and Congress were all to be there. The networks rotated the job of producing this annual event, and each network always put its best foot forward.

Bill Henry, the news reporter and commentator who was handling the show for the correspondents, and I had several meetings at the White House with Robert Montgomery, who was the president's

TV specialist. I never saw the president, but Montgomery filled me in on what he liked. He loved the speech that Abraham Lincoln made when he left Springfield, especially as done by Raymond Massey in Robert Sherwood's stirring play *Abe Lincoln in Illinois*. He also liked Paul Hahn, a trick golfer who hit golf balls into a curtain. I said I would get them both.

We had Jane Froman to sing with the U.S. Marine Band, Sam Levenson, Mary McCarty, and Art Linkletter as the MC. Sid Garfield, a young publicity man at CBS, kept calling to tell me to bring Phil Silvers in from California for the show. He wanted Silvers to do a marvelously funny routine called "The Singing Lesson" that Silvers and Sinatra had done all over the world for GIs. It was always a smash.

First Sinatra sang in his inimitable style. Then Silvers walked up to him and told him he was doing everything wrong. "Okay, Frank, let me show you how it goes. Now sing a few bars."

The minute Frank opened his mouth, Phil pushed his lips together and slapped him on the forehead. He continued to do this until the audience was laughing so hard you couldn't hear a word from the stage.

I said, "Sid, this bit only works when you have a star of Sinatra's stature."

Since Sinatra wasn't speaking to me and vice versa, I figured Phil was wasting his time by waiting with his bags half packed in Hollywood.

At lunch time on Friday, October 19, Sid called and said, "You won't believe this, but Arthur Godfrey just fired Julius LaRosa on the air."

The rudeness of Godfrey came as a tremendous shock to the public and made headlines in every paper. LaRosa instantly became a big star. I got LaRosa for the dinner. Silvers flew in. The two men did the routine, and soon all three networks made immediate offers to Silvers. He accepted the one from CBS, which then hired Nat Hiken, who was writing and directing the Martha Raye show on NBC, and that's how the "Sergeant Bilko" series was born. Bilko and Silvers and Nat Hiken all became heroes, but the real hero was the persistent Sid Garfield, who would not quit.

Jackie came down to Washington for the Eisenhower dinner. We met the president, and when Bill Henry discovered that Jackie had never seen the sights in Washington or toured the White House, he set up a special VIP tour for her. She loved it. On the way back to

New York, she said to me, "You know, doll, you really do pick winners."

That was the better side of the 1950s.

But there was also a more somber side. On May 9, 1951, Jackie and I were at a table at the Waldorf with the Ed Murrows, the Barry Grays, the Sam Levensons, and the Ed Sullivans for the first televised awards dinner of the Academy of Radio and Television Arts and Sciences. We all won in our respective divisions—Ed Murrow for TV reporting, Barry Gray for stimulating radio talk, Ed Sullivan for "Toast of the Town," Sam Levenson for new comedian of the year, and I got the Showmanship Award for TV.

I was very proud, made the usual "Thank-you-CBS-for-the-opportunity" speech, and hoped that my mother and father were watching the broadcast.

A little later, I called my parents' home from the lobby of the Waldorf, but there was no answer. I called again—no answer. I called our hotel for my messages, and there was one from my mother asking me to call her at a number I did not recognize. I called, and my heart sank when the operator answered, "Veterans Hospital." I asked to talk to my mother, and they connected me with her. She was crying and said, "Look, don't worry about pop."

I asked, "Where is he?"

She said, "He had a heart attack watching the show, and an ambulance brought him to the Coney Island Veterans Hospital."

I called my limousine service, and Jackie and I were there in about forty minutes. I wasn't allowed to see my father; he was in intensive care. But I was assured he would be okay. I sent Jackie home with the limo, but first she dropped my mother and me at my parents' apartment on Crown Street. I didn't want my mother to be alone that night.

About an hour later, the hospital called, and my mother jumped to answer it. "Oh, no," she cried. "It can't be." I was an only child who had loved his father very dearly, and now he was gone. Then Jackie's grandmother died, my mother died in 1955, and Jackie's father died two years later, on April 3, the day after our eighteenth wedding anniversary. Robert Susan was seventy, very, very tired by then, still heartbroken over Guy, and, I think, glad to be at peace. Jackie must have realized this because she took her father's death far more calmly than I would ever have imagined.

Since Jackie's parents did not have a cemetery plot, I arranged for Robert Susan to be buried in a plot at a cemetery in Queens that I had bought some time earlier. Jackie never missed visiting her father's grave on the anniversary of his death. If we were going to Europe or the coast, she would sometimes make the trip to the cemetery a few days before or after the anniversary. Then she would stand at the grave and say, "Daddy, I'm a little late, but I'm sure you'll understand. You know that I think of you all the time, and I'll love you always." Then she would scatter a few blades of grass on the grave as a symbol of life renewing itself. And she never spoke a single word as we rode back to the city.

How did we get through the bad times? Sometimes with rueful laughter. One year for my birthday Jackie gave me a croix de guerre she'd bought in a hock shop. I guess we both felt we had been through the wars. But there were three main things that saved us. The first was golf. We had begun while Guy was still at home. All our friends were playing golf. They would go off to the golf course every Saturday and Sunday and have a wonderful time. We usually took Guy to the park on Sunday, but we didn't have anything special to do on Saturday, so we joined the Englewood Club, just across the George Washington Bridge, where Joey Bishop, Dick Shawn, and a number of other friends were already members. I played a few rounds, found I was terrible, and signed up for some lessons at Spaulding's in Manhattan.

The lessons were absurd. The pro made me swing with a rope instead of a club. I quit the lessons, and Jackie took my place. We began playing a couple of times a week and gradually got better. We learned how to hit irons and how to hit woods and how to find balls in the rough. I enjoyed being outdoors, and the exercise was particularly good for Jackie. She could use up some of her coiled-up energy that had nowhere else to go. We became friendly with a couple named Edythe and Tom Kutlow and played with them quite frequently.

We went with them to the Concord several summers. Jackie worked on her swing with the pros, Jimmy Demaret, who won the Master's three times, Cary Middlecoff, who became a very important player, and Jackie Burke, also a famous golfer. I once played in a pro-am match with Ben Hogan, who made a nervous wreck of me. (Have you ever played with a legend?)

From the Englewood Club, we moved to the Alpine Golf Club. There Jackie became very friendly and played regularly with Sheila Bond, Helen Cooper, and a lively Italian girl named Fran Rosenblum, whose husband was a former magistrate. Jackie got to be a fair player—she could hold her own. Her one moment of triumph was a hole in one while she and I were playing with Jan Murray at the Concord. It cost her $136 in drinks in the clubhouse.

One day, I was sitting at the club with Judge Rosenblum, and he mentioned that he was general counsel to a company called Schiffli Corporation. Schiffli was a Swiss process for making embroidered lace by machine. This lace was used on blouses, housecoats, and sportswear. Schiffli was seeking a bigger share of the American market through a new campaign of TV advertising. Judge Rosenblum wondered if Jackie would be interested in doing the commercials for the company. I think the judge and the Schiffli people were impressed that for the last several years Jackie had been in the top ten of the annual best-dressed list for women in television. A strong fashion image was important for them.

Yes, Jackie was interested. She had been doing some commercials for Hazel Bishop, a cosmetics company, and for a full year with Ben Hecht on ABC-TV. She was thoroughly familiar with what was required. Jackie went on TV for Schiffli in 1956 and stayed with them until 1962. Their main program was a live, late-night interview show called "Night Beat," presided over by a brilliant young TV journalist named Mike Wallace and later by John Wingate. Jackie delivered the commercials. After a while, she was editing the commercials; eventually, she was writing the commercials. "Night Beat" was on five nights a week.

It was really an innovative TV show. By placing the host and the guest in an adversary situation, it changed forever the cream-puff interviewing that TV had been doing up to that point. Wallace searched out his guests' weak spots in advance. From newspaper clippings or from back copies of *Time* magazine, he read complimentary and uncomplimentary remarks about them or conflicting statements from their own mouths and then asked, "Now what do you have to say to that?"

They usually had quite a good deal to say, and the show was so lively that it commanded a very large audience for a local show and got more than its share of notice in the press.

Jackie was busy on the show during the late hours every week night. Sometimes we went to the theater or a movie before her broadcast. Sometimes we ate before, sometimes after, she was on the air. While she was at the studio, Billy Rose and I used to wander into a little delicatessen called the Chambers at 58th Street and Sixth

Avenue where, in the back, some of the heavyweight intellectuals and talents of the world gathered and argued over coffee and Danish: Ferenc Molnar, the playwright, Kurt Weill, sometimes Bertolt Brecht, Oscar Levant, Michael Arlen. I mostly listened when I was with this high-brow crowd, but Billy Rose mixed right in and disputed and battled.

Billy never bought his own cigarettes. His arrival was always signaled by a member of the group who warned, "Hide your cigarettes, fellows. Here comes Billy."

Because of Jackie's late show every night and my shows several times a week, we became more night owls than ever. My youthful dream of sleeping late had long since evaporated—I discovered I was a natural early riser. But getting Jackie up on mornings when she had an early appointment was tough going. I would get up first and call to her as I went into the bathroom. She'd say, "Five more minutes."

I'd call her again when I was half shaved.

She'd say, "Just five minutes."

Then, with lather still on my face, I'd grab one foot and start pulling. She'd say, "Okay, just put it on the floor. I'll leave it there and give me five minutes more."

Ten minutes later, I'd come back, and the foot was no longer on the floor—it was back in the bed. Then I'd take both feet and put them on the floor, and she'd say, "Let me be this way for one minute. I'll be up in sixty seconds."

Three minutes later, she'd be turned over, curled up, and sleeping. Then I'd throw off the covers, lift her up bodily, deposit her in the bathroom, and close the door. From that point, she could manage alone.

Doing commercials for Schiffli was not exactly having your name up in lights at the Winter Garden. But it was steady, reliable work, better than sitting home, and it paid very well. Jackie hardly needed the money for herself, but she still had that sense of urgency about putting money away for Guy's future, and the job let her feel she was doing her part. So Schiffli, along with golf, helped her through the low period.

Her third great comfort was a black ball of fluff and personality named Josephine. Josephine was so important in our lives that she deserves a chapter all to herself.

$\mathcal{S}$omebody asked me recently how much of Jackie's book *Every Night, Josephine!* is true. The answer is easy: all of it.

The closest I had come to a dog in my childhood was backing away from a snarling one. Jackie, as a girl, had been interested in a kitten for about two weeks, craved a pony, but never owned a dog. Then Jackie met Tinker, the poodle of her friend Dorothy Strelsin. Jackie watched as Tinker, three pounds of squirming, elated love, saturated Dorothy with adoring kisses, then capered at her heels, squealing with joy.

Suddenly, as Jackie put it, "I wanted a little fanfare of my own. I wanted someone to bounce to the door to meet me, to cover my face with adoring kisses, to follow me around the apartment. And as much as Irving loves me, he just is not the prancing, following type."

When Jackie began thinking about poodles, in her thorough fashion, she researched poodles, visited kennels, and interviewed eccentric ladies who raised poodles. She met Dipper, the stunning silver poodle of her golf friend Edythe Kutlow. She checked out poodles with Joyce Matthews Rose, recently returned from Europe, who loved her year-old poodle, supposedly a miniature but now grown into something resembling an alligator.

Jackie knew exactly what she wanted: a silver-gray male miniature. While she was casing the silver-gray male miniatures in a pet shop, a paw tapped her shoulder. It belonged to a poodle that was everything Jackie didn't want—black, half toy, half miniature, and female. In seconds, Everything-she-didn't-want was kissing Jackie's cheek with its rough little tongue. Jackie had found her poodle, or more likely, vice versa.

So Josephine came into our lives over my fierce objections.

"That dog goes back," I told Jackie in my most final voice. She tried charm to persuade me, then tears, then hysterics, and finally she fainted. We made a deal. We were leaving for California in three months. She could keep the dog until then, but at departure time, she would give the dog to Florence Lustig's son Craig. I made her put the deal in writing. Meantime, I would never walk the dog, never go along when Jackie walked the dog, never clean up after the dog, and never pay any of the dog's expenses—except its funeral.

Jackie agreed, with a look that made it clear I was the heel of the earth. Then somehow, my hand, entirely on its own, found the back of Josie's head and stroked it. When Josie practiced her arias at night, I banished both Jackie and Josie to the kitchen. But I couldn't stand the thought of that poor little puppy sleeping in the kitchen, so I brought them both back to bed. Only it was Josie who crawled into my arms. And that was that. I became more batty over Josephine than Jackie ever was.

We fed her goodies and yummies and sweet cream at meals, between meals, and between the betweens. She dined on room-service leftovers. She rewarded us with adoring wet kisses, wild tail waggings, and a potbelly. She seduced my mother, who thought *all* animals belonged in a zoo. Before long my dog-hating mother was cooking chicken and chicken soup just for Josie, and when she dog-sat, she made sure Josie had her quart of milk a day, laced with cream, coffee, and sugar.

Josephine enlarged our social circle. She got to know Laurence Harvey and his wife, Margaret Leighton, Dame Margot Fonteyn and Rudolf Nureyev, all of whom lived in our building. Richard Burton, who was appearing on Broadway in *Camelot*, was on our floor. Whenever Josephine scratched at his door, he let her in and allowed her to jump on his bed. He saved scraps for her second breakfast— after she'd had her first at home. Jackie used to say, "I wonder what would happen if I scratched at his door. . . ."

I remember the terrible time when Josephine was left at the vet's overnight for a teeth cleaning and it turned out that Dr. White, the sadist, extracted her front teeth for some frivolous reason, like saving her mouth. After Jackie got over her own hysterics, she was afraid to tell me. That evening, I called to Josephine, "Come to daddy, sweetheart. Daddy wants to inspect the pretty pearly teeth."

Sweetheart opened her mouth. I said, "Sweetheart, I've got to pull down your lips because I want to see the gorgeous front teeth."

Then I said, "I must be doing something wrong. I can't find her bottom teeth."

Jackie said, "There aren't any."

I got out my glasses and made a careful study. In a deadly tone I asked how many teeth Sweetheart had left.

Jackie said she hadn't made a count, but 16 were in the possession of Dr. White. Then Jackie was saying, "Stop shouting! You're frightening Josie." I took a Seconal and went to bed.

Josie managed very well with her gums and what teeth she had left. I was the one who had a hard time.

Josephine really was a winner. She had a gorgeous coat, a disposition like three angels, a dancer's gait, the personality of an intelligent cheer leader and limitless supplies of kisses. Jackie and I both became deeply entangled in a love affair with Josie. She brought sunshine into our lives again.

In June 1960 Jackie had to cover the French fashion shows for Schiffli, so we made a vacation trip together. In Paris, while we were sitting at Fouquet's, Maurice Chevalier walked by. We'd first met him in Miami in 1948 and we knew from that earlier encounter that Chevalier in person was as utterly charming as on the screen or on stage. In Miami, he'd kissed Jackie's hand and told her she reminded him of Kay Francis, a stunning, dark-haired movie actress. But we'd learned in Florida, when we'd joined him for drinks and for lunch, that someone must have sewed up his pockets. He never put his hand in them for money. In fact, his stinginess, we discovered from his friends and ours, was legendary.

Now in Paris, he was again all charm and kissed Jackie's hand. "You remind me of someone," he said. "It's Kay Francis." He graciously invited us to dinner at his home outside Paris, and of course we accepted. We thought he'd send a car for us, but since that didn't happen, we took the concierge's advice and hired a limousine. Chevalier had an enchanting house in the country. He looked the perfect, debonair host in his velvet jacket. He introduced a number of other guests to us, but didn't introduce us. I had the feeling he wasn't quite sure about our names. We sat around waiting for two more guests. No drinks were served and no hors d'oeuvres.

When we finally went into the dining room I knew I'd never seen anything like it—Renoirs and Pissarros on the walls—it was incredible.

There were also endless photographs of Maurice—his hands, his straw hat, Chevalier dancing with his hat in his hands, Chevalier with celebrities from all over the world, including Charles de Gaulle.

Dinner was served—very elegant service, but only a thimble full of pea soup to start, then for the main course a piece of meat about an inch and a half by an inch and a half, shaved paper thin, six string beans, a few peas and a few carrots. Jackie asked what the meat was— it was too tough to be anything we were familiar with. Turns out it was venison. There were three tarts for dessert, cut into narrow slivers to serve the nine of us at the table. And finally a half demitasse of coffee.

Then we all got up and went into a lovely den where there were more beautiful pictures. Chevalier turned to Jackie and said, "Jacqueline, ma chere, what would you like to drink?"

Jackie said, "Maurice, I never drink on an empty stomach."

In November 1960 I did the single worst thing to Jackie in my entire life. I forgot to take her to Europe. That's going to take a little explaining. Jackie was still doing Schiffli nightly and Peter Arnell, a bright young man, and I were producing two major TV shows: "The World of Talent" with Dick Clark in New York and "Take a Good Look" with Ernie Kovacs, Edie Adams and Cesar Romero in Los Angeles. One thing that's impossible is to produce two important network shows at the same time.

Well, now I was not only producing two, but at opposite ends of the continent. Every week Peter and I commuted between New York and the coast. Jackie could make the trip with me only rarely and wouldn't you know that once when she came along our plane had lost a wheel and a tire and on arrival at the L.A. airport, we were told to pull down the window shades, take off our shoes, put our eyeglasses in our pockets, place our elbows between our legs and pillows in front of our faces in preparation for a crash landing. I peeked out the window and was shocked to see searchlights, ambulances, fire trucks. Foam covered the runway.

Jackie said, "What do you see?"

I said, "Nothing much, they're just taking precautions." I disregarded the order about putting my elbows between my knees and held onto Jackie's hand.

We circled the airport several times while they dropped the fuel and the luggage. We could hear voices from the shortwave radio in the cockpit telling motorists to stay away from the L.A. airport area. They jettisoned the landing gear and the plane slowed and came in on its belly. Not one person was hurt. When the pilot stepped into the cabin, we all cheered like mad. Jackie and I were both wet with perspiration, but happy to be alive. Once she knew it wasn't curtains for us, she said, "Well, doll, at least we'll be able to go to Ernie Kovacs' party tomorrow night."

My usual schedule was to leave for California on Thursday and come back to New York on Sunday. After a while, I didn't know where I was, where my head was or which script I was reading on the plane. Jackie and I would leave each other notes. Sometimes I'd rush to the apartment from the airport, accept Josie's squeals and wriggles, find Jackie asleep, kiss her and tell her not to wake up because I was hurrying off to the studio, find her gone when I got home and perhaps not see her for forty-eight hours after I got back to New York. By then I was almost ready to fly back to California. It was a crazy time.

One night, I flew into New York, and Jackie and I went to Joyce and Billy's for dinner. By then, Joyce and Billy were living in a sensational townhouse on East 93rd Street filled with the most incredible works of art. During the meal, something came up about plans for the next day, and I said, "I can't make it. I'm going to London with Ernie and Edie."

Jackie said, "You're what?"

I started to repeat what I had just said, and then I said, "Oh, my God, I forgot to tell you. Ernie is doing a movie in Europe and has to tape some shows in London."

"And you're going with him?" she asked in that very quiet voice.

When it was time for us to leave, Jackie said, "You go ahead. I'll stay here."

"What's the matter? Why aren't you coming with me?"

"No, I'll just sleep here tonight."

I couldn't persuade her to come home with me, so I left and phoned her from the apartment. She wouldn't speak to me. Billy got on the phone and said, "How could you do such a thing? How could you not even tell her you were going to Europe?"

"I just didn't think about it," I said.

"What do you mean you didn't think about it. Someone had to make reservations."

"The studio did all that. I was stupid. I just didn't think."

Jackie wouldn't see me or talk to me before my plane took off. I couldn't cancel the flight—I had too much to do in London. I called her from London, finally reached her, and made completely abject

[112]

apologies. I really did feel terrible. My head had been in such a whirl that I had arranged to go to Europe, without taking her and without mentioning it, as casually as I might have made a trip to Brooklyn. It was unforgivable.

Jackie said, "I don't know if I want to continue talking to you. You made me feel terrible in front of Joyce and Billy. They think we're such a wonderful couple, and now they'll never be able to think of us in that way again." She started crying.

I told her to get out her passport—there was already a first-class ticket for her the next day on BOAC—and to make any old excuse to the people at "Night Beat."

I hired a Rolls Royce with a driver and met her at the London airport. I kissed her, and she said, "Listen, I have a friend. Can we drop her off?" Jackie had gotten into a conversation with a woman on the plane, and I don't think that woman ever got over being met by a Rolls.

We stayed at the Mayfair hotel. Jackie gambled at the Palm Beach Casino, won far more than she usually did, and handed her winnings to a sweet little honeymoon couple who had lost their entire stake. We went on to Paris and had a wonderful time there.

So one way or another, with the good and the bad mingled, we got through 1960. The year 1961 opened with Jackie tripping on the phone cord in our apartment and landing in LeRoy Sanitarium for four days. In February, Rose Susan came to visit and was stricken with a heart attack in our apartment. Rose was in Doctors Hospital for eight weeks. Jackie visited her daily and built her whole schedule for two months around her mother's ups and downs.

In June, I was able to give Jackie one of the great thrills of her life. Irving Peiser, a furrier friend of ours, called to say that he had made up an absolutely magnificent sable coat for a customer who had refused it because it was just a little too long. Would I be interested in seeing it? At this point, Jackie had a new mink and a lovely leopard coat, and Josie had a fake leopard to match Jackie's real one. I told Peiser I probably wouldn't buy it, but if he wanted to stop by with it. . . .

He arrived later that afternoon, a Saturday. When she heard who it was, Jackie appeared immediately in a bathrobe. "What has he got?" she asked, eying the big box he was carrying.

"I think it's a sable," I said.

"Who's the lucky lady?"

"It's a problem coat," he told her. "It doesn't fit the woman it was made for, and it's too expensive to redo it."

"Can I try it on?" she asked.

He opened the box, removed the tissue paper, and handed Jackie the most gorgeous coat in the whole world. There is really nothing like sable; it is unbelievably glamorous and luxurious. The worst-looking woman in the world becomes a beauty in a sable. A beautiful woman turns into a Venus. Jackie danced around in front of the mirror and said, "Oh well, maybe next year."

"No, this year," I said, and kissed her. "It's yours."

She screamed. A happy scream. She ordered her name, Jacqueline, put in it in Schiffli embroidery. Peiser left with the coat. Jackie made a beeline for the telephone. That was the end of her for the evening.

Jackie adored that coat—as well she might. I wish the coat story had a happy ending, but it doesn't. The coat was stolen when we were robbed in 1969, and we never saw it again.

That New Year's Eve, Jackie gave me a terrible shock. We were in Miami, staying at the Fontainebleau and planning to go to a big party the Arthur Murrays were giving at the hotel. Late in the afternoon, Jackie went down to the beauty salon to have her hair done. She seemed to take longer than usual. When she walked in, she had platinum hair. I looked at her, then looked back to my newspaper.

She said, "Well?"

"Well, what?"

"You must have a comment."

I said, "About what?"

She said, "Listen, you're going to ruin my whole New Year's Eve."

"How am I going to ruin it?"

"I've spent three and a half hours in the beauty parlor . . ."

"Were you getting a shine or something?"

By this time, she was looking for something to throw at me. "Come on, what do you really think of it?"

I said, "Jackie, are you going to make any New Year's resolutions? Because I'm making one. And it's not to talk to you until the beauty parlor opens so you can get your hair back to its natural color."

"You really don't like it?"

"I hate it."

She had a terrific tan and had looked wonderful just a few hours before. She looked in the mirror and said, "You know what—I hate it, too."

Jackie definitely had a brunette personality and looked right only as a brunette. As a blonde, she looked like a stripper. She went down to the beauty parlor and got a wig to wear that night. She stayed platinum long enough to have her picture taken. You'll find Jackie the blonde in the book's photo section. I think you'll agree—she does look like a stripper.

I've got just one more story to tell before we get back to Josephine.

In May 1962, we were having dinner one night at a very elegant New York restaurant with Florence Lustig and her husband, Harold Crossman. We nodded to Rocky Graziano, the fighter, at another table and to Johnny Carson, who was with his wife and some friends. Jackie had enormous admiration for Carson. She considered him the greatest monologist in the business and was always after me to make him host of one of my shows. He had been a sensational guest star on the Polly Bergen show that I had produced several years before.

Johnny had been drinking that night quite a bit. When Johnny drank, he was not a very good boy. I think things have changed for him now, but that night he was on his worst behavior. He came over to our table, pulled a chair up so he was facing me, and had his back to Jackie and began to talk to me. I moved my chair around so he would not have his back to Jackie. But Johnny moved his chair, too, and over his shoulder, he said something to Jackie that she did not like at all. To this day, I don't know what it was. I don't think Carson himself knows, either.

Whatever it was, Jackie got into a rage and said, "How dare you!"

He growled something at her.

Jackie was holding her drink in her hand—a black Russian, which is a combination of vodka, Kahlúa, and cream. She threw her drink right in his face. He got up as though he were going to punch her. I grabbed him and said, "Come on, Johnny, watch your step."

In a way, I felt sorry for him. He didn't even know what the hell he was doing. That's how drunk he was.

The captain came over. Rocky Graziano came over. I didn't want to see a fight between Johnny and Rocky. Johnny's wife, his second wife, Joanne, and a waiter walked him out of the restaurant.

The rest of us settled down, but Jackie was still seething. Johnny was outside, but suddenly he came running back in and headed toward Jackie. I stepped between them. He said, "Let me at her."

Again, he was hauled off, and someone poured some coffee into him before they took him outside.

On the way back to our hotel, Jackie kept saying, "I don't know what got into him. I don't know what got into me." She felt terrible because she really liked Johnny. We decided not to tell anyone about the incident, and we hoped the others in the restaurant would keep quiet. But no such luck. The next day, a reporter called from the *New York Post* and wanted to know if Jackie had been in an altercation with Johnny Carson.

"Why would Carson have a fight with my wife?" I asked.

The *Post* didn't print anything, but I later read the story in a book or magazine article about Carson.

About a year later, I was giving a party upstairs at Danny Stradella's restaurant for Merv Griffin, who was hosting "Celebrity Talent Scouts." Everyone in town was there, not only the guests we had invited but a lot of the people who were having dinner downstairs at the restaurant. Jackie was at the door acting as hostess. Johnny Carson walked in with Ed McMahon. This was the first confrontation between Jackie and Johnny since the black Russian had smeared up his face and suit.

Johnny said, "Is this a private party, or can anyone come in?"

"It's for friends," said Jackie. "Do you want to be a friend?"

"Yes, I do. No hard feelings."

They shook hands, and that was the end of that. The incident was never mentioned again.

At about the time of the original Carson incident, Joyce and Billy Rose were living in the south of France. To keep them amused, Jackie, in her letters, recounted the adventures of Josephine—the loss of those front teeth, winning over my mother, going on television, Josie's romance with Bobo Eichenbaum, the poodle next door. The letters were sprightly and funny. So sprightly and funny that when the Roses returned from Europe, Billy dropped a large manila envelope on our coffee table.

"Jackie," he said, "here are the letters about Josephine you sent us. They are cute, funny, adorable. With just a little work, they'll make a book. You ought to write that book."

By this time, Jackie had made herself a solemn promise: no more books, no more plays. She had spent years, literally years, at her typewriter, with nothing to show for all that time and hard work except the four-week run of *Lovely Me*. Never again. The typewriter had been put away for good.

But Billy Rose was not a man you said no to.

In addition to Billy's persuasiveness, there was an overheard remark that was rankling Jackie. As we were leaving Sardi's one night, a couple of kids with autograph books had rushed over to me and asked me to sign. Amused and flattered, I gladly signed my name. While I was writing, one kid said to the other, "Who is he?"

"Don't you know? He's a big-shot TV producer."

"Who's that with him?"

"Her? Oh, she's just the Schiffli Girl."

Those words echoed in Jackie's head: "She's just the Schiffli Girl." Was that what the struggle had been about for all these years— the battle to get to New York, the bad plays, the weeks on the road, the look-alike TV shows, the unpublished books, the high expectations, the dashed hopes? Was she to end up as "just the Schiffli Girl"?

Out came the typewriter, and with Josie at her feet, Jackie spent six months in 1962 whipping the letters about Josephine into a book about Josephine. She showed me the chapters as she finished them, and they really were delightful. She had caught all the love and affection that flowed back and forth between the dog and us as well as Josie's special charm and style. The book was warm and witty.

This time, I was sure, Jackie would find a publisher. In fact, Jackie was going to find a publisher if I had to operate an underground press myself. I was not going to let Jackie be disappointed again.

First there was the problem of a title. The obvious one was just plain *Josephine*, but that lacked pizazz. "What was it that Napoleon said to Josephine?" Jackie asked me.

"Not tonight, Josephine."

"That's not right for a title, but what about *Every Night, Josephine!*" That was it, and we knew it right away.

The next problem was an agent. Jackie had not had any success with the William Morris office. I went to Anna Sosenko, who knew a lot of literary people, to get her recommendations. She suggested an agent named Annie Laurie Williams, a woman of considerable age and enormous reputation who had handled many big properties, among them Kathleen Windsor's blockbuster bestseller *Forever Amber*. She was John Steinbeck's agent. Jackie wondered whether she would bother with us.

Anna made the introduction, and Jackie and I went to see Annie Laurie Williams in her cramped, old-fashioned office. There we met her husband, Maurice Crain, and a charming southern woman who was busy making tea. When Jackie asked if she might possibly have a second cup of tea, Annie Laurie Williams said, "You know, that's not the maid. That's Harper Lee—she's up for the Pulitzer Prize for *To Kill a Mockingbird*."

Jackie had thought the woman was a friend. She had not taken her for the maid—or for a literary lion. After all that was worked out, Annie Laurie said she would be happy to read *Every Night, Josephine!* We would hear from her shortly.

She called a few days later. She loved *Josephine!* absolutely loved it, and was sending it right over to Doubleday where she was sure Ken McCormick, the editor-in-chief, would be as enthusiastic as she was.

Jackie was delighted but not ready to let herself go overboard with enthusiasm. *Josephine!* went to Doubleday, and we waited. As days and weeks passed, Jackie got more and more impatient. Why were they taking so long? Why didn't she hear? They must hate it; otherwise, they would have called. Maybe they lost it. She repeatedly threatened to call McCormick to find out what was holding up a decision. I forbade her to do that—the agent was the one to make such calls. And Annie Laurie cautioned patience.

But Jackie didn't have patience. This wasn't a patient period in her life. She wanted action, and fast. She was making my life miserable with her impatience. She called me at the office to ask if I had heard anything. If I called her during the day, she insisted that I call Annie Laurie or Ken McCormick or somebody. She *had* to know what was happening.

The only solution was to get Jackie out of town for a while. I quickly found a way of doing it. The Alpine Golf Club was running a trip around the world for its members. I said to Jackie, "I want to treat you and your mother to a trip around the world."

"Why my mother? If I'm going around the world, I'd want to go with you. You can carry my bags."

"I can't go, Jackie. I have to do my shows and sell your book. Someone has to be here. Don't you want to see the Taj Mahal and shop in Hong Kong?"

I didn't have to work on selling her because several of her friends from the golf club were going on the trip, and when her mother got word of the invitation, she started pressuring Jackie. So it was arranged. By the time Jackie got back, I was sure the book would be sold.

The trip started off with problems. We drove to the airport in Jackie's Cadillac El Dorado. Jackie was driving; Anna Sosenko, who would drive the car back to the city, was next to Jackie; Rose Susan and I were in back. Somewhere on the East River Drive, Jackie's mother asked, "Did you pack that little clock of mine?"

Jackie said, "I don't remember."

"What do you mean, you don't remember?"

"I just don't, but don't worry. I have a clock."

"Jackie, it's important. I need *that* clock."

Jackie said, "Look, mother, I'll buy four clocks at the airport. You can have one for morning, one for afternoon, one for night."

They got into such an argument about that clock that Jackie was almost ready to turn the car around and go home. Finally, Anna said, "Look, Mrs. Susan, you're talking about a little ten-dollar clock. Don't spoil the trip over a little clock."

We made it to the airport, Jackie and her mother joined the thirty or so people from the club, I kissed them good-by, and they were off. Their first stop was Vienna. It had been a long flight, and Jackie wanted to sleep. But Mrs. Susan had booked tickets for the opera, and to the opera they went—all dressed up in evening clothes. They continued eastward around the world. Amusing cards trickled in long after their return.

Jackie's first phone call to me came from Honolulu. "I was just taking a shower," she said, "and I felt this little lump in my right breast."

"Skip the rest of the trip," I told her. "Come right home."

*J*ackie called me when she landed in San Francisco. The lump was still there. Jackie had always had a certain amount of trouble with her breasts. They had a tendency to form cysts that had to be checked out frequently by her gynecologist. In the past, the cysts had always been benign. "How are you feeling?" I asked her.

"I feel fine, but the lump is still there."

"I'm sure it's nothing," I told her. "I'll see you at the airport tomorrow." I wished I was as confident as I sounded.

The same day Jackie called me from the coast, Annie Laurie Williams called. "I've sold the book to Doubleday," she said.

That was wonderful news. I would have something good to tell Jackie at the airport. On December 23, two days before Christmas 1962, Anna drove me out to meet Jackie's plane. Anna wanted to be the one to break the good news about the book, so I agreed to let her do it. Jackie and her mother came through customs. Jackie looked wonderful—but worried. We got in the car, and right away Jackie asked, "What about the book?"

Anna began spinning out the story in the slowest way possible. "Why Jackie, Annie Laurie was just saying the other day that every time she gets a new book, she wants—"

Jackie couldn't stand it. "Skip all that," she said. "What *happened?*"

When she finally heard the good news, she was overjoyed. She hugged Anna. She reached into the back seat and hugged me. She even hugged her mother. As soon as we were home, she called Joyce and said, "What do you think? My book is sold to Doubleday."

Joyce congratulated her and put Billy on the phone. He congratulated her and said, "I want to write the ads for the newspapers."

"That's sweet of you, Billy," she said.

"And Joyce and I want you and Irving to come to dinner on Christmas night."

But on Christmas night Jackie was in the hospital.

The morning after she got home, Jackie went to see her gynecologist. He sent her that same afternoon to a breast surgeon, who insisted on an immediate biopsy. The next day, she was in Doctors Hospital. The surgeon was Dr. Gerson Lesnick, a kind and very compassionate man and a very fine surgeon. Everything moved so quickly that we hardly had time to think. The biopsy was done the day after Christmas. The news was bad. The lump was malignant, and the breast had to be removed.

We were both in a state of shock. I don't think there's a woman in the world who can stand up to such news in a stoic way. Jackie was crying but otherwise seemed calm. Only it was the calm of complete numbness. The full horror had not yet sunk in. I walked down the hall with the doctor and asked, "Does she really have to have the operation?"

"I'm afraid she does," he said.

"What if she doesn't?"

"It will spread through her system and kill her in a couple of years."

"And there's no possibility of a mistake. You're *sure* it's malignant?"

"We're sure," he said sadly.

I went back to the room and found Jackie all dressed in her slacks and black jacket. "I'm going home," she said. "I'm not going to let them do this to me."

"But Jackie, they *have* to do it."

"Not to me. I'm not going to be here. I don't want to live like that—disfigured, scarred. I'm leaving."

The anesthesiologist, a very charming woman, came in, and she got the picture right away. She got Jackie undressed and back into bed. Then she came out and said to me, "Mr. Mansfield, just go in there and talk to her for a while. She'll be all right."

I wasn't exactly all right myself, but I went into the room and talked to Jackie. I said, "Look, Jackie, I know this is a terrible thing you're facing. You feel you'll be only half a woman, but that's absurd. You'll always be you, you'll always be Jackie. I know you don't want to have this operation, but you must. Don't do it for yourself. Please do it for me. Please. I'm not going to love you any the less. I want you around. I want you with me for a long, long time. We still have good, happy years left. We'll have fine times again. Please do it for me."

We held onto each other. She cried. Then, finally, she said, "All right, I'll do it . . . for you."

The resident came in with a paper for her to sign giving permission for the surgery. She looked at the paper, then started to get out of bed and reach for her clothes again, but I held her arm. "Jackie, you promised."

She gave me a long, sorrowful look, took the pen, and signed her name.

They took her up to surgery very early the next morning. Again, exactly as when Guy was born, I was left waiting in the lounge. But this time there were no happy expectations. I waited and waited. A mastectomy is a relatively quick operation—a couple of hours in the operating room at most. But I waited the whole day and well into the afternoon. My mind ran through all kinds of dire possibilities. What was taking so long? Were there problems, complications? Why didn't someone keep me informed?

About four P.M. Dr. Lesnick was astonished to find me in the lounge, still waiting.

"Didn't anybody call you?" he asked. "Your wife's fine. She's been back in her room for hours."

What Jackie had, I learned later, was an infiltrating ductile carcinoma, the kind that accounts for about eighty-five percent of all breast cancer cases. There was no involvement of the lymph nodes in the adjacent armpit, and that was very good news. It meant that the cancer had not spread at all. What Dr. Lesnick had performed was something between a radical and a modified radical mastectomy, quite an advanced operation for that time.

In the traditional radical mastectomy, which most surgeons were still doing in 1962, all the muscle underlying the breast was removed, leaving a conspicuous hollow under the arm. The modified radical, which is now in general use, leaves the muscle intact. The operation performed on Jackie removed half the muscle but preserved the fold at the underarm. Dr. Lesnick told me later that he spent many hours figuring out how to keep the underarm area looking as natural as possible, without a hollowed-out look, so that Jackie could continue to wear the off-the-shoulder dresses she loved.

Jackie had remarkable recuperative powers and a will of iron. And a good thing, because here was a woman who was devastated by the surgery, absolutely devastated. She was proud of her body and had always enjoyed showing it off. Yes, she was vain. She enjoyed being beautiful and being admired. She had wonderful posture and always carried herself like a queen. She had never disguised her breasts or hidden them or tried to flatten them. They were an asset that she wore with pride.

Now, as soon as Jackie came out from under the anesthesia and recovered from her first round of sobbing over the bandages she could see and feel around her chest, she began to fight. The first stage of her fight was an unshakable decision to keep the operation secret.

"I don't want pity," she said to me, holding tight to my hand. "I don't want people whispering and shaking their heads and saying, 'Poor Jackie, she's so brave.' I couldn't stand that. I don't want to be thought of as a cancer victim or a cancer case."

Remember, we're talking about 1962—more than a decade before Betty Ford and Happy Rockefeller and Marvella Bayh and all those other brave women went public with their mastectomies. In the early 1960s, cancer was still something mentioned only in hushed tones. It was coupled in people's minds with death, with slow dying.

Jackie didn't want any of that stigma to touch her. She was going to live. And the best way to do that, as she saw it, was to go on as if nothing had happened.

"How soon can I leave the hospital?" she asked Dr. Lesnick.

"Ten days, two weeks—that's the usual stay," he told her.

"No, I can't do that. I want to be out of here in three days. If I'm in and out fast, nobody will notice. It's the holiday time, and people are moving around. They'll never know I was here. If I stay two weeks, word will get around; people will start to talk."

Dr. Lesnick had never had such a patient. Since there were no complications and she was healing fast, he went along with her wishes. He would come to the apartment and dress her wound there. So Jackie, after losing her right breast on December 27, went home on January 1. She held her head high as she walked through the lobby of the Navarro, and within minutes after she entered the front door of our apartment, she was in bed and on the telephone, chatting away to her friends, wishing them Happy New Year, talking about her round-the-world trip. Yes, she'd picked up a little bug somewhere, but she was fine now, well enough to have a Lindy's cheesecake for New Year's, and her book was sold, and everything was great.

One of her first calls was to Muriel Slatkin in California. Muriel was happy to hear that Jackie had recovered from the bug she had picked up on her travels, and Muriel had good news, too. She had just undergone a breast biopsy—on the same day as Jackie's, it turned out—and it had been negative. "Isn't that wonderful?" she said.

"Oh, it is wonderful," Jackie told her. "I'm so happy for you. We'll have to celebrate together."

I think that the cancer experience brought about some of Jackie's finest moments as an actress, because everything was not great. Yes, the physical part was fine. Dr. Lesnick came over on January 2 to dress her wound. He was delighted with her progress. Mrs. J. K. Lasser, the mother of Louise Lasser, who had founded Reach for Recovery to help cancer patients through their rehabilitation stages, came to the house and gave Jackie a series of exercises for her arm and shoulder muscles. Jackie put a mark on the wall and every day raised her fingers and her arm another inch above the mark.

On Mrs. Lasser's second visit, she said to Jackie, "Let's see how well you raise your arm."

"You mean like this?" Jackie asked and lifted her arm all the way over her head. Mrs. Lasser was astonished.

Jackie never had a bit of trouble with the arm, she never let the shoulder on the mastectomy side droop, and she never, in the succeeding years, had any swelling of the arm. She was lucky in that respect. And, of course, she had a brilliant surgeon.

But the emotional side of her recovery was going less well. Although she tried to be brave and kept telling herself it was "only a breast," she was shattered right down to the depths of her being. After she'd kept up the cheerful front for everyone out there, she came home and cried. Jackie had always been a brief crier. She could well over with tears after she'd read a sad book or seen a tragic play. She often had wet hankies in her purse. But this was different.

Now she cried in that inconsolable way that Guy had screamed. She felt that our lives were wrecked, her dreams were out the window, the good days were over. She was no longer the princess. She no longer walked around in a magic aura. She was just forty-four, but life would be downhill from here on. The downhill had started with Guy. Now the descent would get steeper and faster. And it was all her fault. She had brought this misery on me, on our marriage.

I did everything I could to comfort her, but she was hard to reach in her grief. And it wasn't easy for me to handle my own feelings. I was angry, very angry. I hated everybody. I hated the lab for finding out that she had cancer. I hated the doctors for telling Jackie that she had cancer. I hated them for cutting off her breast. I hated all the cruelty involved. I even hated the word "positive," which until then had been a good word. But now the dictionary was upside down, and "positive" was bad, and "negative" was good.

There was no way for me to vent my anger. I couldn't yell at the doctors. I couldn't scream at God. I could only put my own feelings aside and try to help Jackie in her agony.

I cooperated with her in every way in keeping her secret. We told only Anna, Hildegarde, Bea, Joyce, and Billy. We also told Louise, our housekeeper, who had to know. We didn't tell Jackie's mother. Later, we told Roberta, the woman who came in to give Jackie massages.

Maybe it was not wise to suppress all this information and bottle up our feelings, to add this secret to the secret of Guy's autism. Now we were smiling at the world and telling two sets of lies: "Oh, yes, Guy's fine. The school in Arizona says he's outgrowing his asthma and doing very well. But he can't live in this climate—not yet." And then: "Oh, yes, I'm fine, never felt better. I'm playing golf again. Oh, sure, I licked that little bug I picked up in India."

Yes, she was back at the Alpine golf course in less than a month. But it was different. Now she wouldn't use the shower or walk about in the locker room undressed the way she had in the past, the way all the women did. It made a big difference. We could no longer socialize after a round of golf, play in a foursome with our friends, then go on with them into the dining room for a festive meal. A woman has to shower after taking off her golf clothes and before dressing for dinner. But Jackie wouldn't shower or change. So that meant only a hurried drink on the terrace before we rushed home. We made all kinds of excuses, but there was no way to save our social life at the club. We could only play and run.

It wasn't only in the locker room that Jackie would not let anyone see her scar. At the beginning, she was just as secretive at home. From the start of our marriage, Jackie had been modest about undressing in front of me. It was part of that ladylike Philadelphia background—a nice girl never undresses in front of a man.

Gradually, she lost this sense of modesty. After a while, we took showers together, and by the time Guy was two years old, the three of us were splashing around in the tub like a school of frisky dolphins.

But now, after the surgery, she was covered up again. She wore a breast-shaped prosthesis in her bra during the day, and she kept the bra on at night under her nightgown. Now she always closed the bathroom door. If she got a phone call while she was in the tub, I had to knock on the door before I passed the phone in to her, and she either pulled the shower curtain around herself or covered the area of the missing breast with a washcloth.

After this had happened a number of times, I knew I had to do something about it. Otherwise, the covering up would become an obsession. One day, when I heard her moving around in the tub, I knocked on the bathroom door. She said, "Yes?"

I said, "I want to come in for a second."

She said, "Wait," then, "Okay." She had put the washcloth in place.

I went in, kneeled at the tub, and started to pull away the washcloth. She clutched at it all the harder. I grabbed it away, threw it on the floor, and with my hands pinned her arms to her sides. Then I bent over and kissed the scar. It was not a pretty scar. It was a diagonal red gash from the lower center of her chest upward to her armpit. And, of course, the whole area under the scar was flat against her ribs.

She gasped when I kissed her but didn't say anything. She just looked at me, and then we both cried. Finally, I said, "Jackie, I have to make you understand that this makes no difference. To me you are everything. If I lost a finger, you wouldn't treat it like the end of the world. Well, this isn't the end of the world. And you aren't half a woman. You're a whole, beautiful woman. And I love you."

That night, Jackie got all dressed up, and we went out to dinner with Luba and Victor Potamkin, who later became the biggest Cadillac dealer in the world. They noticed how happy and bubbling Jackie was. "Something special must be going on with you two," Victor remarked.

He was right. We had turned an important corner.

But Jackie still had a long way to go. Several months after the operation, she said, "I think I need some help with this. Do you mind if I start seeing a psychiatrist?"

I didn't mind at all. In fact, I was in favor of anything that might help Jackie come to terms with her feelings. She went to see her analyst three mornings a week for about two years. At first, she went to a man; then she switched over to a woman doctor. There was a period when she was in bad humor and depressed after her sessions with the doctor. But slowly she adjusted and came to accept herself as she was. She saw that she was not changed in any significant way. She saw that I was not going to leave her. She saw that the world was still full of possibilities.

One day, she said, "You know, I think it's time for me to wind up this analysis. I'm paying her seventy-five dollars for fifty-five minutes, but the doctor uses most of the time to tell me about *her* problems with a man who used to be a patient. I think she's sicker than I am." Jackie must have had a very healthy instinct about quitting because a couple of years later we read the psychiatrist's obituary in *The New York Times*. She had killed herself.

$\mathcal{W}$hat sustained Jackie more than anything else through those dreadful weeks after her operation was her excitement over the sale of her book. She was just thrilled at the idea that she was soon to be a published author. Her mind was racing ahead to publication day, and I suspect she had already decided what she'd wear to her publication party and what she'd say to interviewers. But Jackie's path was not smooth. Trouble began on the *Josephine!* book right at the outset.

When the contract was delivered from Doubleday, I read it and didn't like it. "Jackie," I said, "this is not a very good contract. It does not set a date for publication."

Jackie was not in a mood to quibble over small print. She was in such a hurry to get started, she would have signed any piece of paper put in front of her. She was already ignoring the small advance the publisher was offering. I think it was about $3,000. Very, very modest, but Jackie knew she had no bargaining power as a writer. And now here I was making trouble over a technicality about the publication date, and she didn't like it.

"What's the difference about the date," she asked. "They're buying it, aren't they?"

"I know, but they could buy it and just sit on it."

"Why would they do that?"

I had no idea why or whether they would do that. But after all the years I had fooled around with contracts for myself and for performers on my shows, I knew a loophole when I saw one, and I wanted this one plugged up. I called Maurice Crain, Annie Laurie's husband, and said, "Why is there no publication date in Jackie's contract?"

He said, "Let me read the contract. I'll call you back."

A small warning bell rang in my head. How come Jackie's agent had not gone over her contract with a fine-tooth comb?

Crain called back in ten minutes and said, "You know, you're right."

He got in touch with Doubleday, and it turned out that the vagueness about publication was deliberate. Doubleday had paid Bea Lillie, the wonderful English comedienne, a sizable advance, something like $30,000, for a book about her Pekingese, which traveled everywhere with her. She had a very catchy title, *For the Love of Peke*. Naturally, Doubleday could not publish two dog books at the same time, so Jackie's book would come after Bea Lillie's.

"How far advanced is Bea?" I asked.

It turned out she hadn't started yet.

I said, "But she's running all over the world with her act. What if it takes her five or ten years to finish this book?"

The answer was that however long it took Bea Lillie, Jackie would have to get in line behind her.

I said to Crain, "Absolutely no. Either you get a date from Doubleday, or we take this book back."

"Have you discussed this with your wife?" Crain asked. He was well aware of Jackie's impatience.

Crain and I argued about the contract back and forth for weeks, and finally I got the book back. I put off telling Jackie for as long as I could—I knew the kind of scene she would make. She did not disappoint me. She had a fit. When she was coherent enough to talk, she screamed, "But I've told all my friends that Doubleday is publishing my book. What will I tell them now? They'll think I lied to them."

"Tell them there's a temporary setback," I said. "But don't worry, this book is going to be published. I promise you. I guarantee you."

She said, "I don't want a vanity press. I don't want that kind of thing." A vanity press is a setup in which the author pays the publisher, instead of vice versa, for putting out the book. It is not a very classy operation.

"No, no vanity press," I assured her. "The real thing—and a better deal than from Doubleday."

Things were very bitter between Jackie and me for quite a while. I knew I was doing what was right for her. I *was* right because Bea Lillie entered a nursing home some years later and never did write the book. But Jackie was convinced that I had taken away from her the one thing she wanted most in the world.

Now I had to figure out how to get her book published. One night, I ran into columnist Earl Wilson at a party. "I hear Doubleday's publishing Jackie's book," he said. "That's great."

"Not so great," I said, and told him what had happened.

"I know a fellow named Bernard Geis who publishes books," Earl said. "Maybe he'll like this one."

I gave Earl a copy of *Josephine!* He loved it and said he would pass it on to Geis.

Thank God, Geis liked the book, so Jackie had her publisher. Geis was a small but very aggressive operator who had published Helen Gurley Brown's *Sex and the Single Girl.* Jackie was overjoyed. She was back on the phone to her friends, and Jackie and I were once again on good terms. Jackie gathered photographs of Josephine for the book. She read and corrected galleys with her editor, Jackie Farber. She sent biographical information to Letty Cottin Pogrebin, who handled publicity for Geis. She went through all the wonderful preliminaries of being a real, honest-to-goodness published author.

Every Night, Josephine! was scheduled for publication in November 1963. Jackie was booked on a number of TV shows that were taped several weeks in advance of publication. One of the main shows was an interview with Conrad Nagel, which was to be aired on NBC on November 22, 1963. That day, before lunch, we sat down to watch the program.

Jackie had just gone on the air when there was an interruption and a sign came on the screen asking the audience to please stand by for an important news flash. The sign just hung there, so we switched channels. Channel 2 had the same thing. So did Channel 7. I went back to the original channel, and then came the flash from Dallas: President Kennedy had been shot.

I guess there isn't anybody who was alive that day who doesn't remember exactly where he or she was at the first announcement of the Kennedy assassination. Jackie and I started to cry. We left our apartment and walked over to the Bernard Geis office on East 56th Street. Letty was there crying; the whole staff was crying. We started walking again and headed aimlessly down Fifth Avenue.

A huge crowd was gathering at St. Patrick's Cathedral. Jackie had developed a fondness for St. Andrew, one of the lesser-known saints, who rarely had a candle lit at his station. Jackie decided she wanted to light a candle for John Kennedy. We pushed our way into the cathedral to Jackie's saint. Jackie lit her candle, left ten dollars, and felt a little better.

Three or four days later, we flew to California to begin what was supposed to be a small publicity tour for the book. It was a disaster from the outset. The press agent assigned to her on the coast hadn't the faintest idea what he was doing. He had her booked for only one TV show. I knew all the TV people. I could have gotten her on every show in town if I had known in advance it wasn't being done. But it was too late for me to move in once we were there.

The one show he had her scheduled for was with Art Linkletter. "Where's the dog?" the press agent asked as soon as he met us.

"We didn't bring the dog with us," I said.

"They don't want you on Linkletter without the dog." He said, "I tell you what, I'll borrow a dog. I'll get a black poodle, and we'll call it Josephine."

I said, "You won't do any such thing."

He said, "I don't think they'll take Jackie without the dog."

"Would they take the dog without Jackie?" I asked.

He said, "Yeah, they might."

I called the producer of the show. I didn't know him, but he knew who I was. Yes, of course, they'd take Jackie without the dog. Jackie went on, and I lined up a few other shows for her.

We went around to some bookstores. There were no books. No, the manager had not heard of a book called *Every Night, Josephine!* No, the manager had not heard that the author of this book was in town and appearing on radio and TV.

The book business, I decided, must be a pretty funny business to mess up on getting books and announcements to bookstores. But maybe things were confused by the turmoil over the assassination. Nobody was functioning very well.

We went on to San Francisco where Jackie was booked on three shows on station KGO, it said on our schedule: one with Roger Grimsby, one with Jim Dunbar, and one with Owen Spann. Just one thing was wrong. None of these people had ever heard of Jackie or the booking. Before she could tear down the station brick by brick, I found out that the manager was Dave Sachs, an old pal of mine. He fixed it up so that she appeared on all three shows even though there wasn't a single book in a store in all of San Francisco. We knew from having checked the book department at City of Paris, one of the city's fine department stores, which was scheduled to run a major newspaper ad for the book.

That night, just as we were getting into bed at the Mark Hopkins Hotel, Jackie said, "I'm going to call Geis in New York."

"It's twelve o'clock," I said. "That means it's three in the morning in New York."

Jackie didn't care. She called Geis at his home. He woke up and answered very sleepily. When he heard who it was, he said, "Do you know what time it is?"

"Yes, I do," Jackie said. "And listen, you son of a bitch. There isn't one of my books in a store here, and there's going to be an ad in the paper tomorrow, and I'm not going to be able to sleep a wink tonight. So why should you sleep?" And she hung up.

In Chicago, again everything was confused and sloppy. The publisher's representative there had booked Jackie on a show on a five-watt radio station that was so far out in the country Fred Allen would have said the manager was a bear. Jackie went only because she knew the program was run by a blind man. I think maybe four people heard the interview. It cost us thirty dollars by taxi each way.

We weren't even booked on the Kupcinet show, the best show in town, but Kup and his wife Essie were old friends of mine, and we worked things out for Jackie to go on.

In New York, Rosemary and Earl Wilson gave a publication party that got big press coverage, and Jackie appeared on a lot of shows. We sent out complimentary copies of the book to a very long list of prominent dog lovers, media people, even dogless celebrities. Many of these copies were signed with Josephine's "pawtograph." Charming thank you notes came back from Pat Nixon, Elizabeth Taylor, Barbara Stanwyck, Princess Grace, and dozens of others.

Josephine became a celebrity. She began to think that *she* had written the book. When people petted her on the head, she looked up as if to say, "It was nothing—I just dashed it off." The Beverly Hills Hotel relaxed its policy of no pets when Jackie explained, "She's not registered, she's just visiting." A slight rivalry developed between Jackie and Josephine. If someone complimented Jackie on the book, Josephine got a little huffy. After all, *she* was the star. Why shouldn't she get to take the bows?

The two got so competitive that when Josephine kissed me or licked my face, Jackie had to find an excuse for Josephine's affection.

"You must have been going around checking stores today," Jackie would say. "That's why she's loving you."

You bet I checked stores and rode herd on Geis. I even lent him $5,000 to buy paper for another printing when it turned out he was in a cash bind. All I knew was that this book *had* to succeed.

And it did. The reviews were good. What was there to dislike in a funny book about an adorable overweight poodle who dined on room service and knew famous people?

One day, the phone rang, and a very clipped English voice said, "Miss Susann, the Duchess of Windsor would like to give a party for your poodle."

At first, Jackie thought it was a joke, but it turned out to be the real thing. Someone had given the Duchess a copy of the book. She was a dog lover, she loved the book, and she wanted to give a party at the Waldorf Towers where she and the Duke were in residence. Every guest had to bring a dog.

Early on the day of the party, Jackie took Josie to the Poodle Boutique where Josephine went regularly to be groomed and clipped. "Give her something special today," Jackie told Mel Davis, the owner. "She's to be guest of honor at a party given by the Duchess of Windsor."

Mel outdid himself. He bathed Josie, brushed her silky black coat to a glorious sheen, clipped her nails, perfumed her, and entwined at least sixteen ribbons in each ear. She was gorgeous. And when we took her out on the street, she made the whole block smell like the perfume counter at Bergdorf's.

Most of the guests at the party were Europeans with titles in front of their names and much given to hand kissing. Among the few people whose names we recognized were Estée Lauder, the head of the cosmetics company, and Anne Slater, the well-known socialite. The Windsors, of course, had their pugs—very haughty and aristocratic dogs. A lot of the dogs at the party, Jackie and I suspected, were rented for the occasion. Like rented tuxedos, they did not quite fit their owners. The dogs all yipped and yapped at each other but otherwise behaved beautifully. There were yummies for the dogs, hors d'oeuvres and cocktails for the people. Josephine, ignoring the yummies, zeroed in on the people food and practically climbed on the Duke's lap to get at his plate. Jackie rescued the Duke by taking him into another room to compare golf swings.

The party was a huge success, and Jackie developed a warm friendship for the Windsors.

In February 1964, on a plane, Jackie was reading a movie review in *Time* magazine. All of a sudden, she yelled, "Wow!" and pointed to the bottom of the page. *Josephine!* was number nine on *Time's* nonfiction bestseller list. Jackie was so excited she wanted to run up and down the aisle and shout, "That's me, that's my book!"

Jackie's joy was worth everything to me. Getting on a bestseller list was the equivalent to her of having her name up in lights. She had finally made it. I wanted to shout, "Wow!" too, and run through the streets waving *Time*.

But publishing is not a trade in which it is easy to get or keep a swelled head. Some months later, we found that *Josephine!* had been sold in England, so we made the publication there an excuse to take a trip—at our own expense. Geis had gotten only a few hundred dollars for the British rights, and he was in no position to underwrite our trip as a publicity tour. The money for the English rights would hardly pay for a half hour at the Dorchester Hotel.

We checked into the hotel, located a neighborhood with a number of bookstores, and looked through the stores, but we did not find a single copy of *Josephine!* Jackie called the publisher and said, "I hear publication date is next week. How come there are no copies out?"

It turned out that the editor who had handled the book was away at the Olympics and Jackie was talking to someone who was not familiar with the book.

"Is that Napoleon's Josephine you're asking about?" he wanted to know.

"No, it's about a dog," Jackie said.

"Oh, you want our animal section."

Jackie finally found someone who knew what she was talking about and said, "I'd love to see a copy of the book." Why of course, they'd send two copies right over to the Dorchester.

In a little while, there was a knock at our door. A young woman came in with a package. "You'll have to sign for this," she said. Jackie signed. "And that will be four pounds six—it's C.O.D."

Can you imagine? The publisher sent the author two copies, and we had to pay for both of them!

While we were in England, our good friend Bob Musel, senior editor of UPI International for Europe and Africa, took us sightseeing:

Porto Bello Road in Kensington, the Tower of London, Miller's Court, where Shakespeare was stage manager, and the Old Bailey, where Oscar Wilde stood in the dock. He was a wonderful guide.

When we got back to New York, to celebrate the success of *Josephine!*, I bought Jackie a new mink coat. It was delivered with her name embroidered in it, but Jackie took the coat back to the store and had the inscription changed to "Every Night, Irving!" After that, I got a lot of admiring and astonished stares from hatcheck girls.

*O*ne day in February 1963, less than two months after her mastectomy and during the period when it was not clear who was going to publish *Josephine!* or whether the book would appear at all, Jackie sat down at her typewriter and wrote on a sheet of rough white paper these words:

VALLEY OF THE DOLLS
by
Jacqueline Susann

She called me over to look.

"What's that?" I asked.

"It's going to be a novel."

"That's wonderful. What's it about?"

She shook her head and pressed her lips together to show she wasn't talking. "I'm not saying. You'll see it when it's finished."

That's the way it was. I did not read *Valley of the Dolls* until nearly two years later when it had gone through four rewrites and was almost ready to be submitted to the publisher.

My first reaction to the project was overwhelming joy. I was so happy that Jackie had enough faith in the future to launch a long-term project—a novel—that I could have just hugged and hugged her. In fact, I did.

Don't forget, she was deeply depressed about the surgery she had undergone. She had not yet come to terms with the new look of her body or the psychological damage that had been inflicted. She was still wondering out loud how much time she had to live. She was pouncing on stories in the newspapers about cancer victims, counting their years of survival after surgery. She cried easily and for no reason.

She was just starting to see the psychiatrist, and neither of us knew how that would work out. Guy was now in a school in a southern state, always happy to see us when we flew to visit him nearly every other weekend but not making any progress at all.

I think by this time we had resigned ourselves to accept the unalterable—Guy would not change. We would always have a beautiful, beautiful son with a mind that was hopelessly flawed. At a time when the teenage children of our friends were completing high school, talking about college, wondering what careers they would follow, our boy was looking down the years—to nothing. Just nothing. And we were looking at the same emptiness. It's hard enough for a father to face that; how a mother does, I don't know. I've never known how Jackie was able to go on. But Jackie, as I'm sure you know by now, had the strength of an armored division on the attack.

For a while after Guy left home, we talked about having another child. We would both have liked that very much. But the months and the years sped by, and nothing happened. Then it was late for Jackie to be thinking about a baby. And always, I'm sure, since we had no clear explanation of what had gone wrong with Guy, there was deep within Jackie the terrible fear that a second child might bring upon us a repeat of the unbearable tragedy.

So now Jackie threw all of herself into her book, and I went on with my work as the TV producer of "Celebrity Talent Scouts," a show that Jackie had thought up. In 1960, Ford had needed a show to replace a disaster called "Star Time" that had gone something like six or seven hundred thousand dollars over its budget. Sonny Werblin, who was then New York head of MCA, the talent agency, had called me and asked if I had a quick idea. "I'll think of something," I said.

That night, Jackie suggested, "Why don't you do a different kind of 'Talent Scouts'? Instead of having a relative or a neighbor introduce the person who is going to perform, get a celebrity to do the introducing. That will double the interest."

Werblin loved the idea, and "Celebrity Talent Scouts" was a hit. For the first special, Dave Garroway was MC, then, for two consecutive summers, Jim Backus and Merv Griffin. Everybody wanted to be on the show. It was a fantastic showcase, not just for the young people who were breaking in but also for the celebrities, who often wanted to plug a movie or a book or just keep themselves in the public eye. We taped it from the Ziegfeld Theatre, and our rating was sensational.

On that first show, Joan Crawford introduced Colleen Dewhurst, who was then married to George C. Scott and was pregnant. I remember going to Joan Crawford's apartment to arrange for her appearance and being asked to take off my shoes. She did not permit shoes on her white carpets. Richard Rodgers introduced a young singer. Hugh Downs, Ethel Merman, and Frankie Avalon introduced talented youngsters. Everyone had a great time on that show. That included Jackie and me because, always in search of new faces, new performers to put on, we had to cover all the night clubs and out-of-the-way spots where youngsters tried out their acts. Jackie loved that.

The other show that kept me busy at this time was "On Broadway Tonight." In 1964, Jim Aubrey, who was president of CBS, called me from California and asked how soon I could put together another "Talent Scouts."

Aubrey provided me with a challenge I couldn't resist. He wanted me to produce a full-scale, major-network show in less than a week. We were talking on Monday afternoon. The show was to debut on Saturday night.

"There's nobody in the world who can do that," I told Aubrey.

"That's why I'm calling you," he said.

I guess I'm a sucker for that approach. The next morning, Aubrey flew to New York, and by that time I had my idea for the show all worked out.

The MC would introduce the young professional performers who were yet to make their mark, and in the audience would be at least four famous, top-notch Broadway producers. The performers would be auditioning for the hot-shot producers—and also for the TV viewers.

Carol Burnett was his problem, Aubrey explained. She was quitting her show. That's why he needed me so urgently. Carol was doing a Comden and Green show on Broadway called *Fade In, Fade Out*, which got lukewarm notices. She was also doing a weekly Saturday night television show called "The Entertainers." Carol was exhausted from working eight performances a week and rehearsing an hour-long variety show—a backbreaking schedule for anyone.

So the next thing anyone knew, Carol was in the hospital. Her Broadway show had to close. And I was scrambling to get something on the air to replace her TV show the next Saturday.

We went on the second Saturday and for many Saturdays with "On Broadway Tonight." On each program, a spotlight shone on the producer in the audience. I had no trouble getting producers; they loved to go on television.

We had well-known guest stars on the show including Judy Garland, Eydie Gorme, Robert Goulet, Tony Martin, Eartha Kitt, Carol Lawrence, and Louis Jourdan.

Who were some of those unknowns? Well, there was Richard Pryor, a sharp young comic whose act had to be considerably cleaned up by Saul Turtletaub before he could go on the air (he made two appearances), there was Joanne Worley, who later made it on "Laugh In," Bob King, who today is a major star in commercials, George Carlin, Peter Allen, Joan Rivers, Hines, Hines and Dad, which included Gregory Hines who appeared in *Sophisticated Ladies*, and Rodney Dangerfield, who had worked under the name Jackie Roy.

Some of the acts were recommended to me by songwriter Al Kasha and Richard Stenta, who produced the Mitch Miller Show.

While all this was going on, Jackie was home writing.

Writing of course was not new to her. But her earlier projects had all been different—quickies like *Yargo* and that first ridiculous play dashed off in a week; or collaborations with Bea, combining chitchat with the hard discipline of writing; or the reworking of informal, personal letters, like *Josephine!*

Valley was the first long-range, deeply demanding writing that Jackie had ever undertaken entirely on her own. To keep to her self-imposed schedule, Jackie pared her own activities down to bare essentials.

She was no longer one of the ladies who lunch, as celebrated in Stephen Sondheim's song of the same name. Those ladies were serious about it. They went to places like "21," the Russian Tea Room, the Colony, or La Grenouille. First, they usually stopped in at the beauty parlor for a comb out (if it wasn't a day when they were being done) and perhaps a quick touch-up to their manicure. Dressing was no casual thing. It was competitive and up to the minute— "Your new Trigère, darling, it looks smashing"—and was preceded by hours of shopping and fitting.

A cocktail or two before lunch, leisurely service at a pink clothed table, decorated with out-of-season hothouse flowers, perhaps wine with lunch, exchange of gossip, scandal, personal tidbits as delicious as the crab meat salad. "My God, how can it be almost four o'clock already?" A quick scattering to cabs or limousines, home for a nap to sleep off the lunch and wine, time to dress for a cocktail party and the evening's rounds.

Yes, there are women who lead such lives; you read about them in the gossip columns all the time. Jackie was never on this circuit on a day-in and day-out basis, but she usually "lunched" several times a week, and it always killed a whole day.

Now that was out. No time. Jackie held to a tight schedule. She was up about eighty-thirty. No need to go through the foot-on-the-floor routine. When Jackie was writing, she was self-propelled. She got herself up without any difficulty. She dressed, usually in her Marlon Brando black slacks and jacket outfit, to take Josephine out for a quick walk around the block. Some days she stopped at a drugstore with Josephine for coffee and an English muffin.

On other days, she had coffee after her exercise sessions with Kounovsky, a tough exercise teacher who kept dozens of women in the theater and in the public eye in tiptop shape. For a while, she went to early-morning appointments with her psychiatrist. But whether it was the shrink or the gymnast, Jackie was home at her typewriter by ten o'clock.

She worked at her desk in the back room of the apartment at the Navarro, the room that had been Guy's, with Josephine curled up at her feet. She wore pants or a short housecoat. She frequently did her hair in pigtails. Jackie had told Josephine she was writing a sequel to *Every Night, Josephine!* and Josie was so proud of being a heroine all over again that she never let out a whimper or a bark while Jackie typed. Jackie turned off the phone so that the bell would not interrupt her train of thought, but she left the signal light on. That way, she knew whenever a call came in and could check with the answering service after she finished working.

Her lunch was usually a tunafish sandwich—she became a tunafish junkie—either brought up by room service or served by Louise, our housekeeper.

I suppose that if firemen had chopped down the front door and one of them had slung Jackie over his shoulder, she would have left the apartment. But I don't think anything else could have tugged her away from her typewriter before five in the afternoon.

Jackie wrote from ten to five every day.

That is, every day she was home. During the two years she worked on *Valley, Josephine!* was published, we made that disorganized cross-country trip for *Josephine!,* we celebrated *Josephine!'s* triumphal appearance on *Time's* bestseller list, and we went to Europe in the summer of 1963 and 1964. We made frequent visits to Guy and Jackie's mother, played golf, and at the end of 1964, we spent a lot of time with lawyers setting up a company we called Sujac. Our accountant thought that was the way to go just in case whatever it was Jackie was putting through her typewriter might someday earn so much money it would have to be handled in a sophisticated, businesslike way.

At the start, Sujac was more for Jackie's morale than anything else. The $4,000 in earnings she had jotted down one year on the wall calendar was about average for all the years she had been knocking herself out in the theater and on TV. We never saw any real royalties from *Josephine!* Now, to be setting up a company to take care of the royalties and foreign rights and movie sale of a book that no one but the yet-to-be-proved author had read was insanity. But it was cheerful insanity.

The stacks of paper on Jackie's desk grew taller and more varied in color. The rough run-through was on cheap white sheets. The next rewrite was on yellow, and in that draft Jackie concentrated on her characters. The third version was on pink, and it stressed story and motivation. The fourth draft was blue, and on this version Jackie cut and cut again.

The color changes were a trick Jackie had learned in the theater where a different color paper is used for every revision in a play script and the director can easily say to the writer and the actors, "Let's go back to the second version, the lilac one, for the love scene. I think it plays better." The colored sheets helped Jackie keep track of her corrections.

She bought a large blackboard, propped it against the wall, and plotted out time sequences, interrelations of characters, and twists of story line. She used chalk in different colors to match her typing paper to coordinate her changes and adjustments.

I used to watch her staring at the board, her chin in her left hand, her fingers over her mouth, lost in thought as she followed the jottings on the board. Then she would reach out, erase a name or a connecting line, think some more, make another change, and finally turn back to her typewriter.

When I got home around six or seven, Jackie would close up the typewriter and come have a drink with me. In the past, she had always been in the habit of asking me what had happened during the day and loved to pick up the thread of some unfinished business—how had I worked it out with the stubborn agent of the temperamental star, or did the network really think it could get away with whatever injustice in programming it was trying for that week?

Now she asked the questions as she always had, but she didn't always seem to be present when I answered. There was a body next to me showing interest, but the body was only half there. The other half was lost in some intricacy of plotting or character development.

"Hey, you're not listening," I'd say to Jackie when I saw that glazed look in her eyes.

"I am so," and she'd repeat my whole last sentence, word for word. Her memory was fantastic. The words I had spoken were just sinking in now as she repeated them. She hadn't heard them before; her head had been too busy elsewhere. She could do this kind of double take perfectly. She was going along on two tracks and switching from one to the other without losing a beat on either.

She did it sometimes at a restaurant or when we were with other people. I don't think they noticed, but I was so attuned to her that I could tell when her mind was freewheeling in another direction even while she was smiling and nodding and saying whatever polite things were required.

While we had our drink after her day's work, Jackie made a few catch-up phone calls. Then we'd go out to dinner and on to a movie premiere, a theater opening, a sporting event. We'd come home before midnight, get into bed, and watch Johnny Carson's monologue. If we knew someone on the show or if one of the guests was a writer, we'd stay with Carson until the end.

But even while Jackie was watching television, she'd be on the phone. This was girl-talk time. She'd check in with her friends, find out who had done what to whom that day, how romances were progressing, double-crosses were being revenged, wrongs repaid with greater wrongs. Nearly all of Jackie's friends led very intense emotional lives that they shared with their half-dozen closest friends. I think we were the only people we knew who consistently stayed married. Everyone else divorced, remarried, circled, and talked. How they talked!

Jackie had one friend who had a single response to every newly reported outrage: "No shit!"

"Time to check in with 'No shit,' " Jackie would say, and dial her number.

Sometimes Jackie's voice on the phone and her hoots of laughter drowned out the TV program I was listening to. I'd tell her she was making too much noise. "Oh, pipe down," she'd say, as if I were at fault. But I didn't care, not even if she ruined the punch line of a great story someone was telling on Carson. It was so good to see her cheerful and laughing, I was so happy to see her enjoying herself that I gladly let her get away with murder.

There were nights she slipped out of bed at two or three in the morning, and I could hear her typewriter going in the other room. Once in a while, toward the end, she stayed up and worked right through the night. I'd look in on her at some wild hour like four in the morning, sometimes still in her daytime clothes, her half glasses slipped down her nose, her eyes bleary from hour after hour of concentration. "Can't it wait until tomorrow?"

"No," she'd say. "I'm hot now, and I don't want to lose this streak," or, "No, it's not working, but I have to stay with it," and she'd wave me back to bed. Jackie believed she had to keep working until the juice ran out.

So it went for two years. Can you imagine the discipline it took, the faith in herself, the sheer will to pound out that book that was shaking the bars inside her head. It was as if the book, imprisoned within her, was imprisoning her in order to escape.

I had many fearful moments. What if it doesn't work? I'd ask myself. What if it's a failure? How would Jackie react to such a defeat?

I knew the answer to my questions. If Jackie failed again this time, I was sure she would not survive. But I loved Jackie too much to let that happen. So I said nothing, but I made a resolution, a promise to myself: I would stop at nothing to make Jackie's book a success. I loved her too much to let her face another failure. There was no way Jackie was going to lose this round.

Then one Thursday night, when we got home later than usual, Jackie said, "Go into my study, doll, and look at the typewriter."

In the typewriter was a white sheet of paper rolled halfway up and just six words arranged on three lines:

THE LOVE MACHINE
by
Jacqueline Susann

"What's that?" I asked.
"It's a new novel I'm starting."

"What happened to the old one?"

"Oh, I finished it. There it is." She pointed to a stack of blue paper at the edge of the desk. "You can read it tomorrow night. It's too late now."

I kept staring at the piece of paper in the typewriter. I was stunned by the title. It was sensational. Was there anyone on earth who would *not* want to read a novel called *The Love Machine*?

"Where did you get the title? It's wonderful."

She shrugged. "It just came to me—from watching television."

I wasn't sure just what that meant, but I decided not to push it at that time.

The next night, Jackie held onto her stack of *Valley of the Dolls* until we got into bed. Then she said, "Welcome to the Friday night fights. Here's the book."

There must have been a thousand typed pages.

I read the first five pages and started laughing. "What's so funny?" she demanded.

"It's your spelling. Look at this d-e-f-i-n-a-t-e-l-y."

She made as if to take the script away from me. "Look, there are a million people out there who can spell. But how many can write a book? I don't want to hear about the spelling."

I kept quiet and turned page after page. She was sitting at my side, propped up against a pillow and following my eyes with her eyes. If I read a page too fast, she said, "What are you skipping?" If I read slowly, she said, "What's bothering you?"

I was afraid to show any expression, afraid to vary the speed of my reading. Josie jumped on the bed, and I absent-mindedly scratched her head. Jackie ordered her away from me. There were to be no distractions. She made Josie go to the foot of the bed, and she said, "You stay there," and Josie stayed, swiveling her head like a spectator at a tennis match to watch both of us.

I read about half of it and put the manuscript down.

"Do you know what you have here, Jackie?" I asked her.

"What?"

"A blockbuster. A real blockbuster."

Jackie let out a breath that sounded as if she'd been holding it for twenty-five years. "You mean I didn't waste my time? You think it will sell?"

"It won't just be on the bestseller list, Jackie," I told her. "This book is going to be number one. Now move away. I want to read the rest of it."

"Do you have to be anywhere in the morning?"

"Stop interrupting. I want to finish."

By the time I finished the book, it was nearly daylight.

"Is it still number one?" she asked.

"You bet—all the way." And I really meant it. I was not just trying to make her happy. I had never read anything like it. This book, I knew, would be a winner. A smash. Jackie had really done it.

We got up, had breakfast, and walked around the corner to the Park Sheraton Hotel where there was a public stenographer. We gave her the manuscript to type in a final draft on good white paper. I think we gave her about two hundred pages each time. Remember, this was the only copy, and we did not want to let the whole thing out of our sight.

The typist was having a wonderful time. Each time I showed up with the next two hundred pages, she'd practically snatch them out of my hands. "I can hardly wait for the next part," she'd say. "I'm really hooked on the story."

That was the best omen we could possibly have.

When it was all typed and I was writing her a check, the typist said, "Boy, you really got a helluva book there. Who wrote it?"

"My wife," I said.

"Jackie Susann is your wife! Wow! Two first names and she wrote *this*?"

Then Jackie and I took the freshly typed script around the corner to a place on 57th Street where we had three copies made. We stood there while the manuscript was being copied. Again, we would not let that precious stack of papers out of our sight. It took several hours. Xerox machines were not so speedy then, and collating was a slow, manual process.

The next day, we gave the book to Annie Laurie Williams.

$\mathcal{W}$hat was this novel that we gave to the agent early in 1965? It was really an amazing document. It was a book that changed popular fiction from then on. It was a book that was as revolutionary in its way as the winds of change that were sweeping through the student movement and the women's movement and the gay rights movement in that turbulent era of the 1960s.

On the surface, it is a simple enough narrative. Anne, a small-town girl, a very good girl, comes to the big city to make a life for herself. While succeeding beyond her most glowing dreams, she meets Neely, an ambitious young hoofer; Jennifer, a gorgeous show-girl with a monstrous mother; Helen, a major Broadway musical comedy star; an assortment of Mr. Wrongs; and a large cast of Broadway and Hollywood heels of both sexes. The characters slide in and out of each others' lives over a period of twenty years.

All the women in the book are deeply involved in their careers. This in itself is pretty remarkable in the year 1965 when the feminist upheaval is barely under way. No one would describe *Valley* as a novel about working women, yet it is. For all of them, Anne, Jennifer, Neely, and Helen, are deeply committed to their work, their talent, their success as performers.

Going a step further into the newly emancipated world, these women take for granted that they are entitled to an active sex life, whether in or out of marriage. At that time, this, too, is a relatively new notion both in American society and in fiction. What's more, there is no guilt attached to extramarital sex and very little to adultery. The only one you don't tell is your mother. Even so, the women seek marriage. The older, traditional forces are still powerful, and only marriage provides emotional and financial security. Except that marriage almost never works.

In fact, in this book, almost nothing ever works. Success corrupts. Power destroys. Love fades. Marriage breaks up. Money undermines. Health fails. Youth and beauty erode away. Only death and pills prevail.

Pills! They are the key to everything, for *Valley* in many ways opened the window onto the world of drug use and drug abuse in which we live today. *Valley* did not launch that world, but it was the first widely popular book to acknowledge and explore it. And Jackie's sharp insight into the role of drugs in contemporary life certainly sparked some of the astonishing appeal of this book and much of the abuse that was heaped on it.

Jackie and I had been taking sleeping pills for years. Most of our friends used sleeping pills. We had both taken bennies or uppers on occasion but were not regular users. Many of our friends, however, were on a constant seesaw of uppers and downers, wake-up pills, go-to-sleep pills, don't-eat pills, clear-the-head-from-the-other-pills pills.

The drugs in use then were chiefly prescription barbiturates and amphetamines. Heroin had not yet entered the middle class. Cocaine was something you heard about but no one you knew used. Marijuana was big among musicians, just starting in a major way with kids, still undiscovered by the general population. LSD was just beginning to get headlines. Valium was not yet on the market. Miltown was around and widely overused.

Jackie used the word "dolls" to describe the pills her characters took. It was a word Jackie made up—an absolutely brilliant invention, for it reduced something that was inherently lethal and deadly to the friendly, comfortable level of a toy or a plaything. And it turned adult pill takers into grown-up children.

Dolls were definitely in the news. Marilyn Monroe had died of an overdose of "dolls" in August 1962, Edith Piaf in October 1963. Janis Joplin and Judy Garland were fast destroying themselves. "Dolls" were starting to take their toll; but they were not yet a subject for polite conversation—until Jackie made them so.

And when Jackie finally pulled aside the curtain on drug use in high places, among the stars, the achievers, the high livers, then everyone, but everyone, rushed to have a look. At that point, of course, the book critics and the social critics did the classic thing: they opened fire on the messenger who brought the news.

Jackie never set out to write a sociological tract. But her insights into the destructive factors in our society gave her story a solidity and importance it would not have otherwise had.

And what a story it was! Jackie was always a great story-teller—at parties, on the telephone with her friends, with me. On all those talk shows, whether as guest or as host, she had honed her skills so that her timing, her tone, her buildup, were perfect. In *Lovely Me* and her other plays, she had taught herself to write sprightly, fast-moving dialogue.

In *Valley* she translated her great story-telling ability and her ease with dialogue into an unstoppable narrative. No wonder the typist couldn't wait for the next batch. No wonder Noel Coward later said, "Jacqueline Susann has the greatest narrative drive of any modern writer." This book was what the trade calls admiringly "a page turner." No quitting once you start.

Where did she get the elements for this nonstop narrative? It was as if she had taken one of those writing courses in which the professor pounds out again and again his basic advice: "Write about what you know. Write about what you know."

Jackie did that—with a vengeance. She knew about getting away from a small town. (Philadelphia happened to be a small town with a lot of people.) She knew about struggling to break into show business. She knew about agents and deals and double-crosses from twenty years of conversation around dinner tables. She knew about tangled love affairs, some of them unbelievably twisted and snarled, from years of gossip on the phone, at lunch, around the pool at the Beverly Hills Hotel. She knew about loss and heartbreak from Guy, from her own surgery, from the tearful outpourings of friends.

Jackie took what she knew—stories, people, places, anecdotes, attitudes, scenes—altered them, enhanced them, shifted them, breathed her own form of life into them. *Valley* is a patchwork quilt of Jackie's own life and world. The setting is the New York Jackie knew, south of 59th Street, north of Times Square, with many way stops at El Morocco, the Barberry Room, the Stork Club, the Copa, Toots Shor. The action shifts to Hollywood, which Jackie also knew well, and briefly to Switzerland, London, and France, where we had gone on our travels.

The only unfamiliar setting is a mental hospital where Neely goes to dry out. To get the details of daily life in such a place, Jackie arranged to have herself admitted for several days, under an assumed name, to a major psychiatric institute near New York. She came home pale and shaken but full of intimate knowledge of hospital procedures and patient reactions.

Jackie herself, of course, is Anne, arriving in New York on a steamy September day, escaping from Lawrenceville, named for the prep school that all those solid Philadelphia boys attended but transferred to Massachusetts near Cape Cod where Jackie had often visited Bea Cole in her home town of Windsor. Anne has escaped from the pressure to marry one of those home-town boys, from the orderly, emotionally stifling life of her mother, from a place where everything is assumed.

Critics and reporters always insisted that Neely O'Hara was Judy Garland. Jackie thought of her more as a combination of Piaf and Janis Joplin. But she could be any of the dancers or singers who shot like meteors across the sky and fell to earth in a shower of drugs and booze. At the beginning, when she is just starting, Neely says, "My big social life is going over to Walgreen's Drugstore and talking to the other out-of-work actors." Jackie didn't waste a thing.

The gorgeous Jennifer is introduced in a "white dress, shimmering with crystal beads, cut low enough to prove the authenticity of her remarkable cleavage." Her face is described as perfect, with a childlike beauty and innocence. This could be Joyce Matthews Rose or Marilyn Monroe or even the young Jackie herself. But Jackie gives Jennifer a prince as an ex-husband, suggesting Rita Hayworth, and when Jennifer enters a room, Jackie wrote, you would have "thought Rita Hayworth was making an entrance." Later, Jennifer falls in love with a senator who wants to marry her—in a spooky prophecy of Elizabeth Taylor's marriage to Sen. John Warner.

That was Jackie's technique—a little of this and a little of that.

Helen Lawson was often compared to Ethel Merman, but again she was a composite of all the musical stars who lived in terror of the talented youngsters coming up behind them and eager to shove them out of the spotlight.

Jackie put me in the book—so literally that I had to laugh. She made me a Broadway press agent named Mel Harris, said I looked a little like George Jessel, went to NYU, had a devoted family in Brooklyn, worked for a comedian named Johnny Mallon (otherwise known as Fred Allen), and didn't try to get fresh on early dates with Neely, whom I eventually married. Again, no waste.

I don't think there was any specific prototype for Lyon Burke. He was a composite of all the charming, lying, conniving Broadway agents who eventually rose to become heads of major Hollywood studios.

The little touches were everywhere. For Ronnie Wolfe, the gossip columnist who hops from table to table, substitute the real Leonard Lyons, who often mentioned Jackie in his column. For Jennifer's breast exercises, there were the calisthenics of the luscious Christine Ayres back in Jackie's J. J. Shubert days. Anne becomes the "Gillian Girl," representing the products of cosmetics tycoon Kevin Gillmore. Jackie had represented Hazel Bishop and had been the "Schiffli Girl," and the famous model Suzy Parker had made headlines as the "Fire and Ice Girl" for Revlon. No waste.

On the darker side, there is Tony Polar, a singer with the magical voice and appeal of a young Sinatra. But Tony has a congenital brain disorder that will doom him to the back ward of a mental hospital. His devoted older sister, who raised him, explains how the doctors "warned me he would never be normal, but he was just a year old and so beautiful. I refused to understand. But when he was seven and couldn't get past first-grade work, I began to understand." The sister then tells how she stashes away every cent she can to make sure Tony won't land in some terrible charity place after she's gone. I can only suppose that in creating Tony, Jackie worked out some of her own rage over what happened to Guy. But we never discussed it.

Then there was Jennifer's mastectomy. The frank, outspoken discussion of breast cancer was surely a first in a popular novel. Again Jackie was working out her rage. The scene in which, on the eve of her surgery, Jennifer slips out of her hospital bed, down the dimly lit corridor, and past the nurses' station with the clock ticking in her ears is an enactment of the escape Jackie almost engineered for herself. Jennifer's death by pills is a replica of Carole Landis' death, maybe Marilyn Monroe's and Lupe Velez'.

Jennifer's funeral, so frenzied that it blocks traffic on Fifth Avenue, is an eerie preview of Jackie's own funeral less than a dozen years later.

Valley came to be described as a sexy book, hot, steamy, shocking. By today's standards, it is not. Far from it. Yes, there is a lot of sex. It's on everyone's mind. It's talked about constantly. But it is not at all the kind of raw, vivid, graphic, sadistic sex that has become standard in today's novels and films. There is no cruelty, no viciousness, no ugliness.

A lot of the sex action takes place off-stage and is only talked about by the characters. The powder-room discussion between Neely and Anne centers on their careers, until Helen Lawson arrives and Neely and Helen get into a donnybrook of a fight that ends with Helen's wig being flushed down the john. Jackie must have recalled from *The Women* how much the public adores a good, old claw and scratch battle between two women.

The language is frank for the 1960s, but most of the well-known, short swear words are used by Helen Lawson, who is depicted as a character in urgent need of having her mouth washed out with soap. The four letter word most used by Anne is "love." She is very hung up on love—true love, lasting love, real love—and she takes an appallingly long time to get it into her otherwise bright head that most men are vastly more interested in sex than love. Jackie gives to Anne much of her own early naïveté—that lovely freshness that I found so appealing. Through Anne, she touches lightly on her concerns about virginity and frigidity, but she is not prepared to deal with these matters more fully until several years later in another strongly autobiographical character, January, in *Once Is Not Enough.*

Mothers are the people who come off worst in *Valley.* Jackie really dumps on them. Anne's mother is narrow, stiff, "emotionally virginal." Jennifer's mother is grasping and whining. Jennifer at one point exclaims, "Damn all mothers! Even in death they reached out and loused you up." Tony's sister speaks of "their lousy tramp of a mother." Neely is a neglectful mother. It is never Mother's Day in *Valley of the Dolls,* and I think this was harder for Rose Susan to accept than all the unladylike words and the less than proper behavior.

Critics rarely talked about the dark underside of *Valley,* but the pervading pessimism is what most strikes today's reader. The good people, the bad ones, the indifferent ones, the vicious ones, are all punished equally. Success is always hollow. At the summit of achievement you are too weary to enjoy the victory. What little joy you can get is snatched away by time. And time, the implacable enemy, strikes early. Still in their twenties, the young women feel that life is slipping away from them. Everything is finished at forty. "Age became a hatchet that vandalized a work of art," Anne says of Helen. "Time is the most precious thing," says Lyon Burke. "Because time is life."

Of course, the critics had no way of knowing that this was Jackie's own cry of pain, her own fear that she would not have time to get to the top of Mount Everest, to feel the rush of exhilaration at the peak. And since she might not get there, why not proclaim the climb not worth the struggle. That reduces the pain. Or you take the dolls to lessen the pain. As on the final page, Anne, the girl who has done everything right, who has befriended everyone, who has hurt no one, takes a red doll because she now knows, when she sees her husband in another's, a younger woman's, arms, that "one day there would be nothing left—no hurt, and no love."

Jackie sensed the loneliness and isolation at the top. She recognized that stardom demands its price. Again and again, she asserted in the book that the price is far too high. You pay—often with your life, nearly always with your love, frequently with your integrity—for scaling the topmost peaks.

Yet even so—knowing how almost unfailingly winners turn into losers—Jackie herself wanted to get to that mountain top more desperately than anyone I've ever known, than anyone you've ever known.

Strange that a book so black in mood, although vibrant with life and drama and sensuality, should achieve the greatest sales ever recorded by a work of fiction and bring Jackie the blazing stardom that had been her life's goal.

$\mathcal{W}$e delivered *Valley* to Annie Laurie Williams in January 1965. She read it and loved it. Jackie was delighted at her reaction. Annie Laurie was a very genteel woman of very advanced age. She could easily have been too horrified and offended to touch *Valley*. But she promptly sent it on to Bernard Geis, the publisher of *Josephine!*

Nothing, as I've said, ever came easy to Jackie. *Valley of the Dolls* proved no exception.

After Geis got the book, there was a long silence. We didn't hear from him for weeks. Jackie was seething with impatience. She had put two years into the book. And now she had to wait weeks for a reaction from her publisher. Finally, she called him and said, "Look, if you don't want this book, then send it back."

Geis asked for a little more time. His publishing house had never before handled a novel that had the potential to become a bestseller. This would be a first. Jackie made a second call and asked to have the book returned. Maybe she'd send the book directly to a Hollywood studio and sell it as a movie, bypassing the whole publishing hassle. In that event, Geis would not receive the one-third of the movie sale that would be due him under the book contract.

At that point, Geis decided to go ahead. Annie Laurie worked out the terms of the contract. Jackie was to get $1,000 on signing, $1,000 on delivery of the manuscript, and $1,000 on publication. It was not glorious in any way, but at least it would get the book published and into the stores. The contract also included an option clause that required Jackie to submit her next two books to Geis. An option clause is printed in all publishers' contracts. Its purpose is to keep, or try to keep, a successful writer in a publisher's stable.

What I did not know then is that in many, many instances,

agents cross out that clause, leaving writers, especially beginner writers, free to offer their work to any publisher.

After being incensed at the Doubleday contract for *Josephine!*, I should have made a strong objection to the option clause in the *Valley* contract or Annie Laurie should have quietly drawn a line through it. If we had done that the publisher might have accepted the change without question, Jackie and I would have later avoided enormous grief, and—you may find this hard to believe—we would have saved in the neighborhood of $400,000. But that comes later.

Jackie signed the contract on April 15, 1965. The next day, she sat for a new set of photographs by Bruno of Hollywood for the book jacket and publicity. For the photographs, Jackie wore the beautiful suit Chanel had given her. She had on pearl button earrings. Her hair fell in soft bangs over her forehead. She was forty-seven, but looked at least ten years younger.

Once the contract was signed, we left in high spirits on a trip we had been planning for a long time. Billy Rose had given his vast and valuable sculpture collection to the State of Israel; in April 1965, the Billy Rose Sculpture Garden was to be dedicated in Jerusalem. Joyce and Billy had asked us to join them for this memorable event.

We flew to Israel and stayed at the Sharon Hotel in Herzlia, on the Mediterranean. We had to wait half a day to get into our room—until Marlene Dietrich packed and moved out. Jackie and I were both excited by this new country. We were awed by its energy and its fast pulse beat. We went to a kibbutz, to the Rothschild winery, to ancient tombs and new hospitals. Jackie loved the beach at our hotel. I think the *idea* of swimming in the Mediterranean, a sea so full of history and legend, delighted her even more than the warmth and gentleness of the water.

We met many high Israeli officials at a huge reception at the King David Hotel two days before the dedication of the Sculpture Garden, which contained magnificent pieces by Jacob Epstein, Rodin, Henry Moore, and sculptors from all over the world. At the reception, Billy was introduced to Menachem Begin, the leader of the Irgun, the daring shock troops that had spearheaded Israel's war for independence.

Billy noticed that Begin was looking around the handsome dining room with great curiosity. "Haven't you ever been here before?" Billy asked.

"Oh, yes," Begin replied quite calmly. "Unfortunately, the last time I was at this hotel, I blew it up."

Billy's health worried us. The year before, the famous Dr. Michael DeBakey had performed vascular surgery on him; he was still in great pain and not feeling at all well. But the thrill of the ceremonies and the joy of being able to give art of such beauty and enormous value to a country to which he felt strong emotional ties sustained him at a high level of excitement.

From Israel, we went on to Rome where Jackie forgot all about her dieting when we tried the pasta at her favorite restaurant, Piccollo Monde. In Paris, we could not get into the George V or the Ritz and stayed at the Crillon. But dinner at Fouquet's, La Tour d'Argent, and La Coupole and shopping for perfume made up for everything.

We had a wonderful time in London, and Jackie had a great visit with her old friend Joan Castle and her husband Bill Sitwell. In New York years earlier, when Joan and Jackie were both young actresses, Joan had been thrilled when Bill, a member of the famous Sitwell family, proposed to her and had quickly phoned the great news to her parents.

But Jackie had said, "Don't rush into this, Joan. We don't know much about Bill." Then Jackie had buttonholed the young man and asked, "Now tell me, what are your prospects?"

"Wait a minute," Bill had protested. "Why are you asking me a question like that?"

"I have to find out these things," Jackie explained, "because Joan is an orphan."

One thing in particular I remember about that trip to Europe. Jackie was trying to give up smoking. And it was murder. Jackie had not been a smoker in the early days of our marriage. She had taken it up gradually and through the times of trouble escalated herself to two and sometimes three packs a day. After the surgeon general's report on the health dangers of smoking, Jackie talked about giving up cigarettes but never quite got around to it.

I suspect she made one of her bargains with God on a trip to the Wishing Hill while *Valley* was under consideration at the publisher's. She must have promised to quit smoking if her book found a publisher. Once she signed the contract, she was under obligation to hold up her end of the deal. She did not smoke during our trip. But oh! how she carried on. She glared at people who smoked. She cadged cigarettes, lighted them, then put them out. She talked constantly about how horrible it was not to smoke.

She'd say to me, "Doll, how about getting me some cigarettes."

I didn't smoke, and of course I didn't make a move to get any for her. I think she could have killed me. She managed to stay off cigarettes for quite a while but eventually drifted back to using them again.

When we returned to New York, Jackie got a copy of the changes made in the book by Don Preston, her editor. She hit the ceiling. In no uncertain terms, she told Preston, "Look, you can make cuts, and you can tell me to make cuts. But don't tell me how to write the book. And don't rewrite it for me."

We had a harrowing time for a while. Jackie and I wanted him taken off the book. When Geis said he'd edit the book himself, we both felt more comfortable.

I'll never understand why it takes so long after delivery of the manuscript for a book to get published. It seems to be just one of those laws that almost a full year is usually required. For Jackie and me, it was a year of suspense, a year of waiting and hoping.

And while we waited, life went on. Jackie checked in with Dr. Lesnick in April and September. Everything was fine. She went steady with her dentist who was always tinkering with her teeth. We went to see Guy at least every other Saturday. We played golf. We went to Philadelphia in May, and Jackie's mother spent a week with us in July and again in December. We were in Beverly Hills in November and Florida in December.

In October, the excitement about the book began to build. Letty Cottin Pogrebin, the extremely capable publicity person at Geis, was sending out releases describing *Valley* as "the most talked about bestselling novel of 1966." Publishing trade papers were touting *Valley* as a very hot book.

Then we got word that Twentieth Century-Fox was interested in buying the film rights. Jackie was out of her mind with excitement. This could be the really big break she needed. If movie rights could be sold from the galleys, before publication, that would guarantee a successful launching of the book. A major movie sale, combined with proper promotion, could give the book a head start toward the bestseller lists.

Jackie had only one thing in mind. She wanted to be number one on *The New York Times* fiction list. Nothing less would do.

When we went to a meeting at the Twentieth Century-Fox New York office to wrap up the details of the movie sale, Henry Klinger, in charge of the literary department, represented Fox. David Brown, head of Fox in the East and married to Jackie's friend Helen Gurley Brown, stepped in from time to time. Our attorney Arthur Hershkowitz, Annie Laurie Williams, Lucille Sullivan, Jackie and I, and a Mr. Colby from Fox made up the rest of the group.

Klinger made an offer of $50,000.

"I don't think Jackie will feel very successful with that amount," I said.

Annie Laurie looked eager to take the $50,000. She thought it was a good offer.

David Brown came in and said, "Suppose we make it sixty-five thousand up front, and if certain amounts of books are sold, we can escalate it to two hundred thousand."

"Make it eighty-five thousand," I said, "and I want the TV rights."

"We don't give the TV rights," Klinger said.

"Let's forget the whole thing, then," I said.

David Brown was kind enough to work out an arrangement that would give us the TV rights in ten years.

"Is that all right with you, Annie Laurie?" I asked.

There was no answer. I looked more closely at our agent. She was asleep.

We made the deal. Later, when we were on the way home in a taxi, Annie Laurie said, "Why did you make such a big fuss about the TV rights? None of my authors bother about that. Mr. Steinbeck doesn't care about TV."

I looked at her. I knew that TV was already paying big money for literary properties and would be paying even more in the future. And here was an agent who couldn't be bothered with securing TV rights for her clients. (I might point out that Steinbeck's books are still being dramatized for TV, and I wonder if Elaine Steinbeck has received any money from the productions.)

"Look, Annie," I said. "You would have settled for fifty thousand dollars. I got eighty-five thousand, and with any luck at all, it'll run up to two hundred thousand."

Jackie was thrilled out of her mind with the movie sale. She called at least a hundred best friends to tell them. She danced around the room. She even called her mother with the news. I think Jackie was already working out a strategy to minimize the shock of the book to her mother. If she could dazzle her with enough dollars and other proofs of success, Rose might not notice all those four letter words.

While Jackie enjoyed her first tastes of success, I was doing some hard thinking.

Annie Laurie Williams was a woman with a fine reputation, but she was really not doing a good job for Jackie. Jackie needed someone who would fight for her, really fight. I knew that as soon as Jackie hit the truly big time, she would be in shark-infested waters. You don't wear white gloves to deal with sharks. You don't nap while crucial numbers are being argued back and forth. With sharks, you outtough them, outmaneuver them, outbully them if you want to stay alive.

Who could do the job for Jackie that really needed doing?

Even as I asked myself the question, I knew the answer.

I was the only one who could do it. I loved Jackie. I wanted success for her as fiercely as she did, maybe more fiercely. I knew how to fight the sharks.

I was the only one who could put in all the time, effort, and in-fighting that would be required to make *Valley* number one. And do the same for *The Love Machine*, the book with the fantastic title that Jackie was working on whenever she got a few free hours.

I was going to have to do it myself.

I had already had my success. Fame in my field, acclaim, money, had all come to me. Now it was Jackie's turn. She had waited all these years. It was twenty-eight years since she'd come to New York with those stars in her eyes. Almost anyone else would have given up. But not Jackie. She was going to make it or die trying. Now she was on the verge of what I felt would be huge success. But she needed someone at her side every minute to maneuver and fight for her.

That night, after the movie contract was signed, I made a contract with myself to devote, from that moment on, all my energy and cunning and intelligence to ensuring Jackie's success. If it meant dropping my career as a producer, well, I'd had my turn. Now it was Jackie's. I wanted her to have every reward that was due her.

I kept my decision to myself. There would be time enough to discuss it with her.

$\mathcal{I}$ learned very quickly how right I was in my decision.

Completely by accident, I found out that in November, six weeks before the Twentieth Century-Fox deal, Geis had sold the paperback rights to *Valley* to Bantam Books. The basic price was $125,000 for the American paperback rights, $17,000 for the British hard-cover and paperback rights, and bonuses based on the number of books sold that could bring the total to a minimum of $217,000.

It was not a bad arrangement at all for a book by a relatively unknown writer who was getting a mere $3,000 from the publisher. It was completely within Geis's right to make the sale to Bantam. Jackie would get half of what Geis got for the American rights and sixty percent of the British rights.

But there were two horrifying things about the sale. First, Jackie and I had not been told, which meant that I was at a terrible disadvantage in my negotiation with Fox. If I had known at my meeting with Brown and Klinger that the paperback rights had already gone for a hefty $217,000 (you always use the maximum price when you negotiate) and to a publisher as important and promotion minded as Bantam, there is no question that I could have gotten better terms from Fox. I would have been in a far stronger bargaining position.

Second, Geis had gotten the entire $125,000 at the time of the contract in October and had control of our half share. When would we see our money? The sharks, I suspected, were already gathering.

Then we began hearing rumors that Geis was in financial difficulties. Jackie said, "Hey, wait a minute. What happens to money that should come to me as royalties if the company sinks?"

It was a real fear. Book authors are usually paid an advance against the money to be earned after publication. Then they get a percentage of the retail price, known as a royalty, for each book sold. But accumulated royalties are distributed to the author only twice a year. The royalty on a book sold in a bookstore in May may not reach the author until December or even later. If the publishing company gets into serious financial difficulties, those royalties can easily vanish between May and December.

So we had Arthur, our attorney, work out a new arrangement that would require the publisher to hold in escrow any money that was due Jackie.

We thought that would protect us, but just wait.

In November, after Jackie corrected galleys, we flew out to California to meet the people at Fox. The studio laid out the red carpet for us all the way from the airport. Jackie had her own designated parking space at the studio. She was wined, dined, lionized. They asked her views about the film. She had a hunch they weren't listening to a word she said. But at least the trip out there in November was a triumphal tour.

Believe it or not, even during those exciting days in Hollywood, Jackie was working on her next book. Beginning back in July, she had started spending at least two days every week on *The Love Machine*. She wrote in New York. She wrote in California. Back in New York early in December, she hit a fast stride of twenty pages on a good working day. She even wrote beside the pool in Florida at Christmas time.

In Florida, she once again gave up smoking. We were there with our friends Lily and Joe Cates, and Jackie had made a bet with Joe that she could stay off cigarettes during the entire vacation. Now her pride was on the line. She suffered but grimly held out for the duration of the bet. Then she gave up and was right back where she had started.

It seems almost symbolic that the year ended with a robbery. Just before New Year's, our room in the Thunderbird Motel in Hollywood, Florida, was burglarized during the night while we slept. We never heard a sound, but in the morning we found that a cat burglar had made off with three hundred dollars in cash from Jackie's wallet and left her emptied pocketbook on the floor.

But the day wasn't a total loss. Jackie wrote another twenty pages.

On a New Year's card to me, she wrote:

"I hope I'm going to make it as a writer.

Will I ever give up cigarettes?
Will I have my full victory?
I love you."

In January 1966, Joyce and Billy invited us to come with them to Jamaica where they had a beautiful house near Round Hill. It was a wonderful house; we knew because we had been there once before— and that was enough.

On that visit, Jackie had nearly died of terror over the huge moths and bats that flew through the unscreened windows and the giant lizards that slithered in and out of the swimming pool. To defend herself against the flying creatures, Jackie had closed the heavy wooden shutters on the windows in our room. But the shuttered room became dark as a cave, so as soon as decently possible, we had made our escape.

This time, we used publication of *Valley*—the official date was February 10—as our excuse for not going to Jamaica. Instead, Jackie sent Billy an advance copy of the book and asked him to read it. When he finished, he said to her, "You know, Jackie, I've known you for—what is it?—twenty-five years, and I have to apologize. For twenty-five years, I thought you were just one of those lightheaded girls. But now, after reading this book, I find I underestimated you all that time." Then he added, "Coming from me, that is a very big concession."

Jackie smiled sweetly and said, "Thank you very much."

"And any help you want on launching the book, I'll give it to you. I'll write ads for it if you like."

As we approached publication day, the excitement mounted. Publishing trade papers heralded the book as "a big, spicy exposé of the nightmare world of love and hate among the rich and famous." Column items reported the movie sale, often using inflated numbers for the sale price. Invitations piled in.

One was for Jackie to be an honored guest at the Book and Author Luncheon presented by the *Philadelphia Inquirer* at the Warwick Hotel. Jackie always got strong press coverage in her home city, so now she could no longer put off sending her mother a copy of *Valley*. Don't think Jackie wasn't worried about her mother's reaction.

Rose Susan read a few chapters and called me instead of Jackie. She was completely hysterical. "How can I show my face among my friends? I'll be disgraced."

"Rose, I think you've gained a writer and lost a city. Move," I suggested, not very helpfully. Rose was extremely upset for quite a while. But Jackie was absolutely right about her mother. Her bitter complaints ceased as soon as the book became a success and people were saying to her, "Oh, Mrs. Susan, isn't it wonderful about your daughter's book!"

"Yes," Rose would murmur, "I'm so proud of her." Or, "Oh you know important writers have to write like that. It's called the new realism." Or, "Jackie doesn't use those words—it's the people in the book who talk like that." So that problem was eventually taken care of.

On February 6, columnist Earl Wilson and his wife Rosemary gave Jackie a publication party at their penthouse in the Parc Vendome apartments which included Perle Mesta, Walter and Betsy Cronkite, Anna Sosenko, Rona Jaffe, Jim Aubrey, Suzy, Peter Falk, Pat and Victor Lasky, Joe E. Lewis, and Noel Behn.

The New York Times reviewed the book before publication—a very hopeful sign—even though the review was not exactly a rave. Eliot Fremont-Smith wrote, "Did you ever see 'A Star is Born'? This book is that film (plus snippets of 'Stage Door,' and 'All About Eve') as it might have been 'recreated' in print form by a slightly bashful fan of Harold Robbins."

We weren't sure exactly what that meant, but it was good "selling" copy, and that was fine.

Publishers Weekly said before publication: "a big, savage, sexy, gamy, poorly written, but powerful and sometimes fascinating novel about show business and the up-and-down love affairs of three girls who star in modeling, acting or singing."

Jackie was pretty mad about the words "poorly written," but she knew she was going to have to take the bad with the good.

We woke up on the morning of February 10 full of happiness and anticipation. This was to be Jackie's big day. The apartment was full of flowers. Telegrams were stuffed under the door. The phone never stopped ringing. Congratulations. Invitations. Calls about interviews, photographs, the publicity tour Jackie was soon to take.

And then came another phone call—totally unexpected.

It was a call from Jamaica. Billy Rose was dead.

We had lost our best friend—on the publication day of Jackie's book.

What should have been a time of total joy was turned into the deepest grief. We really loved Joyce and Billy. We were so happy that they had worked out the problems in their stormy relationship. Over the years, they had married and divorced, married and divorced, and Billy had married and divorced Doris Warner Vidor in between. In recent months, Joyce and Billy had been living together again and were about to remarry. But now it was all over. Billy had never really recovered from the vascular surgery. Finally, pneumonia had taken him. Billy was only sixty-six—much too young to die.

The funeral was at the Billy Rose Theatre on West 41st Street. The casket, completely covered with flowers, was placed at the center of the huge stage. Jimmy Cannon, a popular newspaper columnist, and Abe Burrows delivered the eulogies. Later, we all went to Billy's townhouse. I'll never forget how it rained that day. It was a Noah's flood rain. Billy's friends and some of his enemies, too, remembered him by exchanging anecdotes and tall tales about this brassy, driving little man who had led such a colorful life. As we listened to the stories, Jackie and I turned to each other, and our eyes met. I knew exactly what she was thinking. She would have given anything for me to tell at that moment the greatest Billy Rose story of them all. She had been there when Billy took us into his confidence, and she knew he had sealed our lips. Poor Jackie, even at this dire moment, she hated to miss out on a good story. Now, after so many years, with everyone involved long gone, I think it's time to tell that story.

Billy Rose had made a fortune with his French Casino and Diamond Horseshoe, with other show business enterprises, and with his shrewd investments. In 1944, he and Ben Marden decided they wanted to buy the Ziegfeld Theatre at 54th Street and Sixth Avenue. It was an ornate palace of a theater erected by the late Florenz Ziegfeld as a showplace and then, after his death, turned into a movie house.

Billy's dream was to restore this monument, rename it the Billy Rose Theatre, and change it back into a premium Broadway theater. The building was coming up for auction, and through their sources, Billy and Ben learned that the top bid would be around $600,000. They planned to put in a bid for about $25,000 more. Then they heard that Joe Kennedy, a wealthy businessman who owned the Merchandise Mart in Chicago plus a lot of real estate all over the country and had been named ambassador to Great Britain by President Roosevelt, was coming into the bidding.

Trying to figure out how they could outbid Kennedy, Billy,

never shy, got on the telephone, introduced himself, and said, "May I ask you a very personal question. Are you going to bid for the Ziegfeld Theatre?"

Kennedy said he was thinking about it. Billy then said, "Mr. Kennedy, I have one great ambition in my life, and that is to own the Ziegfeld Theatre. To you, it's only another building. But to me it's the fulfillment of a lifelong ambition."

"What do you want me to do?" Kennedy asked.

Billy said, "I can only buy the building if you stay out of the bidding."

Kennedy thought a minute and then said, "All right, Rose, I'll stay out, but I have a call on you. Remember that. Someday, somewhere, I may call you."

Billy and Ben got the building; eventually, Billy bought Ben out. Billy started taking steps to rename the place the Billy Rose Theatre, but there were protests. Ziegfeld was a tradition, a legend. Billy, for once, listened to reason and left the name alone. He later bought the National Theatre on 41st Street and called it the Billy Rose Theatre.

The years passed, and there was no word from Kennedy. Then it was 1960, and Richard M. Nixon was running against John F. Kennedy for the presidency. Billy, an ardent Republican, was bringing together fifty of the richest men in New York for a major fund-raising event for the Republican party. He had sent out invitations and scheduled a spectacular program. One day, Billy and I were shooting pool in his house, and Jackie and Joyce were watching. The phone rang. We could hear Billy say, "Hello, Mr. Kennedy, yes, sir . . . yes, sir . . . yes, sir."

When he hung up, there was a very peculiar expression on his face. "That was Joe Kennedy," he said. "He wants me to forget about the fund-raising dinner for Nixon." Then Billy told us about his conversation with Kennedy back in 1944, sixteen years earlier. This time, Kennedy had said, "Remember, Rose, when you told me it was your lifelong ambition to own the Ziegfeld Theatre. Remember, I had a call on you. Well, now it's my lifelong ambition to have my son the president of the United States."

That same day, Billy canceled the fund raiser for the fifty rich Republicans.

Jackie was fascinated by the story. She thought it revealed so much about the way power is wielded invisibly by men in high places. She told me that she tried several ways to work it into *Valley of the Dolls*, but it never quite fit. Some years later, she tried again to use it in *The Love Machine*, but again it didn't work.

The rain was coming down even harder when we left Billy's wake. I can still see Jackie's face as we stood in front of his house late that afternoon waiting for the car that was to take us home. Between her tears and the rain, her makeup was washing down her face in dark, wavy streaks.

"It's not fair," she said. "It shouldn't have happened to Billy. And it certainly shouldn't have happened today. Why does something have to kill my joy every time?"

I really had no answer for her. President Kennedy's assassination on publication day of *Josephine!* and now Billy's death.

But fair or unfair, Jackie and I had a job to do to promote *Valley*. I was spending more and more of my working hours on the promotional and, later, the legal aspects of Jackie's book in those hectic, crowded weeks as we pushed in every way we knew to make *Valley* a bestseller.

Jackie went on every radio and TV talk show that Letty or I could book her for. On some, she appeared more than once. She was a big favorite of Long John Nebel's, who had a late-night radio show on WNBC every week night from midnight until five in the morning. Several days after Jackie's first time on the show, a man stopped her on the street and said, "I'm Irving Berlin's lawyer, and I want you to know that Mr. Berlin listens to you all the time on Long John. He thinks you're sensational."

Jackie said, "Oh, that's very nice of Mr. Berlin. Please thank him for me."

The lawyer then sent us tickets to the opening of Berlin's next show. Jackie was thrilled to have such a famous admirer.

If Long John's regular guest canceled or he needed someone to liven up the proceedings, he'd give Jackie a last-minute phone call, and she would rush over to the studio. They talked about everything—politics, gossip, weather—and somehow she always managed to turn the conversation to a character or an incident in *Valley*. Long John was very helpful to Jackie in launching her book.

On March 3, less than a month after publication, *Valley* made its first appearance on *The New York Times* bestseller list. It appeared in fifth place. James Michener's *Source* was number one. Geis ordered a fifth printing of 20,000 copies, bringing copies in print up to 86,000. We celebrated only briefly, pushed on even harder. Geis had set up a tour through the midwest for the end of March. Jackie did radio and TV programs, newspaper interviews, and store appearances in Detroit, Houston, Cincinnati, and Chicago. In Cleveland, we became very friendly with Anne Yudin, the book buyer at Higbee's, and her capable associate, Richard Gildenmeister. She gave a lovely party for Jackie.

Sometimes when we arrived in a city, there were no books in the stores. Jackie was instantly on the phone to Geis—never mind whether it was day, night, or weekend. With each complaint, Jackie threatened to end her promotional tour right there, or she threatened to sue. Jackie was becoming as feisty as I was about promoting the book. She would not let Geis get away with erratic shipments.

In Chicago, we got a terrific break when Carson, Pirie, Scott, a major department store, announced that the book was too dirty to keep on open display. It would be stored under a counter and produced only on demand. We quickly brought a suit in Cook County Court to force the store to sell *Valley* openly, in a normal fashion. The story of our suit hit the wire services and made headlines all over the country. That was great. We wanted people to talk about *Valley*, to say to each other, "Have you read that book the store banned in Chicago?"

Valley, as I've already pointed out, was not really a dirty book. But every time a reviewer or a critic called it dirty, we noticed a spurt in sales. So when *Time* magazine named it "Dirty Book of the Month" and a reviewer for King Features wrote, "The language is filthy, the clinical depictions are filthy, and almost all the characters are filthy," we cringed and secretly said, "Thank you."

The only way they could hurt us was by ignoring us. But there was no way that was going to happen. Geis placed teaser ads in *The New York Times* and other papers that said things like "What a movie it's going to make! But how will they handle that scene in the Plaza ladies' room on page 298?" Louella Parsons trumpeted in her widely syndicated column, "It makes *Peyton Place* look like a Sunday picnic."

When the papers and commentators got tired of hitting the "dirty book" theme, they could always shift to the guessing game. In the *Washington Post*, staff writer Winzola McLendon speculated, "Who are the main characters in Jacqueline Susann's just-out novel, 'Valley of the Dolls'?" Louis Sobol wrote in his syndicated column, "The identities of at least four of the characters are so thinly disguised that two of them, I hear, have placed Jackie on their drop-dead list." "Big Question Game Raging over Dolls," headlined the *Houston Chronicle*.

And, of course, there was the drug theme, which was endlessly fascinating. "Craze for Pills," "Dangers of Drugs," "*Peyton Place* with Pills," "A Way of Life—and Death," "Novel of Hooked, Hyped, Hip Set," and "How to Get High with a Book on Pills" were some of the headlines on reviews and interviews.

Oh, the press had a field day with Jackie. She was pretty to photograph, quick to offer lively, colorful quotes, skillful in bringing any subject back to *Valley*. She could hold her own in any kind of conversation and even sparkle up a dull interview show. She learned how to do this on one of her early interviews when the host made the mistake of saying, "You know, Jackie, I just loved your book."

What could she say but "Thank you." After that, there was a lot of dead air. In that instant, Jackie learned that a challenge from the interviewer such as "How dare you write such a book" offered her a better chance to get in her innings than a bland compliment.

The next time a host said, "Oh, I loved it," she was ready. "Why thank you," she said, "but tell me. Do you think I went too far in the underwater sex scene in the swimming pool that everyone's talking about?"

If the poor guy hadn't read the whole book and had to ask, "What scene is that?" Jackie was off and running. If he had read it, he couldn't avoid talking about it. Either way, Jackie won.

In April, we went to the coast—more interviews, more teaser items about which stars were in or out of the book, which stars would play the roles in the forthcoming film. Was Judy Garland in or out? Would Bette Davis be named to play Helen? What about Ann-Margret?

Valley was climbing the bestseller lists all over. On April 3, it placed number one on the list in the *New York Post*. But we were still waiting for the big one—number one in *The New York Times*.

At the end of April, we were in Miami, at the Fontainebleau, when I made my regular call to Nat Goldstein, the circulation manager of *The New York Times*, who was able to tell me where *Valley* would stand on the list on the second Sunday following. This time, he said to me, "You did it."

"Are you sure?"

"Absolutely."

Valley of the Dolls hit first place on the *Times* list on Sunday,

May 8, its ninth week on the list, and stayed number one for a record-breaking twenty-eight weeks. It toppled James Michener's *Source* out of the number-one spot. Jackie wrote, "A dream come true!" at the bottom of the list and had it framed for her study. I can't tell you how happy she was.

To celebrate, we had a wonderful dinner at the Colony with a new friend of Jackie's, Carol Bjorkman, a brilliant writer for *Women's Wear Daily*. Jackie and Carol had met just the month before when Carol did a profile of Jackie for the publication. The two became very close friends—in a tragically short-lived friendship. But that night was a time of sheer, unalloyed joy as Jackie at last realized her dream. After all the years of struggle, all the failed hopes, all the near misses, she had written a book and taken it to the very pinnacle. She finally had top, top billing. Her name was all the way up there in the brightest possible lights, just as she had always known it would someday be.

Did everything go smoothly after that? Was it an easy streak ever upward?

The answer is both yes and no.

Yes, book sales and publicity took off with new momentum. Stores simply could not keep *Valley* in stock. Clerks would pile a counter high with books in the morning and pile it again at noon. By the end of the day, everything in sight would be sold out.

At the beginning, Letty and I had had to put real effort into getting Jackie on TV and radio shows. For some of the top shows, it was often necessary to make a dozen calls. But after Jackie was number one, the tables were turned. Shows called us. "Could Miss Susann . . . ?" "Would it be convenient for Miss Susann . . . ?" "How can we persuade Miss Susann . . . ?"

Stores, which had not exactly rolled out the red carpet when we were on the publicity tour, began calling. Hudson's in Detroit, Wanamaker's in Philadelphia, Shillitos in Cincinnati, Marshall Field in Chicago, wanted her for a personal appearance, an autographing party, to judge a contest.

Jackie said, "We've been all over the country. Who's ever done two tours?"

I said, "Who's been asked a second time? Come on, let's go again."

"But the publisher won't pay for it."

"The hell with the publisher," I said. "I'm interested in you and your future. I think we should go again."

So we were off on a second round and eventually on a third promotional tour. Once, we took a morning plane to Chicago, did the Kupcinet show, did a CBS show, made an appearance at Marshall Field's, and flew right back to New York—on the same day.

As the door opened wider and wider, I was the one who shoved a whole foot through, and you couldn't close that door unless you amputated my foot. Jackie was going to get what was due her—and more. I had completely turned my back on my own TV career. In fact, I had just been offered a major network post, but without even consulting Jackie, I'd said, "No, thank you." I knew I had more important work to do closer to home.

I didn't want to take credit for her success. I didn't want people saying I was responsible for what she did. I just wanted to make sure that this terrific book she had written did not get lost or undersold or undernoticed because of the craziness of the publishing industry and the tendency of just about everybody to say, "Oh, yes, I've heard about the *Valley of the Dolls*, but that was yesterday. What's *new* today?" I wanted to keep Jackie's book *new* for as long as possible, and that was going to take a lot of work.

Everywhere we went, we checked bookstores. Even before we unpacked in a new town, we would hire a limo and tell the driver to make the rounds of local bookstores. Was the book in the window? Was it displayed prominently inside? If we didn't know the store manager, we'd introduce ourselves to a clerk and ask to talk to the manager. People who run bookstores are always happy to meet writers, so we'd usually have a friendly chat. If the books weren't out in full view, the manager would promise to get them on display immediately. "And into the window, too," Jackie would remind him.

Then Jackie would buy a book—at retail, right then and there— and autograph it to the owner or the manager. Sometimes she bought several books—one for the day manager, another for the night manager. We did it for good will. We knew the store people would remember us. And they did.

In New York, we got friendly with Lillian Friedman, who managed the Brentano store on Fifth Avenue. We became friendly with Max Coulson, the manager of the Doubleday retail department, and with Jerry Chase, John Donovan, and Louis Jenkins. They were all wonderfully helpful to us. In the beginning, when Jackie was home writing, I was the one who walked up Madison Avenue and across 57th Street and hit all the bookstores.

"Hey, you're having all the fun," Jackie said. "Why can't I come along?"

After that, we both made the rounds, usually in the evenings. We were like night watchmen. It got so I think the stores posted lookouts, and when they heard we were in the neighborhood, they loaded up the counters and windows. Fine. That's what the whole thing was about. The trick was to saturate the public with *Valley*, remind people at every turn that this hot, important, talked-about new bestseller was right there in easy reach, to be bought, read, given as a gift.

Then two lucky things happened at once. One night, we were watching Bette Davis on the Carson show chatting about this and that when she suddenly said, "You know, Johnny, I just read the most marvelous book. It's called *Valley of the Moon*. It's about people in show business and drugs and what happens to them."

"Don't you mean *Valley of the Dolls?*" Johnny said.

"Of course, that's it—*Valley of the Dolls* and it's a terrific book."

Jackie let out a scream you could hear in Connecticut. "Listen to that," she said. "Wow!"

That was the first mention of the book on the Carson show.

Jackie grabbed the phone and called Viola Rubber, an agent she knew, to get Bette Davis's phone number in California. Viola refused to give out the number, but Jackie was so persuasive she managed to get it.

Bette Davis answered the phone herself. Jackie said, "This is the author of *Valley of the Moon*."

"Oh, I'm so sorry I got the title wrong," she said. "I loved the book."

"I just want to thank you," Jackie said. "It was wonderful of you to mention it on the air."

Jackie went on to tell her that we would be in California shortly and that she hoped she could meet Miss Davis. That was a very happy night. And sales spurted after the important plug on Carson's 220 stations.

About this time we got a call from Jane Howard, a writer for *Life* magazine. They wanted to do a piece on Jackie. Jane said she would like to follow Jackie around in New York, Hollywood, wherever, to report on the daily life of the number-one bestselling author.

Now, a major piece in *Life* was something an author could only dream about. Press agents could angle and scheme for months and make no progress at all. But if *Life*, on its own, decided to do the story, then you just had to count your blessings and shout hooray!

But Jackie did more than that. She said to Jane, "We're going to the coast in a week or two, and you know that Bette Davis loves the book. You might want to take some pictures of us together."

Jackie then called Bette and told her the people from *Life* would be with us in California and could she bring them around? Of course, Bette would love it. For lunch. For anything. And she'd like to include her sister in the group. *Life* was a magic word. We figured that Bette was interested in playing the part of Helen Lawson in the movie. Fine.

Jane Howard turned out to be wonderful to work with. The piece ran in *Life* on August 19, 1966. Book sales took another upward spurt.

While on the coast, I decided we ought to have our own press agent for *Valley*, someone who would be working 100 percent for us. One day in the lobby of the Beverly Hills Hotel, we ran into Harriet Parsons, daughter of the famous columnist Louella Parsons. With her was a gentleman named Jay Allen, who was in the publicity business. "Did you ever publicize a book?" I asked him.

He said, "No, you don't get much of that business out here."

I asked him which people he knew on the newspapers, at the wire services, on radio and TV. He had good contacts. And, of course, I knew a lot of people. From the way he talked, I could see he was very honest. He seemed like an industrious and square-shooting guy. He was very impressed that we had done the *Life* story on our own. I said, "Okay, I'm going to make a deal with you."

Jay Allen became the publicist for Jackie's books and did a terrific job on all of them. His reputation spread, and his client list expanded. In fact, he became the leading book publicist in the West. We always had a wonderful relationship with Jay, and we knew we could trust him in any situation.

I think it was the *Life* magazine piece that really united the literary establishment against Jackie. What right did this interloper have to top the bestseller lists and get herself a big spread in *Life* magazine? Yesterday she was Miss Nobody. Today she was number one. They couldn't stand it. Since she was too important to ignore, they had to snipe and shoot, and they did so at every turn.

One of the sharpest snipings came from Gloria Steinem. Jackie had always admired Gloria as a writer, so when we got a call from David Brown asking how we would feel if Gloria Steinem wrote the adaptation of *Valley* for the screen, we said, "Fine. If she can do a good adaptation, we'd love it." Brown said they would make a flexible arrangement with her to see what she could turn out.

Several weeks passed, and then Brown called to say that Gloria was off the screenplay and that it was now being done by Helen Deutsch, a veteran screenwriter who later shared credits with Dorothy Kingsley, who had written the screenplays for *Seven Brides for Seven Brothers*, *Kiss Me, Kate*, and *Pal Joey*. Mrs. Kingsley, a dignified white-haired woman, wrote the script in longhand, and because of *Valley*'s reputation as a racy book, she earned for herself in the trade papers the dubious nickname of "Dirty Dotty."

On April 24, 1966, in the *Herald Tribune* Book Review, the last issue before the newspaper folded, there appeared a review of *Valley* by Gloria Steinem under the headline "A Massive Overdose." It was not a kind review. She wrote, "For the reader who has put away comic books but isn't yet ready for editorials in the Daily News, *Valley of the Dolls* may bridge an awkward gap," and concluded, "Her first work, *Every Night, Josephine!*—billed as 'a charming and witty account of her life with an almost human poodle'—was for many months the only book on display at the Sixth Avenue Delicatessen in New York."

Jackie, of course, was seething mad. "Can you imagine," she said after reading the review. "I wasted all that time admiring her." But if Gloria wanted to play meeooow, Jackie was perfectly capable of playing back—and then some. When Jackie went on the Merv Griffin show a few days after the review, she began talking about Gloria and said, "I'd like Miss Steinem to know that the Sixth Avenue Delicatessen is not the only place where *Josephine!* is on display. It's also at the Colony, at Danny's Hideaway, and at '21.' I feel sorry for Miss Steinem that the only place she gets taken to dinner is the Sixth Avenue Delicatessen."

I said before that some things went well and some did not go so well after *Valley* hit first place. What went badly was our relationship with our publisher. We had not received any of our half share of the $150,000 that Bantam Books had paid Geis for the paperback rights back in October 1965, and here it was nearly the end of 1966. You can be sure it was not for lack of asking. We asked; our attorney asked. There were many explanations but no money.

Then two things happened. I ran into Groucho Marx one day at the posh Bistro in Beverly Hills. I had known Groucho for years. He, along with Art Linkletter, Cowles Communications, Inc., Goodson-Todman Productions, and Esquire, Inc., was associated with Geis as a limited partner in the publishing venture, but he was clearly not an admirer of Mr. Geis. Groucho said he hoped we were keeping two eyes open as far as our publisher was concerned and offered to send me a copy of the firm's latest accountant's statement. I knew right away he was telling me something important.

The statement from the accountants, Phillips, Gold and Company, was an eye opener. Bernard Geis Associates owed more than $386,000 in current and back royalties to writers—money that it did not have since it was $383,000 in the red. Among the writers owed back money was former President Harry S Truman. What's more, the partnership was subject to two lawsuits in connection with the publication of *Harlow* by Irving Shulman.

I decided not to burden Jackie with this unhappy news.

Then Bennett Cerf, whose Random House distributed Geis Books, mentioned to Jackie that she must be selling about 11,000 books a week, since she was holding in the number-one position. Jackie was astonished. Her reports from Geis indicated much lower sales.

What was going on? It was time for us to talk to our attorney. We asked Bantam not to pay over any more money to Geis. All through the second half of 1966 and on into the next year, there were endless and often acrimonious meetings with attorneys and accountants.

At one point, Geis insisted that the only way he could pay us what was due us—$100,000 by his accounting—was for him to get a big paperback advance on Jackie's next book, which, under our contract, we had to submit to him. He figured the advance should run between $300,000 and $400,000, and that would straighten out everything. He would need an outline to show to paperback editors.

I couldn't believe it. How in the world, acting in good faith and with a good agent, had we gotten ourselves into such an insane position? It was outrageous. Jackie was walking around with murder in her eyes.

But she did the prudent thing. With everything else going on— *Valley* soaring away, the film getting under way, everyone in the world wanting her to write something, go somewhere, appear for

[173]

some cause—she sat down and wrote an outline of *The Love Machine*. Jackie had been working on the book all along, but she had never done a formal outline.

The scheme for bailing out Geis with the new book came to nothing as a new and nasty element entered the controversy. We found that Geis had commissioned a writer to write a searing, sexy, sensational novel about a Sinatra-type male singer that he hoped would have the same impact as *Valley*. This was outrage on top of outrage. Not only was he not paying Jackie, he was inventing competition for her.

Eventually, after protracted unpleasantness, we had to sue Geis for an accounting. He stated he wanted $200,000 for the cancellation of his option on *Love Machine* and the third novel. Know what? He eventually got $400,000. That's what he had to be paid to free us from this entanglement. The payment was made by Bantam against our future royalties, and as a result of this transaction, Bantam became the owner of the right to publish *The Love Machine* and the third novel in paperback.

I guess Jackie and I were supposed to consider ourselves lucky that we did not have to put up the entire $400,000, which, of course, we did not have. But it was money that really should have been ours as an advance on the two books after *Valley*. What's more, this advance could have been twice as large, maybe three times, if we could have offered the books on the open market without having to be rescued from the sharks that I had suspected all along would be lurking out there.

If anyone tells you that publishing is a gentleman's profession, I suggest you just laugh.

But Jackie was a lady right to the end. When she finally was ransomed from Geis, she insisted that as part of the settlement her friend, Helen Gurley Brown, who had also been shortchanged, be paid $60,000 in back royalties for *Sex and the Single Girl* and that Hugh Schonfeld be paid $39,798 in delinquent royalties for his novel *The Passover Plot*. Jackie didn't even know Schonfeld; she just admired his book.

here were two major events in our lives in the year 1967 and at least a million minor ones. The big ones were the filming of *Valley of the Dolls* and the publication of the paperback. Both were resounding successes, but in very different ways.

The movie went before the cameras at Twentieth Century-Fox in April after intense advance publicity. Studio publicists turned the casting into a major national guessing game, interweaving the excitement of who-will-play-what-role with the other long-running guessing game of who-was-who in the book. Columnists and feature writers went along with the charade as if their very lives depended on it. The publicity was endless and unrelenting—fine for the movie. And for the hard-cover book, too, which was still holding its number-one position.

About this time, ABC television decided to do a TV special about Jackie and the unprecedented success of *Valley*. That was fun for everyone. For weeks, cameramen and technicians were underfoot and leaning over our shoulders wherever we went. Jackie was filmed at her typewriter at home, in the park in her black slacks and jacket with Josephine, at glamorous restaurants, at Twentieth Century-Fox in California. She talked about her childhood and how she devoured movie magazines and dreamed of Grauman's Chinese Theatre and Schwab's Drugstore. She told about pretending to adore canneloni, because it was the cheapest item on the menu, when she dined at Sardi's with other young hopefuls in her early days in New York. She talked about meeting me and the first years of our marriage. She talked about Josephine and how she became the Dr. Spock of poodles. She showed the typewriter and the blackboard she had used in writing *Valley*.

[175]

Everyone had his innings on the show. Victor Lasky said, "She had the product." David Brown said, "She's a hypnotic story-teller." Jim Aubrey described *Valley of the Dolls* as "the biggest presold book in history." Jackie said, "I love all my characters," and reactivated the guessing game of who might be the real person behind Anne, Neely, Helen, and Jennifer. She talked about the emptiness and loneliness at the top and the search for comfort and oblivion in pills.

Then she paid me a lovely tribute. She said, "I can accomplish anything as long as I know Irving Mansfield is my husband. None of this would have happened if I was not Mrs. Irving Mansfield first."

It was happening, as Jackie had always known it would. As individuals, we each had strength and drive. But as a team, our energy was multiplied in a fantastic way. Together, we could take on the world.

The ABC special was shown in January 1968, right after the release of the film. Do I have to tell you that it helped zoom book sales and movie box-office receipts right off the charts?

Going back to the filming of *Valley*, Jackie and I learned very quickly how little influence we would have on the making of the movie. Our education began in 1966 when *Life* was photographing Jackie. On that trip to the coast, we had had dinner with Mark Robson, the film's director. Mark had directed the very successful film version of *Peyton Place* and *The Prize*, from Irving Wallace's novel.

Jackie said to him at dinner, "Wouldn't Bette Davis be wonderful for Helen?"

Robson said, "I don't think so."

We were about to lose fight number one.

"She's a big name and a wonderful actress," Jackie persisted.

"We're thinking of someone else," Robson said. "Judy Garland."

"Judy Garland!" Jackie and I both exclaimed at the same time.

It seemed an absolutely wrong choice to us. Judy was far too vulnerable to play such a tough, strident performer. And with all the trouble Judy had had, it hardly seemed likely she could stand up to the demands of the role. But Robson was insistent. "Judy can do it," he said with finality.

Then Jackie asked him who would play Anne.

He said, "Barbara Parkins." Barbara had been playing the lead in

"Peyton Place" on television. Jackie liked her and thought she was a good choice.

"What about Jennifer?"

David Weisbart, producer of the movie said, "There's an absolutely beautiful girl named Sharon Tate." We didn't know Sharon then, so we had no comment. Later, when we met Sharon, we were both delighted with her. She was wonderful.

"I think Neely is the best part," Jackie said. "Who will get it?"

"Everyone in Hollywood wants to play Neely," Robson told us. "We're testing a lot of people. We're even testing Patty Duke."

"Patty Duke?" Jackie couldn't believe she'd heard right. Patty Duke seemed completely wrong for the part. She was a fine young actress. But she had none of the gamin quality of Neely, none of the quicksilver. But that was Hollywood, we were learning quickly. Forget about logic.

Jackie was to play a cameo part in the film as a reporter. She had five lines to speak, and our plan was to stay only three days. We traveled light on that trip at the end of April 1967—Jackie took two Pucci dresses, a bathing suit, and a raincoat. We checked into the Beverly Hills Hotel. The whole town was abuzz with the shooting of *Valley* and the big comeback of Judy Garland.

At the studio, Jackie was given a dressing room of her own, her name was painted on her parking space, and everyone made a huge fuss over her. But nothing happened. Day after day, we waited. The story was that Judy's scenes were going so great the director didn't want to lose momentum. He'd get to Jackie's scene later. For two weeks, Jackie alternated her two dresses. She didn't even have a chance to wear the bathing suit—it rained all the time. Every day, she called the studio and asked, "Are you ready for me?"

"No," they'd say, "maybe tomorrow." That's why she didn't buy any other dresses—it was always tomorrow. When she asked how Judy was doing, the answer was always, "Fantastic!"

At the end of the third week, Jackie received a rush call to do her scene. Judy was out of the movie, and Susan Hayward was in.

Jackie did her scene in half an hour. As she was leaving the set, she stepped into Judy's dressing room. In *Judy*, his moving biography of Judy Garland, Gerald Frank describes the scene:

> *Jackie saw a little white pill on the floor in a corner of the closet. She picked it up and put it to her tongue. She recognized the bitter, telltale taste. Demerol. The maid saw her with the*

pill. "Oh, that must be one of Judy's nerve pills," she said. "If she knew she'd dropped it—when she drops one, she tells me, 'My God, they're diamonds, find them.' "

Poor Judy, thought Jackie.

Jackie came back to the hotel, packed her two Puccis—I think by then people believed they were tattooed on her—made a phone call to Judy but was told Judy was not taking calls, and we got on the plane to New York.

The "no smoking" sign was on in the 707, and the pilot was waiting for his signal from the tower when there was an announcement on the speaker: "Miss Jacqueline Susann, there's an urgent phone call for you. You can take it at the desk outside. We'll hold the plane."

My heart turned over. Was it Guy? Was it Jackie's mother? Had something terrible happened? Jackie walked off the plane, with 103 passengers staring at her with hate in their eyes. They had to sit and wait while this one took a phone call!

It was Judy Garland on the phone. Jackie had not left a flight number with her hotel or even the name of the airline. There were a dozen flights for New York every day. Not only had Judy tracked down Jackie, she had the clout to get her off the plane.

"I was sleeping when you called," Judy explained. "I had a virus."

"That's all right, Judy. I just called to tell you how sorry I am that it didn't work out."

"What are they saying about me, Jackie?" Judy asked plaintively.

"I think they'll just say you've withdrawn."

"I didn't withdraw. I was fired."

"Let me call you from New York," Jackie said. She was afraid the plane would take off without her.

"Jackie . . ." The voice was urgent. "You're the only one who called."

"What do you mean?"

"I tried to reach Mark Robson, Dick Zanuck, Darryl Zanuck. No one takes my calls. I'm a star, aren't I?"

"Of course you are, Judy."

"Then where did everybody go?"

Jackie repeated the conversation to me word for word when she got back on the plane. *Where did everybody go?*

It could have been a line from *Valley of the Dolls.* It could have been Neely wailing her hurt when she was taken off her picture. Now here it was in real life—Judy Garland, once a blazing star, little Frances Gumm, who became the beloved Judy Garland, now ruined by pills and booze, tossed off her comeback film, crying from the gut, *"Where did everybody go?"*

There are two sequels to the Judy Garland incident. The only thing Judy got out of the film was the handsome sequinned pants suit that had been made for her and that she wore in her stage comeback concert at the Palace in New York some months later.

Not too long after that, Jackie was just leaving the Navarro when a distraught-looking woman in a T-shirt called to her and said, "Hey, author, hello there."

Jackie looked more closely and realized it was Judy Garland. "How are you, Judy?" she asked, although it was perfectly clear that Judy was not in very good shape.

"Do you remember in California when I called you and asked you if I wasn't a star, and then I asked, 'Where did everybody go?' "

"I sure do."

"Well, this big star is locked out of her hotel room. I can't even get in there to get my clothes."

"How much do you owe them?" Jackie asked.

"I don't know." Judy was like a lost little girl.

"Come on upstairs with me for a second."

Jackie took Judy up to the apartment and went to look for her purse. I guess she had just been going somewhere in the neighborhood and didn't have any money with her. Jackie pulled out what was in the wallet—eight $100 bills—and handed them to Judy. "Here you are," she said.

"You're a great lady. But I don't know when I'll be able to pay you back."

"Who said anything about paying back?"

Jackie saw Judy eying the bottles on the bar. But she wasn't going to let anything get started. They said good-by at the door. Jackie never saw Judy again.

During the weeks we were in Hollywood waiting for Jackie to do her scene in *Valley*, we had expected to be invited to the daily rushes—the showing of the film that had been shot each day. We were not. We tried, we requested, we angled. We got nowhere. They would show us nothing. You can imagine how Jackie felt about being excluded from *her* movie. But there was nothing to be done. We weren't even invited to company screenings. Hollywood makes its own rules.

Back in New York, we followed the progress of the film by reading the columns and the trade papers. The reports were all wildly enthusiastic. Shooting was completed on June 20. (Films were made more quickly then than now.) Suddenly, there was distressing news. On July 21, while the picture was being edited, David Weisbart died of a heart attack at the Brentwood Country Club. We were shocked and saddened. We had liked David.

But in a sense the movie was already behind us. Life was swooping by at such dizzying speed it was all we could do to concentrate on each day's demands. The hassle with Geis was still sizzling along. I remember one day we were reading the complaint and summons in connection with our suit for fraud and breach of contract when Jackie looked up and said, "Do you think George Eliot had to go through this sort of thing?" On the plus side, Jackie was in greater demand than ever to talk about her book and her movie. It was a struggle to find some free hours now and then to work on her next book.

But mostly, that summer, the paperback occupied center stage. Bantam, we learned very quickly, intended to go all-out for *Valley*. From Oscar Dystel, the president and chief executive officer of the company, to Marc Jaffe, the editor-in-chief, to Esther Margolis, in charge of publicity, and her assistant, Arnold Steifel, and Fred Klein, head of promotion, everyone was set to break all publishing records with *Valley*.

It's a wonderful thing to be working with a publisher who believes in your success even more enthusiastically than you do. We realized right away that there was never going to be any worry about enough books in the stores. We were not going to have to battle about advertising budgets. We were all on the same wavelength.

Publication date was officially July 5. Bantam used a Fourth of July theme in trade-paper ads. The book would blast off like a rocket—and it most certainly did. By July 10, less than a week after publication, there were 4.1 million copies in print and more than 1 million reorders pouring in from stores. Bantam took a full-page ad in *The New York Times* to play up the fantastic launching.

It should have been Jackie's most joyous triumph. But once again tragedy struck. I've told you that Jackie became a close friend of Carol Bjorkman, who wrote a column for *Women's Wear Daily*.

Carol was sensitive, delightful, and funny. She took Jackie to fashion openings and introduced her to the world of designer clothes. Late that spring of 1967, she was feeling ill. She thought she was overworked and anemic. But she had leukemia.

Her friends knew her illness was fatal, but Carol never knew. When she went into Memorial Hospital, her friends brought her beautiful things she loved—Porthault sheets, lace nightgowns, bone china. Her close friend, designer Seymour Fox, and Jackie were with her almost every day in the hospital, helping her open packages and making plans for after she was out and up and around again.

Carol died on July 4. Her funeral was held on publication day of the *Valley* paperback. Jackie was inconsolable. Poor Carol was just thirty-eight, at the start of her career. She had so much living to do. Her death was a terrible tragedy, especially so for Jackie because it reminded her once again that her days, too, might be numbered. The thrill of her success and the reassuring checkups with her surgeon four times each year had tended to soothe away her fears. Now the terror surfaced again. She was sleeping badly, smoking more than ever, scanning the obituaries of strangers for the causes of their deaths.

Valley hit number one on the paperback bestseller list right after publication. I think it was the fastest-selling paperback book ever. It sold 1,000 copies in O'Hare Airport in Chicago in two days. It sold 62,000 copies in Toronto in two weeks. Bantam packed the bookstores and the usual paperback racks with copies. Bantam found new outlets for books and put them on sale in butcher shops and shoeshine parlors. I used to say that the only thing you could turn on and not have Jacqueline Susann talking about *Valley of the Dolls* was a faucet.

In Chicago, Jackie had a brilliant idea. "How do the books get into the stores?" she asked.

"They're delivered by distributors," I told her.

"Okay, let's go see the distributors."

We got up at four in the morning and went to Charles Levy and Company, the biggest wholesaler of books and magazines in the city. The drivers were just loading up their trucks. We brought coffee and a big pile of Danish. Jackie gave a brief pep talk to the drivers. "We're all in this together," she said. "This is going to be our big day for *Valley of the Dolls*." Then she took books and signed them for the drivers and said to the foreman, who also got a book, "Please have the office put these on my tab."

The drivers loved her. They loved it that she cared so much that she was willing to get up early and that she thought they were important. The distributors became our friends. They rooted for us. When you have the distributors, the store buyers, and the sales people on your side, you're really way ahead.

In July we went to Detroit, Minneapolis, Denver, and on to California. This time, there was no trouble getting on any show we wanted. Between Jay Allen's and Esther Margolis's skill and Jackie's magic name, programs were fighting for her. At each stop, she was interviewed by the newspapers, photographed, invited to luncheons, teas, autograph sessions. At each stop, we visited bookstores on our own, had early-morning coffee with distributors and their truck drivers. No stone went unturned.

"We're in this together," Jackie told the drivers. "We're a team. I've worked hard to give you the book. You work hard now to move it into the stores and sell it."

"Sure, coach," they'd shout back, "we're with you." They most certainly were.

In August, *Valley* finally slipped off the hardcover bestseller list—after sixty-eight weeks, twenty-eight of them in first place. I hesitated to break the news to Jackie, knowing how emotionally involved she was with *The New York Times* listing. But I should have known how much of a realist Jackie was. She shrugged at the news and said, "The paperback's number one, doll, so don't bother me about that old thing."

By the way, our favorite *New York Times* listing was on October 23, 1966, when a crazy printer's error placed *Valley of the Dolls* in first position on both the fiction and the nonfiction charts.

By autumn, *Valley* in hardcover was selling heavily all over Europe. There were editions in England, France, Germany, Spain, Italy, and eventually, for the world market, in languages we'd never heard of. We made our first European promotional tour in the fall of 1967. France was not our hottest spot. In fact, we couldn't find a single book in a store. Therese de St. Phalle, the representative of Presses de la Cité, Jackie's publisher, was mainly concerned that Jackie should not wear green when we met the head of the company and his wife at a luncheon. The wife thought green meant hard luck. When we tried to tell Mme. de St. Phalle how dismayed we were about the lack of books in the stores, she told us not to worry, everything was fine.

"But where are the books?" I asked.

"They're all sold," she said. "Isn't that wonderful?"

Presses de la Cité, it turned out, had printed about 5,000 or 7,500 copies in hardcover; they'd all been sold, and that was that.

"But aren't you going to do another printing?" Jackie asked.

No, that wasn't the custom with this publisher. The edition had been sold out, the book was pronounced a success, and when was Jackie's next book arriving? We made up our minds that instant to find a different French publisher for the next time around.

In Germany, Jackie was welcomed with headlines of a size usually broken out only to declare war. The Germans were insane about Jackie and *Valley*. The German title of the book was *Das Tal der Puppen*, which always sounded very sinister to us. We went to Munich where we met with Dagmar Henn, Bantam's German agent. On to Hamburg and Berlin, with wild welcomes everywhere.

In Hamburg, we visited the notorious Hebertstrasses, where depravity of every persuasion was offered with supermarket efficiency for both participants and spectators. We saw very young girls, some of them very beautiful, wearing almost nothing, standing in windows with whips and other accoutrements of their trade, beckoning the passers-by. A lot of them beckoned to Jackie: "You can come in, too, you know." Jackie was appalled to learn that the older girls, those who were about thirty, were in the back where customers could get group rates. That was too much even to think about—only thirty and demoted to group rates.

We went to a café where the dancers sat naked, each at a little table with a number above her and a telephone in front of her. There was a telephone on each of the tables for patrons. You could pick up your phone and dial the girl you wanted. Jackie told me to pick up, so I tried until I found a girl who spoke English. I said I was a stranger in town. She asked what table I was at. When I told her, she said, "Who is the pretty girl you're sitting with?"

I said, "She likes to watch."

"Good," she said. "Good." It would cost twenty-five dollars.

I told her I'd be back later, but, of course, I knew I wouldn't be. I sent her a five-dollar tip.

We went to another place where, for the first time, we watched women wrestling in the mud. There were often six or seven of them, topless, wearing only G-strings, jumping all over each other. Since then, mud wrestling has come to this country, but when we first saw it, we found it shocking and, well, filthy.

In Berlin, we went to see the female impersonators at Chez Nous, a club that presented what seemed at first glance to be a normal floor show. The master of ceremonies was charming and energetic, and the girls were really beautiful and graceful. Only when they sang did you realize from their rather masculine, or falsely feminine, voices what was going on. One of the performers, a stripper with incredibly beautiful breasts, kept winking at me and making gestures in my direction.

"Who's your new friend?" Jackie asked, laughing.

I told Karl Heintz Scheffler, the representative of Twentieth Century-Fox, who was there with us, that I would like to buy all the people in the show a drink. They all came out after their act, and we were introduced. Then Lola, the one with the incredible breasts, said, "Irving, my God, it's been a long time. About ten years, isn' it?"

I turned white. I could see Jackie's eyebrows shoot up under her bangs. Who could this be? What had I stumbled into? It was the worst feeling in the world.

Then Lola mentioned her former name. She, as a he, had been a dancer on the Polly Bergen show which I had produced. Lola was a transexual and had switched genders from male to female. Now she wanted to know what had happened to all the people from the old days, so we had a fine time catching up with the last ten years.

Jackie, I could see, was making furious mental notes wherever we went in that Brechtian world. If you want to follow our tour of perversities more closely, you can do so with Robin Stone in his descent into decadence in *The Love Machine*.

Meantime, word reached us that the film of *Valley* had been previewed in several cities in California with not altogether happy results. Audiences had laughed in the wrong places. More editing was under way.

Also under way were plans for the wildest launching of a film in Hollywood's gaudy history. No ordinary premiere would do. This one had to be sensational. Are you ready? The luxury liner M. V. *Princess Italia* was to make its maiden voyage from Venice to Los Angeles—yes, Los Angeles, right through the Panama Canal—from November 14 to December 14 with *Valley* stars aboard and relays of the world's press boarding and debarking at various ports to attend the premiere of the film and enjoy the festivities.

Jackie and I joined the cruise in Venice on November 14 at the end of our promotional circuit in Europe. It was marvelous to leave

Cause for celebration as Valley of the Dolls, *America's number one bestselling novel hits twenty three weeks.* ENRICO SARSINI, LIFE MAGAZINE © TIME INC.

In front of the camera, Jackie playing a bit part as a reporter in the film version of Valley of the Dolls. *Barbara Parkins played Anne.*

Judy Garland with Jackie at a press conference for Valley of the Dolls.
Judy was replaced by Susan Hayward early in the filming.

We're in Times Square cautiously checking out audience reaction to the Valley film opening.

ABOVE:
*An example of her indefatigable promotion
sense. Jackie meets with wholesaler booktruck
drivers in Long Beach.*

ABOVE:
*Believe it or not, Jackie tries out as a
blond.*

LEFT:
*A moment of clowning as Jackie takes
time out from the publicity tour for the
paperback edition of* Valley.

Clint Eastwood chatting with Jackie at an El Morocco party.

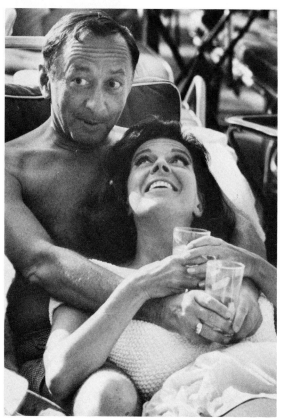

Celebrating my birthday at the Beverly Hills Hotel pool.

JULIAN WASSER, LIFE MAGAZINE © TIME INC.

A *typical scene at home, Jackie working on the plotting for* The Love Machine.

Jackie boarding Gene Klein's National General jet rechristened The Love Machine *for the paperback publicity tour.*

ABOVE:
Joan Crawford and Jackie surround Leo Jaffe, then Chairman of the Board of Columbia Pictures.

RIGHT:
A smiling Cary Grant and Jackie at a Friars Club dinner.

LEFT:
*Jackie and another dog
lover.*

BELOW:
*Close friend Helen Gurley
Brown and Jackie at an
art exhibition.*

Jackie and her new poodle, Joseph Ian, walking through Central Park.

A typical nightly scene as Jackie plays solitaire.
COURTESY PHOTO MEDIA

Chatting with Melina Mercouri and Carroll Baker at a party in London during the filming of Once Is Not Enough. U.P.P.A. LONDON

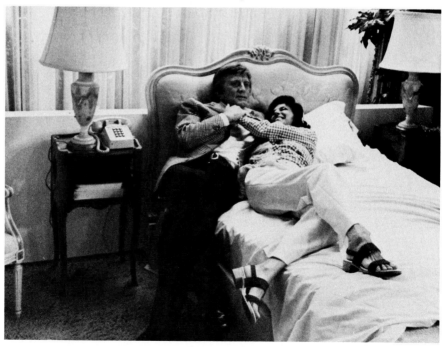

Hamming it up with star Kirk Douglas on the set of Once Is Not Enough.

Chum Doris Day and Jackie arriving at London's Heathrow Airport.

Jackie chatting with friends Muriel Slatkin, owner of the Beverly Hills Hotel, and film producer Howard W. Koch.

Mae West and Laurence Harvey visiting with Jackie at the Beverly Hills Hotel.

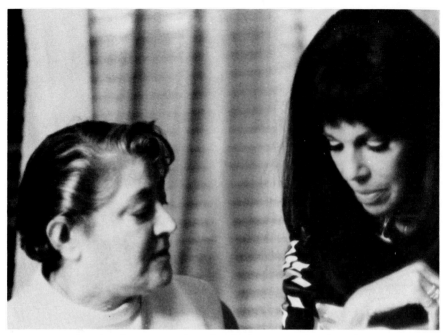

Best friend Anna Sosenko and Jackie having a serious discussion.

Our dear friend Rex Reed and Jackie at a party.

The two of us.

May 1974, the last picture taken of Jackie, as she visits the Wishing Hill with Deborah Raffin, star of Once Is Not Enough.

Venice by ship, to sail out of the lagoon and watch from the deck the receding shore line, the towers and spires and campaniles floating on the mist, the gondolas and vaporettos scooting across the water. Jackie always felt very romantic about Venice and hated saying good-by to that enchanted city.

That night, the lights went dark in the ship's theater, the credits for *Valley* came on, and we saw the wonderful opening scene of Mt. Vesuvius sideways, pumping out pills instead of lava. But from there on, nearly everything went downhill. Jackie hated the film. She hated it passionately. When the lights came on, she got hold of Mark Robson, took him into a corner, and said to him, with fire in her eyes, "The picture is a piece of shit."

Then Jackie burst into tears, ran into her cabin, and cried her heart out. The stewardess knocked on the door, entered, and said, "Miss Susann, I just want to congratulate you on your triumph."

"Get the hell out of here," Jackie screamed. Later, she apologized to the poor woman.

Why was Jackie so enraged? I think it was mostly the tone of the movie. It was a picture about junkies, she felt, not about the price of success and the loneliness of standing out from the crowd, as she had intended. All the nuances were lost, the subtleties of character she had worked so hard to develop. She thought, as she had at the beginning, that Patty Duke was very badly cast as Neely, and as a result of that miscasting, the entire picture was out of balance.

Once Jackie washed her tears away, she decided to play it cool except among intimates. She never bad-mouthed the film publicly, but she never extended herself to publicize it. I think it was one of her really big disappointments that the major motion picture made from her sensationally bestselling book fell so far short of her dream of what the movie should be. It was so inferior to the movie that Jackie had unreeled in her head in those long days at the typewriter when the story was a motion picture in her mind before it was a book on paper.

At any rate, we left the cruise ship at the Canary Islands, flew to Madrid, and then returned to New York. Two weeks later, we rejoined the ship in Miami to meet the American press. Susan Hayward, Patty Duke, and Sharon Tate were aboard this time, along with every notable from Miami who did not suffer from seasickness and some $175,000 worth of dresses created for the film brought together for a fashion show. Jackie sat in a corner most of the time. When a reporter from the *Miami News* approached her, Jackie talked about Josephine.

We flew home, then a week later jetted to Acapulco to rejoin the floating circus and meet the Latin American press. We stayed on board for the trip to Los Angeles, but both of us were sick most of the time. We figured it was from ice made with bad water taken aboard in Mexico.

Can you believe that there were cruise passengers on the *Princess Italia* who survived all those unveilings from Venice to L.A. and lived to tell their children about meeting the stars in person and gasping at Sharon Tate's micro-mini evening dress that covered only a little more area than a bikini.

At the end of November, we toured the West Coast, flew off to Europe for more appearances, and got back to New York on December 15, a bitterly cold and icy day—the day of *Valley*'s opening at the Criterion Theatre on Broadway.

"Let's go see if there's anyone at the movie," Jackie suggested.

"There won't even be a doorman at the theater," I said. "It's too cold. If you're hoping to see a line of people, forget it."

I don't think there was ever in all of history such a penetratingly cold day in New York. But Jackie insisted. We asked our driver to take us downtown—we owned our own limousine by then—and we came through 44th Street. At six P.M. we saw eight hundred people standing out there in front of the Criterion in that arctic cold in a line that stretched around the corner, waiting for the eight o'clock performance.

"Could we be wrong?" Jackie asked. "Will people like it?"

Jackie thought then, and I still do now, that *Valley* could have been a far better movie. But it certainly was a roaring success. The film set box-office records that were not broken until a year later by *Butch Cassidy and the Sundance Kid*.

*J*ackie and the critics were the only ones who didn't like the *Valley of the Dolls* movie. The picture grossed somewhere between $70 and $80 million, and that was in the days when admission to a movie was about two dollars. It's staggering to think what it would earn today. In fact, the movie is still popular on TV. Whenever it plays, it always gets a high rating. It once outrated "Saturday Night Live," when the latter was a hot show.

As Fox totaled up all those dollars earned by *Valley*, the company decided it wanted to do a sequel. Jackie came up with the title *Beyond the Valley of the Dolls*. Jackie was asked to write the script of the new film but declined. Writing a screenplay, she thought, was a thankless job.

"Look what happens," she explained once. "You turn in your script. Even if they say they like it, they get another writer who always changes everything. Then they get someone else to polish it and make more changes. In the end, it isn't yours, and you don't have anything to say about it."

Jackie would never stand for that kind of editing and mutilating. She always wanted to be in control of what she did.

After many meetings with Fox and many hours of discussion, it was decided that the new story should begin where the film version left off—Anne walking through the New England countryside after she has rejected Lyon Burke, with the *Valley of the Dolls* theme sung by Dionne Warwick playing on the soundtrack. I was to be the producer, and Jean Holloway, who had written a number of soap operas, would write the screenplay.

Mrs. Holloway came to New York to soak up the atmosphere where the action would take place. She, Henry Klinger, and I held a number of conferences to talk over the plot. She was not sure yet how many of the surviving original characters she would include. But Anne would still be the focal point. Jackie was writing *The Love Machine* and was only marginally interested in *Beyond the Valley*. I guess she herself was beyond the valley and didn't want to look back.

Mrs. Holloway mentioned one day that she had never been to the Côte Basque, so I took her there for lunch. When I came home that night, Jackie asked me what I'd done that day. I told her I'd taken Mrs. Holloway to the Côte Basque for lunch. Jackie stared at me and then said, "You never took me there for lunch."

She said it in a very cute way, so I said, "Well, you never asked me."

"What do you mean I never asked you?"

I said, "Okay, we'll go tomorrow."

She said, "I don't want to go on that basis."

I wasn't sure how this discussion had escalated, but I figured maybe Jackie was mad because she had been sitting all day at her typewriter with her tunafish sandwich and I had taken this lady to the Côte Basque. I couldn't blame her.

I asked Jackie if she wanted to go to a movie. She said she'd rather get dressed up and go to the Copa. That was all right with me, if she wanted it. She thought maybe not that night, maybe some other time. In the next two days, she mentioned the Copa about fifteen times. I knew she was pretty mad. I also knew I had to get it out of her system.

That Saturday night, the two of us went to the Copa. We had dinner, we saw the show, and we went on to Sardi's afterward. When we came home, she said, "I think I wasted half the day. I took a bath at five-thirty just to go to that damn night club, and the show wasn't that hot." Now she was blaming me for all the wasted time!

Anyway, the writer was having a lot of trouble with *Beyond the Valley*. I read some of her material and didn't think it was strong enough. Henry read it and said, "It's not bad, but you're right, it doesn't have muscle. But I think we can put that in later."

We sent the material on to David Brown. He sent it out to California. In February 1968, we got the following telegram from Dick Zanuck at Fox: "Dear Jackie and Irving: I am delighted that everything has worked out on the sequel. Looking forward to seeing you when you come out here."

With such good news to celebrate, Jackie and I took off for Paris—a holiday trip for a change instead of a promotional whirlwind.

Darryl Zanuck, the head of Fox, was in Paris at the same time, and when he invited us to dinner at Les Moustaches, of course, we accepted. I don't remember what we talked about, but somehow the conversation never got around to *Beyond the Valley*.

Imagine my astonishment the next morning when I picked up the *Paris Herald Tribune* and saw an article reporting that *Beyond the Valley of the Dolls* was being produced and directed at Twentieth Century-Fox by Russ Meyer as an X-rated film. Zanuck had not said a word about this the night before. I read the item again. I couldn't believe my eyes.

Not only had we not been consulted, we were being subjected to the indignity of porno treatment. At that time, major studios did not do X-rated films. Such films existed, of course, but in a kind of porno underground that was kept a safe and sanitary distance from Hollywood's main operations.

When we verified the item and learned that the script was being written by Roger Ebert, a television critic, we contacted our lawyer. We sued because we owned the copyright to *Valley of the Dolls*, and by doing an X-rated *Beyond the Valley of the Dolls*, Fox would most definitely be taking Jackie's property, damaging Jackie's reputation, and humiliating both of us. Our suit was brought while the film was in production. But the film went right on being made as the legal action dragged through the court system.

Jackie underwent a lengthy examination before trial, and so did I. Meanwhile, the film was completed and distributed. Although it got absolutely terrible reviews, it was widely shown, sometimes as a double feature, back to back with *Valley*, sometimes with *Myra Breckinridge*.

The suit did not come to trial until after Jackie's death. Our attorneys were Rosenfeld, Meyer, and Susman and for the trial, John Davies and Robert Dudnick. We had sued for $4 million. We won a $2 million verdict against Fox.

I never actually got the $2 million because every day there was a threat that Fox was going to appeal and that the appeal would take another four or five years. It was finally settled for $1.4 million.

The only time I saw *Beyond the Valley* was at the trial. It was my idea to show it to the jurors on the theory that it would turn their stomachs. My lawyers worked it out so that the judge, the jury, and all of us went to a viewing room two days in succession. On the first day, we saw *Valley*, and on the second, *Beyond the Valley*. The jurors could see that there was no connection at all between the two movies. The characters were different, their names were different, the plot was different. The only similarity was in the titles.

The turning point, I think, was when my lawyer, John Davies, had Dick Zanuck on the stand and asked him if Fox would have released this film if it did not have the words *Valley of the Dolls* behind the word "*Beyond.*" Zanuck said, "No," and that was the ball game.

Beyond the Valley was one of the most deeply embittering experiences of Jackie's life. She was always a very straight and honorable person. In spite of their differences, a lot of her mother's uprightness had rubbed off on Jackie. It never crossed her mind to take what was not hers. It never occurred to her that anyone else would seize what was rightly hers.

That an important film company, a company with which she had had friendly dealings, could take her property, pervert it, degrade it, and profit from it was simply outside Jackie's imagining.

When it did happen, she felt violated. "It's like being raped," she once said. I don't think Jackie was ever as open or as trusting with people after that. She always held back a little. There was always a residue of suspicion. I especially regretted that the court victory did not come while she could have enjoyed the vindication. It would have restored some of her lost trust.

he Love Machine was the longest aborning of any of Jackie's books. She had typed out the title in January 1965 just as she finished *Valley of the Dolls*. She began writing the book toward the end of that year, wrote during odds and ends of time all through 1966 and 1967, and was still working on it early in 1968.

"You're going to get a really big advance for this one, Jackie," I said, "and it's sure to be a smash." While it's not possible to copyright a book title, there is a procedure for registering it. I quickly made sure that the title was available, and I went through the legal procedure of registering it along with a brief synopsis.

The words "love machine" signified to Jackie first the television set itself, then the television executive, Robin Stone, who never quite figured out the difference between love and sex.

Jackie thought it was terrible that generations of children were growing up in front of the box, mindlessly following whatever was on the tube, not reading, not writing, not playing games as children always had but just passively absorbing what was coming at them from the machine.

Even worse, she thought, were the adults who let the stories, the characters, the events on the box wash over them, comfort them, lull them, seduce them. Life on the tube became more real than life itself. "That damn box just pours out love," Jackie once said. "You turn it on, and it loves you endlessly." The box became the love machine.

And so was Robin Stone, another of those devilishly attractive villain/heroes like Lyon Burke, only more powerful, more ruthless. Robin was gorgeous and desirable but incapable of real human warmth and unable to make lasting connections. When I hear young women today complain about the men in their lives and the men's fear of relationships and commitments, I always think of Robin Stone. Jackie really invented the contemporary man.

Amanda, the beautiful model who dies of leukemia, was obviously Carol Bjorkman, to whom *The Love Machine* was dedicated. Christie Lane, the comic, was a combination of half a dozen comics I had worked with years earlier.

The cast of characters included a full range of TV hot shots with whom I had done battle during most of my career (you've met some of them in recent pages), newscasters Jackie had gotten to know in her TV appearances, a girl in the network publicity department who could only be described as a celebrity fucker—we had known dozens like her—assorted writers, agents, press agents, doctors, secretaries, actresses, sisters, mothers, ex-wives, roommates, photographers. In short, the world as Jackie knew it.

The story was more complex than in *Valley*, the number of characters much larger, the focus on individuals not quite as sharp. Many of the same themes were repeated: the drive for success, the escape from a small town, the loneliness of achievement, the fleeting nature of love, the burden of virginity, the fear of age (which sets in at about thirty-eight), the wastefulness of death.

The narrative drive was stronger than ever—the action simply pelts along. There was sex in every corner and crevice, every possible variety, variation, and perversion of it, but the sex seemed less shocking, even if more prevalent, possibly because the characters were less naive. Or maybe because we were all a few years older.

Looked at in any way, it was one whale of a book.

But nobody had been allowed to look at it.

Bantam owned the paperback rights but had never seen it. Bantam had taken it on faith in the course of buying us out of the Bernard Geis disaster. Now arrangements had to be made to sell the hard-cover rights. Oscar Dystel introduced us to a number of major publishers, to whom Jackie made an oral presentation. But her price was too high for them. She wanted $250,000 in advance plus another $200,000 for advertising. Plus limousines and suites when she traveled.

Publishers shook their heads and said, "Great book, but no thank you."

It was my idea to withhold the book from potential purchasers. I figured it gave a mystery and an excitement to the sale that we could not achieve in any other way. "You're the only one in the country who can do this," I told Jackie. "You're the author who will not show her book."

"Do you think I can get away with it?" she asked.

"Sure you can get away with it. You can get away with anything you want. If a publisher wants to be number one on the bestseller list, you're the only one who can guarantee it for him."

Then Simon and Schuster arrived on the scene in the person of Leon Shimkin, president of the company. He came up to our apartment at the Navarro in the spring of 1968 and listened to Jackie's summary of what was in the book. Mr. Shimkin thought a while and then said, "I'm afraid you're too rich for our blood."

He then walked to the door and put his hand on the knob.

I said, "Mr. Shimkin, once you open that door, you'll never get back in."

His hand started to twist the knob, then he turned to us and said, "Okay, it's a deal."

We all shook hands, and it was a deal.

"When is it going to be finished?" he asked.

Jackie was on a yellow or a pink version by then. We gave him a date toward the end of the year. When we got our first money from Simon and Schuster, I walked into the office of Annie Laurie Williams. I think her husband, Maurice Crain, was in the office that day. They both knew that I had made the book sale without them. "I hear you've sold Jackie's book," Maurice said.

"Yes, and here's your check." I handed him a check for ten percent of what we'd gotten.

"But we didn't make the sale."

"I know, but you're our agent." I figured it was worth the ten percent not to have had them at the meeting with Shimkin. Annie Laurie might have fallen asleep again.

Before the book was in final form, Shimkin sent over two of his editors, Michael Korda and Jonathan Dolger. We put one in the living room and the other in Jackie's den and gave them each a copy. Korda, who reads like lightning, finished and said, "Congratulations, you've got a great book."

Jackie said, "I'm glad you like it."

He said he'd like to have a chat with her in a few days because he thought the book needed a big cut.

"Cut? Cut? Where?" Jackie asked, her voice coming up not a decibel. But I could hear the unspoken decibels.

Korda told her he'd be in touch with her.

When we finally took the manuscript to the publisher's office, Korda got out a green pencil and showed where he wanted a cut of about fifty pages.

"Do you know what you're cutting?" Jackie asked. "That's the whole Democratic National Convention." There was a long section in which Robin Stone acted as floorman for his network at the presidential convention. "I spent six weeks in the public library going through newspapers and reading about the convention. I worked hard to make it absolutely accurate," Jackie said.

Korda said, "Jackie, when I'm editing a book, I don't care how much time an author has put into a scene. I have to preserve the continuity and the pace. You're the only one who really cares about the convention. The reader isn't that interested, and all the details slow the story."

Korda turned to me and asked, "Do you care about the convention?"

I said, "Not particularly."

Jackie gave me one of those odd looks, the kind of look that Al Pacino in *The Godfather* gave his brother when he butted in and later Pacino told his brother, "Remember, family never argues in front of anybody."

We walked home from Rockefeller Center without saying a word to each other. Finally, she said to me, "Why did you agree with him?"

I said, "Because he's right."

She said, "I'm not so sure."

When we got home, she was still testy toward me. When I say testy, I mean she was giving me one-word answers. I asked her if she wanted to go to the movies. No. To a restaurant? No. Watch television? No.

I said, "Jackie, the editorial process is not undertaken solely by the writer. It's undertaken by someone who has a good, objective view. I don't have an objective view toward you. My emotions are colored by my love. You tell a story better than anyone tells a story, whether it's the first time or the fifteenth time."

"I never tell a story for the fifteenth time," she said.

"Yes, and sometimes for the twentieth time."

She said, "Are we going to start an argument about how often I tell the same story?"

I said, "No, we're going to argue about whether Michael Korda was right."

"You think he's right?"

"Yes, I do."

She said, "Okay, let's go get something to eat."

We went out to dinner, we saw a movie, we came home. There was still a chill in the atmosphere. I didn't blame her. We all have our egos, we all put our own mark on what we do, and we don't want to be wrong.

We went to bed. I watched Johnny Carson while she read a script. Josephine was sitting there between us. Finally, we both fell asleep. In the morning, Louise made breakfast, and Jackie joined me at the table for a toasted English muffin and coffee.

Jackie said, "I changed the script last night. I made a bridge. Do you want to see it?"

I said, "Sure." She showed me the fifty pages she had taken out. Then, in ink, she had written in, "The seasons melted into one another." We never said another word about the cut, but Jackie recognized that Korda was a fine editor and that the book was leaner and tighter with the convention deleted.

When *The Love Machine* was nearly finished, we were in California, and Oscar Dystel took us to a garden party at the home of Gene Klein, who was chairman of the board of National General and is now the owner of the San Diego Chargers. He had recently built a beautiful house behind the Beverly Hills Hotel. At the party, we met Janet Leigh, who was wearing a little ring with an odd circle on it. Jackie said, "That's an interesting ring."

Janet said, "It's an ancient Egyptian love symbol called an ankh. It means undying love." She took the ring off her finger and gave it to Jackie. "I want you to have this," she said.

Jackie asked her where she got it, and she said it was from Marvin Himes, the jeweler on Beverly Drive. The following day, Jackie went to Marvin Himes' and bought a ring for Janet. She wrote in a note, "You gave me yours, now I want you to have mine."

Jackie decided the ankh would be the symbol of her book. She inserted a reference to it into the text and wanted to get it on the cover. We knew that the creation of a book jacket often presents some very odd problems. For *Valley*, we had asked the photographer to scatter pills of various colors over a mink coat. Great idea, but the pills fell through the fur and disappeared. We had to scrap the mink coat.

Milton Charles, who was doing the jacket design for *The Love Machine*, brought us proofs for our approval. The design showed the backs of a man's and a woman's hands clasped together. The woman was wearing an ankh ring. But the proof I saw looked more like two women's hands than a man's and a woman's.

Charles said, "You're crazy. Those are the two best hand models in New York."

I said, "I'll tell you what to do. Get the second best hand models in New York." I wanted the man's hand to be more aggressively masculine. I didn't want any question about who was holding hands. That's how we got the final jacket design for *The Love Machine*.

In the meantime, Jackie had adopted the ankh sign for her own. She wore it around her neck. We used it in the logo for the movie that was eventually made from the book. We used it on a sign for *The Love Machine* at the Cannes Film Festival. It was put on the huge billboard on Sunset Boulevard. She gave little gold ankhs to TV hosts wherever she went, to bookstore owners, to everyone who worked with her at making *The Love Machine* a success. To this day, I have a tiny one on the front door of our apartment.

In November, Simon and Schuster created a sensation in the book trade by taking a front-cover ad in the book trade magazine *Publishers Weekly* and using only Jackie's picture. No book title. No author's name. No publisher's name. Just Jackie. It took nerve—and style. We loved them for it.

When we left to rest and recuperate in Florida at the end of the year, we were cheered by the good news that *Valley*, in paperback, fighting off all competition, was still holding the number-one spot and selling at an unheard-of rate.

*W*hen Jackie was a little girl in Philadelphia, dreaming of being a star, setting the world on fire, electrifying a room as she walked in, she probably sketched out in her fantasy the life the grown-up Jackie actually did lead in the summer and early fall of 1969. Into those five magic months were packed just about the maximum of excitement, drama, adventure—and misadventure—the human system can tolerate.

In May, *The Love Machine* was published to colossal fanfare, with full-page ads in major newspapers and a first printing of 150,000 copies that by June was up to 300,000. The book hit number-one in *The New York Times* on June 24, just five weeks after publication. It dislodged Philip Roth's *Portnoy's Complaint* from first place and sent *The Godfather* into third place. The publisher ran another full-page ad, shouting, "Welcome back, Jackie, right where you belong." Sales were phenomenal.

Jackie went out on tour again—Chicago, Cleveland, Cincinnati, Detroit. By then, these places were like regular pit stops to us. Book buyers and store managers were old friends. They showed us snapshots of their children and grandchildren. They sent their love to Josephine. We should have had an interest in a liniment company. Thousands of clerks were spraining their backs as they lifted heavy cartons of books and piled displays higher than the tallest reader's eye. Jackie basked in the warmth of hugs and applause.

The book reviewers were no kinder this time around, but who cared. Besides, there were some bright spots. In contrast to the sneers ("Sex saga sags," *Tucson Citizen*), Nora Ephron gave the book a good notice in *The New York Times* Sunday Book Review and it was placed on page three.

On June 27, just three days after the book hit number one, we drove to Philadelphia in Jackie's new El Dorado with the little portrait of Josephine painted on the side door and Jackie's regular license plate, JSM 5. We checked into the Warwick Hotel, went to see Jackie's mother, who never noticed a dirty word in *The Love Machine*—by this time she was feeling sorry for Philip Roth's mother—and went to Wanamaker's downtown store. Vince Rivers, a very charming man who was head of the book department for the whole Wanamaker chain, had set up an autograph session.

When Vince took a half-page ad in the *Inquirer* to announce the event, at my suggestion, he had listed the time as 12:30 to 1:30. "That way," I had pointed out to him, "they'll probably come at twelve and keep coming all during lunch time. But don't advertise a two-hour session. If nobody comes, it looks awful. Wherever Jackie is, there has to be a crowd. If there is a crowd, she'll stay until five, or until the books give out."

At this time, I was in heavy negotiation with our west coast agent George Chasin on the movie sale of *The Love Machine*. I knew that on the day of the Wanamaker autographing, Chasen was seeing Mike Frankovich, who was in charge of production at Columbia Pictures. I had been told that Frankovich had a very interesting proposition to make. Chasin had asked me where I would be that evening. He was to call me in our suite at the Warwick before we went out to dinner.

The autograph session was mobbed and lasted all afternoon. We went back to the hotel and Jackie took a nap. Vince and his sister, whom we were taking out to dinner, arrived around seven-fifteen. We had some wine and hors d'oeuvres in the living room of our suite, planning to go to dinner at seven-thirty at a marvelous little Italian restaurant the Rivers knew and loved.

The phone rang. Jackie said, "Take it in the other room."

I said, "Okay."

It was Chasin calling from California and saying, "Irving, this is going to be a conference call. I'll be on one line, Mike Frankovich on another, and Leo Jaffe, the chairman of the board of Columbia, on another from New York."

The connection was made, and there were a lot of hellos back and forth. We talked a bit about the weather, and then I said, "We have some people here, and we're going out to dinner, so maybe you should tell me what's happening."

George said, "Well, I have told Mike that if he pays us one and a half million dollars, he can have the screen rights to *The Love Machine*. Is that right, Mike?"

Mike said, "That's right, but you must take the rights off the market immediately."

Leo Jaffe said, "Yes, that's the deal."

Taking the book off the market means that you cannot keep it up for sale and use Frankovich's bid to start an auction with someone else. (Remember Walter Winchell and his switch to CBS?)

I said, "Okay, then, we have a deal."

Frankovich said, "Listen, do you want to come out here, or should I fly to New York to work out the details."

I said, "Whatever you want, but we do have a tight schedule of TV shows . . ."

At that moment, Jackie poked her head in and glared at me. "You're keeping our guests waiting," she said in a loud stage whisper.

I put my hand over the phone. "Tell them I'll be right there."

Frankovich was saying, "Well, I have to be in New York, anyway, so I'll see you there."

I said, "Fine, we'll take you to lunch and have a bottle of wine together."

George said, "Okay, now, it's a million and a half, and we take it off the market. Right, Irving?"

"Right, George."

"Mike, do you agree?" George asked.

"Yes, I do."

"And you, Leo?"

"Yes, I do."

I thought for a minute the three of us were getting married.

Then Mike said, "Now I am the owner of the screen rights?"

We all said, "Yes."

"How do you want me to break the news?" Mike asked.

Jackie stuck her head in again with one of her fiercer scowls. "Irving, you're embarrassing me. What's going on?"

I waved her away. Then I said to Mike, "Look, you're paying a million and a half dollars, so you certainly have the right to break it to anyone you want."

He said, "Fine. In that case, I'll give it to Joyce Haber of the *Los Angeles Times*."

I said, "That's fine with me. All we're interested in now is selling more books. I know you'll do a great job with the picture."

We exchanged compliments for a while—Frankovich was a really good picture maker. He had done *Oliver* and *A Man for All Seasons*.

Jackie's head was in the doorway again. I didn't even look up.

Mike and Leo said good-by, and George and I continued the conversation, clearing up a few details and congratulating each other. I had to ask him about his wife Eileen, and we talked for another five minutes.

"For God's sake, will you get off that phone." It was Jackie with blood in her eyes.

I finally hung up, apologized as best I could to the Rivers, and we went out to that little Italian restaurant. We had a nice dinner, said good night to Vince and his sister, and walked back to our hotel.

Jackie didn't say a word until we were in our room. As soon as we shut the door, she let me have it. "How could you be so damn impolite? Leaving me to talk to the Rivers and say the same thing over and over again while you yakked away on the phone. Who were you talking to?"

"George Chasin."

She said, "Oh," and already her tone was a little different because Jackie loved George just as I did. "What did George have to say?"

I said, "Well . . ."

She said, "Did he sell the book?"

"Yes."

"That's wonderful. For how much?"

I said, "A million and a half."

It's the only time I ever saw Jackie's mouth fall open and no words come out. Finally, she said, "A million and a half?"

"That's right."

"You mean to tell me that we sat in there for one hour talking and you never told me you were talking to George Chasin?"

"That's right."

"And we went to that lousy Italian restaurant and ate that terrible food (all of a sudden the restaurant was lousy) and you did not tell me you sold the book for a million and a half dollars."

I said, "Yes."

She said, "Was that fair? Why didn't you tell me?"

My mind was working at double speed. I said, "Jackie, this was something I wanted just the two of us to share alone."

She started to cry and said, "You're terrible, you're just terrible."

I said, "Well, I didn't want to interrupt you."

"Interrupt? This is something you really want to be interrupted for. You could have let me get on the phone and say hello to them."

I said, "Frankovich is coming to New York in a couple of days with the contracts. You can say hello then."

I had been undressing all during this conversation, and by this time I was stretched out on my bed, with my back to the door. Jackie was still in the living room. She was mad. Mad and happy. Happy the book was sold but mad that she wasn't the first to know.

Jackie took the wine bottle out of the cooler. There was still some ice and water from melted ice at the bottom of the cooler. She picked up the bucket and boom! dumped the whole thing on me! "Now we're even," she said.

I said, "No, we're not. How could you do such a thing?"

I got up. She ran into the other room. "What are you going to do?" she asked.

I said, "You're going to sleep in the living room." With that, I stepped back into the bedroom, closed the door, and locked it behind me.

She banged on the door and said, "Let me in."

I said, "No. I'm going to take a warm bath."

She banged some more. "What am I going to do?"

"Go downstairs and get yourself a room and sleep in it."

She said, "I'm going to scream."

I said, "Go ahead."

Instead, she banged some more. The telephone rang. Someone had complained about the noise we were making. "Better cool it," I called to her through the door. "That was the management. They say we're making too much noise."

"I'm going right on making noise."

"No, you better get a room."

"I'm supposed to sleep on a couch while you have the bedroom!"

I said, "You're right, that's unfair. So come on in."

I opened the door, but in the same instant, I scooted into the dry bed. She came in and said, "Did you really sell the book for a million and a half?"

I said, "Yes."

She looked at the wet bed and asked, "Who's sleeping there?"

"You are."

"How can I sleep in a wet bed?"

"You're the one who wet it."

She went into the bathroom, took off her makeup, put cream on her face, and got into the bed with me. She said, "You think I'm terrible, don't you?"

I said, "Yes. How could you do such a thing to me?"

I had her apologizing for throwing the water and ice at me when the whole scene was really one of those wonderful things you remember all your life.

The announcement of the movie sale was made in the *Los Angeles Times*, and after the Columbia Pictures press department went to work, it was in every paper in the world and on the front page of many. Simon and Schuster was ecstatic. When you sell a book to a film company for a million and a half dollars, you better start printing more books. Everyone is saying, "A million and a half? I have to buy that book and see what it's all about!"

There was another printing, another round of broadcasters pulling at Jackie's skirt, asking her to go on the air. There were five calls from Jackie's old friend, Long John Nebel. Whenever Jackie finished the Long John show, she said, "Good night, Irving."

Everyone thought she was telling me good night. But it was for Irving Berlin, who was always awake and listening.

Mike Frankovich came to town, and I set up a lunch for us at "21." Jackie had a certain corner table upstairs that was her favorite. She had often lunched there with Carol Bjorkman. When Jackie, Mike, and I walked in that Tuesday, we saw Aristotle Onassis, who lunched at "21" nearly every day, waiting for someone near the entrance to the dining room.

Jackie had never been formally introduced to Onassis, but she had a nodding acquaintance with him. He approached Jackie and said, "Miss Susann, I've been reading about you in the papers. Is it really true that you sold a book to the movies for a million and a half dollars?"

Jackie said, "Yes, it's true, and this is Mr. Frankovich, who bought the book. Mr. Frankovich, it's my pleasure to introduce you to Mr. Aristotle Onassis. Mr. Onassis, this is Mr. Frankovich."

Onassis said, "You really gave this lady a million and a half dollars for her book?"

He said, "I sure did."

"Oh, boy," said Onassis, "I think I'm married to the wrong Jackie."

All that happened early in July. There was more to come later that same month. July 23 was my birthday. We made a dinner reservation at Danny's Hideaway, but first Jackie had to tape a show with David Frost for future TV airing. The show, built around *The Love Machine*, had three guests who had read the book and were ready to discuss it.

One of the guests was Rex Reed, chosen by Jackie, presumably to be in her corner. Another was Nora Ephron, who was expected to be more or less neutral. The third was Jimmy Breslin, who was supposed to come out swinging. Jimmy Breslin, however, was replaced at the last minute by John Simon, a critic who wrote for the *Hudson Review*.

The three critics sat in the front row of the studio, facing Jackie, who was on the edge of the stage. Jackie was wearing a dress and having a hard time making sure the dress was properly pulled down. First David interviewed Jackie. While Jackie was talking, she noticed that Simon was making sounds like "Grrrrr."

Rex and Nora started asking Jackie questions about the book. Simon said nothing. Then, suddenly, he blurted out, "Miss Susann, vhy did you write such a book, vhy?"

Jackie was aware of David's sense of humor, so she figured this was a setup, some kind of a Dutch comedy. So she came back with, "Vat did you say your name vas—Goebbels, Goering?"

He screamed back, "My name is John Simon."

Jackie said to Simon, "I've heard of Neil Simon. I've heard of Simple Simon. But who are you?"

Now he said, "Don't you sit there with your whorish ways and your long phony hair."

This was cut from the show when it was broadcast.

Jackie retorted, "Don't get so excited. You look like a nice fellow, and your hair must be your own—it's too thin not to be."

Then Rex explained that Simon had been waiting for three years to get at Jackie and that he had only read thirty-three pages of her book.

"You've only read thirty-three pages!" Jackie said. "You didn't do your homework."

With that, he screamed, "Bitch! I would rather see dogs fornicating than read your stuff!"

At that point, a man came running toward the stage, shouting, "I've read her stuff. Don't you dare talk that way to her."

Then another man jumped up and said, "I breed dogs. Seeing them fornicate is more beautiful than this kind of shit."

Everyone went crazy at this point.

Jackie started to laugh and said to Frost, "I should be very angry. You've used me to stage this circus."

Only the printable part of the show could be aired.

Later, Frost sent Jackie flowers and a telegram, saying, "You'll sell more books. I'm still your pal." It was a year before she spoke to him.

At my birthday dinner, Jackie didn't know whether to be amused or furious. But we both agreed that what had happened was probably good for the book. People would be talking about the outrageous show, which meant they'd also be talking about the book.

We didn't know it, but the evening was still young.

We got home in time to watch Johnny Carson. Truman Capote was one of Johnny's guest. He is a short, pudgy man with a nasal, high-pitched voice and a southern drawl.

We were only half listening, but then we snapped to attention because suddenly Capote was talking about Jackie, and we heard him say, "A-n-y way, she looks like a truck driver in drag!"

In his memoirs, *Reflections without Mirrors*, Louis Nizer, the celebrated attorney, recounts what happened next:

> *Words are like chemicals. Some combinations fizzle. Others explode. The laughter which burst across the nation drove Jackie and Irving Mansfield, her husband and gifted partner in the dissemination of her works, right into my office. They insisted on an immediate suit. I advised them that in my opinion a slander had been committed . . . and although I was not unaware of the hurt and humiliation they had suffered, I advised them against suit.*
>
> *Wasn't she still on the bestseller list? Did she really believe Capote's snide comment would affect her popularity as an author?*
>
> *They were determined to attack. Fees were of no conse- quence. She was fabulously successful. She wished revenge. She wanted to see the day when "the little worm would squirm under cross-examination."*
>
> *In the course of the friendly argument, I learned that*

*they were leaving for Europe I seized the opportunity to gain
time . . .*

*When she and her husband sat again in my office, I redou-
bled my effort to have her drop the matter.*

Nizer thought we were close to giving up, but then, in a publication called *After Dark*, Capote renewed the attack, saying that all his
attorney had to do was to get a dozen truck drivers and put them in
drag and have them parade into court and that would be it. He also
attacked her on "Laugh In."

Jackie, of course, was more determined than ever to sue. Nizer
wrote a strong, scolding letter to Capote. Capote wrote back that his
original comment was "bitchy, yes; malicious, no." He apologized in
a roundabout way by saying that as one professional to another, he
admired what Jackie did in her field of literary endeavor, although he
reserved judgment on the virtue of the field itself.

A few days after the Nizer discussions, I called my good friend Al
Rylander, who was vice president, news and information, for RCA.
We discussed the Capote slur. Al told me that if I got into litigation,
it would be a long and expensive procedure for all concerned. Would
I mind if he talked the matter over with Robert Sarnoff, chairman of
the board and chief executive officer of RCA.

A day later, Rylander called and asked me what kind of settlement I had in mind that would allow everyone to walk away happy.
"An appearance for Jackie on the 'Tonight Show,' " I said, "a future
appearance on the 'Today Show' for Jackie's next book, and an
appearance on one of the five-times-a-week daytime game shows."

"No problem," Rylander said.

Two weeks later, at the Beverly Hills Hotel on a sunny Saturday,
Jackie and I wandered down to the pool where we saw Sarnoff,
Rylander, and David Tebet, vice president for talent at NBC. We
joined them, and after making small talk, Sarnoff said to me, "Have
we resolved the Capote problem yet?"

I repeated the conversation I had had with Rylander. Sarnoff
then said, "Okay, we're all squared away."

Just then, the cabana phone rang. It was Tom Ervin of the NBC
legal department. After a brief discussion, I heard Sarnoff say, "I'm
sitting with Irving Mansfield now, and everything is settled." I am still
grateful to Sarnoff and Rylander for resolving a very thorny situation
with such speed and professionalism.

When Jackie went on the "Tonight" show, Johnny reminded her

that everyone was waiting to hear her side of the incident and said, "Suppose you begin, Jackie, by telling us what you really think of Truman."

"I think," said Jackie demurely, "that Truman will go down in history as one of our greatest presidents."

That was quite a birthday I had that year.

Two weeks later, Jackie and I came within a hair's breadth of being involved in one of the bloodiest mass murders of our time. I have to get to that story by telling you that during the shooting of *Valley*, we had both become terribly fond of Sharon Tate, who played Jennifer. She was a beautiful and adorable young woman. But you couldn't trot out the compliments for her boy friend, Roman Polanski. We found him unpleasant. But he was reputed to be a brilliant film maker.

In January 1968, Jackie and I had been in Liverpool for a series of store appearances and interviews for our English publisher. I called the hotel in London daily to get our messages. On January 19, the messages included an invitation the next day to the wedding reception of Sharon Tate and Roman Polanski at an apartment in London. If we were to attend, we would have to cut short our time in Liverpool and skip a couple of TV interviews.

We debated what to do. Jackie, the total pro, always hated to leave a city if there were three books left to be autographed or a night-owl program to do on a ham radio station for Insomniacs, Unlimited. "But then," she said wistfully, "how often does a friend get married?"

We flew back to London and went to the reception. It was a great party. Leslie Caron was there, Barbara Parkins, Warren Beatty, Richard Harris, Tony Curtis's wife, and a lot of British film people. At one point, Sharon called Jackie into another room. Suddenly, her eyes were filled with tears. "What'll I do?" she asked. "Roman wants me to go home and change my dress. He hates this dress."

It was the dress she had been married in less than two hours before.

Jackie shook her head. "You're not going to have an easy time with him, Sharon," she said. "But if I were in your place, I wouldn't let him start giving orders like that. I'd stay right here and keep on wearing the dress. It's a perfectly lovely dress." Sharon kissed her and rejoined the party. Who knows what happened after we left.

Now we go to August 9, 1969, right in the middle of that

incredible summer. It was a Saturday, and we were at the pool at the Beverly Hills Hotel. We looked up, and there was Rex Reed, who had just gotten into town. We chatted with him, and Jackie said, "Why don't you come with us. There's a party tonight at Sharon Tate and Roman Polanski's."

Rex had a script with him—he was going to test for *Myra Breckinridge*. Why didn't we have a quiet dinner and all go to Sharon's together some other night.

I said, "Jackie, is that okay with you?"

To my surprise, she agreed. I was always surprised when Jackie was willing to skip a party. We had our quiet dinner, and the next morning, a beautiful Sunday, we went down to the pool. Johnny Carson was standing there, and he said to us, "Have you heard what happened? Isn't it awful?"

"What? What?" Jackie asked.

"A maniac got loose at Sharon Tate's house last night. He killed Sharon and several others. I can't believe it."

Jackie fell into a deck chair. "My God, we were supposed to be there." Her face was as white as her bathing suit. Mine must have been the same color. We were in shock for days. Shock and mourning for poor, lovely Sharon.

"You ought to buy that saint of yours a whole bunch of candles," I told Jackie.

"Never mind the saint. It was Rex who saved us." We both felt that Rex had saved our lives.

But nothing, not even near murder, stopped *The Love Machine*. It just winged along in first place. Jackie was absolutely on top of the world. I was deliriously happy for her. The only thing that troubled her was that she had no time to write. The next book in her head was screaming to come out. She even had a title for it, a marvelous title.

Jackie's favorite comedian was Joe E. Lewis, whom we both loved. He was a wonderful guy, and whenever he played the Copa or the El Rancho in Vegas or Chez Paris in Chicago and we were in town, we took a ringside table as his guests. We could never pay a check when Joe E. Lewis was playing anywhere. Maybe I didn't tell you, but Josephine was really named for him. He used to say, "I'm the father of the dog."

Joe E. had a favorite line. He said, "You go through life once, and if you work it right, once is enough." That's philosophical and funny. Jackie used to love that line. She could imitate Joe E. and his whole act. He'd fall on the floor laughing when she did his routine in his voice. A time came when Joe E. was very sick. Jackie and I went to see him in the hospital. He had all that apparatus sticking out of him, and the nurse would let us stay only a minute or two.

Joe E. looked at us and said, "You know, Jackie, once is not enough."

When we came out of his room, Jackie started to cry. But in the middle of crying, she stopped. She said, "Wait a minute. That's a wonderful title for my next book."

I quickly registered *Once Is Not Enough,*" but Jackie had no time to write it—not for another two years. *Love Machine* had us going at too bewildering a pace.

All through August, September, and October 1969, we were on the road: California, Las Vegas, the Midwest, England, France, Italy, Germany. We hit them all. At each stop, Jackie was mobbed, lionized, showered with gifts. She hardly had time to wash her face, let alone set her hair. Her falls and wigs saved her; she could always look terrific even after all night on a plane or a day-long book signing under a leaking tent.

We were away from home so much that someone must have decided it was open season in our apartment. We came home one night in September—I think it was over the Labor Day weekend—and everything of value was gone. We were cleaned out. The sable coat Jackie adored was gone. Her mink coat. An 11.1-carat diamond ring that she was wild about. I had bought it for her in Las Vegas, of all places.

I lost a watch Al Jolson had given me. Jackie lost a watch from Eddie Cantor. She lost a gorgeous aquamarine that had been given her by one of her European publishers. She lost a lot of beautiful gold jewelry from Cartier's and Tiffany's. Chunky gold bracelets, pins, earrings. The jewelry had been in a forty-pound safe—they'd carried away the whole safe. We figured we'd lost about $200,000 in the robbery.

The police were sympathetic but only mildly interested. To them, it was just another heist. There was insurance, but you know insurance—it never covers everything. And what good is insurance for irreplaceable treasures like the watches from Cantor and Jolson?

Jackie was terribly upset. She had worked hard for all the beautiful things she had cherished and lost. When we were robbed again some months later, she decided she wanted no more material things in her life. She did not replace any of the lost jewelry or ever again buy expensive furs or fancy decorative items.

"If you can't protect the things you love," she said, "why bother having them? Why get attached?" After the second robbery, Jackie collected only tiny animals of Steuben glass. She loved her little elephant and koala bear and frog and pussycats. "Nobody steals glass," she said. And she was right. I still have her miniature animals.

The Frankfurt Book Fair in October wound up that supercharged season. The fair is a ninety-ring literary circus. Publishers gather from all over the world to show off their wares. There are Soviet publishers, South African booksellers, publishers, authors, and booksellers from big and little countries. You have to make a hotel reservation at least a year in advance. Everyone tries to get into the Intercontinental, but that's impossible. So you scramble and scrape for second best. We stayed at the Airport Hotel.

We were promoting the hard-cover and preselling the paperback of *The Love Machine*. We were there with the people from Bantam, including Oscar Dystel, Marc Jaffe and Mildred Hird. Everyone at the fair wanted to meet Jackie. She was the star. The line at her booth was longer than any of the others. She smiled and nodded and trotted out her limited stock of German words. And tried not to wince.

Because, naturally, at the very moment she was to occupy center stage under the most powerful spotlight, trouble struck. On the day we arrived in Frankfurt, Jackie twisted her high heel in a crack in the sidewalk, fell, and sprained her foot. That night, when her ankle swelled up alarmingly, the hotel sent a woman doctor to our room. The doctor said, *"Nicht gut,"* and indicated that Jackie should go to the hospital.

Knowing Jackie, I was sure there was no way we could get her to a hospital. I speak a little German, so I asked the doctor to tape the foot. Jackie said to me, "Tell her to give me something for the pain."

"You really should go to the hospital," I told Jackie.

She didn't even bother to answer me. The doctor gave Jackie a shot then and another in the morning. I think Jackie liked to live dangerously. A shot and a shrug for the pain. Some tape around the ankle. Jackie smiling bravely. No crutches, thank you. I can walk.

In the morning, one of those giant six-door Mercedes came to pick up our Bantam group, along with Alun Davies, a vice president for foreign sales, and Pat Newman, then head of Corgi, the Bantam paperback affiliate in England, to take us to the festival hall.

There was only one such monster car in Frankfurt. Along the road, we passed pickets. When we got to the hall, the pickets closed in around our car. They were hollering and trying to shove their heads through the windows. The people we were with said, "Don't open the windows or doors."

But Jackie, the desperado, was still on her danger kick. She rolled down her window, and a young man stuck his head in. He was the leader. "What's all the yelling about?" she asked him, and as he started to explain, she hobbled out of the car. Pretty soon she was talking to the young man in French.

It turned out he was Danny the Red, the young revolutionary who had led the French student uprising in Paris the year before. Jackie said, "I'm going inside to do my job. Are you going to let me?"

He said, "Aren't you Jackie Susann?"

She said, "Yes, would you like me to autograph your picket sign?"

She autographed the sign, then reached into the car for some books and autographed *The Love Machine* to Danny the Red. I think Jackie liked the irony of that gesture.

Jackie was a sensation with the German press. She gave a mass interview for forty reporters at one time, then a little later talked to another twenty. The next day, her picture and stories about her wiped everything else off the pages. Jackie was the only thing happening in Germany that day. I never saw anything like it. There were reporters in Frankfurt from all over the world, and Jackie was gracious to them, with and without interpreters, in at least seventeen languages.

Hundreds of booksellers attended the fair. Jackie took everyone's name and address and stuffed her purse with business cards that people pressed upon her. Over and over, she said, "If I ever get to Venezuela, of course, I'll look you up . . ." "You're from Indonesia? You must call me when you come to New York . . ."

When we returned to New York, she slept for two days. Then, on a Saturday, she called the public stenographer in the Park Shera-ton Hotel. She wanted the woman to come to our apartment. No, she didn't do that. "Oh, I'm sorry, this is Jackie Susann." Of course, she would come.

For two days, the stenographer typed ninety-five individual let-ters to the people Jackie had met in Frankfurt. While all the letters were basically the same—how much she enjoyed meeting the person, how much she appreciated his or her efforts on behalf of her book—

each had a personal touch. One letter referred to a bookseller's new baby. Probably named Jennifer. Because of Jackie, Jennifer had come to replace Mary as the favorite name for baby girls. Another letter inquired about a wife who had been too ill to travel to the fair. Another made a reference to the bookseller's pet dog.

Jackie was the ultimate pro when it came to her career. Nothing having to do with the writing, publishing, or selling of her books was handled sloppily or casually. Every detail was seen to, every contingency planned for—and every thank-you note signed in her own writing. Yes, it took time. Lots of time. But you don't short cut what is most precious to you. You build a writing career with love, care, precision, and whatever bullying might be required to bring those around you to your level of perfection.

$\mathcal{S}$ixteen is the average life span of a poodle. Josephine was approaching seventeen and disastrously overweight. We never checked her cholesterol, but we always suspected the worst. I think she stayed alive on kisses and love. And on hope, because soon after *Every Night, Josephine!* was published, Jackie started her second book about Josephine, *Goodnight, Sweet Princess*. Josie, naturally, expected to be a celebrity all over again. But a couple of other projects intervened and somehow claimed Jackie's time and attention. Despite the delay, Josephine, the optimist, never gave up hope.

Then, in January 1970, the poor little thing seemed to be in desperate trouble. Jackie and Bea took her to the vet, Dr. Raphael Meisels. He said he would operate on the dog and try to save her, but he was afraid it was her heart—and hopeless. Jackie and Bea went home and waited. An hour later, the call came—Josie had died.

Jackie was inconsolable, and I was not doing much better. We had Josie cremated at the Marble Hill Crematorium for Pet Animals and her ashes placed in a bronze urn the shape and size of a small book. The inscription reads:

JOSEPHINE
1954–1970

The death of Josephine was treated by the press like the death of a celebrated person. There were announcements and obituary notices in the newspapers and on the air. We received hundreds of condolence notes from all over the world.

One of those who heard the news was Mel Davis of the Poodle Boutique, who had groomed Josie all her life and fallen under her spell. On her visits to his place, Josie always occupied the booth—I suppose in some circles it's called the cage—next to her friend Victoria, the Nixons' cocker spaniel. Knowing how terrible Jackie must feel, Mel spent the entire night running around New York to find the perfect replacement for Josie.

The next morning, Mel came up and lifted out of a box a tiny, three-pound ringer for Josephine. Only this dog was a boy and toy size. "I didn't want to get you another girl," Mel said. "This is a real prize poodle. He's got his kennel-club papers, and he's had his shots. He's my gift to you."

He put the dog on the bed. The dog walked toward Jackie, stuck his head up, and kissed her full on the mouth. Jackie stopped crying long enough to say, "He's cute. Thank you very much, Mel." By then, the dog was licking the tears off Jackie's face.

Jackie didn't know what to do. Her heart was really broken for Josephine. She didn't want another dog to take Josie's place. But how could she send back a dog like this tiny one who was already so expert at kissing and licking?

"Irving," she said, "do you like him?"

"Yes, he's darling."

"Should we keep him?"

I said, "You don't have a choice anymore. The dog has already selected you as its mother."

The little dog was now jumping up and down with joy, fighting to be charming, fighting to stay with these people who obviously knew how to be gaga over a dog. He won, of course.

We named him Joseph Ian—for Josephine and for Ian McKellan, the English actor Jackie adored. Joseph was not entirely housebroken, but we worked that out. Because he had grown up in a kennel, without proper instruction from his mother or his peers, Joseph was a little slow about lifting his leg when he went against a tree. He tended to squat down a bit. When he did that, Jackie lifted one of his back legs—until he got the hang of the thing.

In the next four and a half years, Joseph must have made forty or fifty trips to California with us. We could just pop him into a pocket and take him along on the plane. He never made any trouble, not even when he stayed with us at the Beverly Hills Hotel where dogs are not officially welcomed. "Joseph adores it here," Jackie once wrote Bea from California. "He leaves tootsie rolls all over the green velvet grass."

So we began the year with mourning and rebirth. Then, in February, it was my turn to cause problems. I needed an operation for the removal of abdominal polyps. I was in Mt. Sinai Hospital for more than a week and was enormously uncomfortable. Jackie, the worrier, was frantic before I went into the hospital, while I was there, and afterward, until I was fully recovered.

Jackie worried about my health the way any loving wife worries. But with Jackie there was a far deeper fear. There was absolute terror that something might happen to me and she would have to deal, all alone, with the problems relating to Guy.

We had long since become accustomed to the emotional wrench of our visits to our son. He was in the South at this time, and we got to see him about every two weeks. It was the between-visit emergencies that required urgent attention, because no news from Guy's school was ever good news.

Each call invariably meant another misery. Either he was ill with whatever infection was sweeping the school, or there was a change in doctors and he was not getting along with the new one, or an absconding orderly had stolen all his clothes, or another patient had smashed his new TV. Between our regular visits to our son, we were constantly on the phone straightening out the latest crisis, sending more money, assuring the director that he and the school were doing a great job—but why should my boy's TV need replacing so soon again?

No wonder Jackie worried excessively even if I had nothing more than a hangnail. Well, we got through the polyps, and then it was Jackie's turn to give me something to worry about. She was going back on the stage.

Early in 1970, Jackie was invited to appear in a production of *The Madwoman of Chaillot*, which would play for two weekends in March at the Sokol Hall in Yorkville with Blanche Yurka in the starring role.

Now Jackie needed this job, with everything else going on in our lives, about as much as I needed two weeks in Alcatraz. But even at fifty-two and programmed to the limit with projects and obligations, she was helpless when she heard the siren song of the theater.

"Why are you doing this, Jackie?" I asked. "It's not Broadway. It's not really off-Broadway. It's a Czechoslovak gym up there among the goulash restaurants. Their food is wonderful, but you're a world-famous writer. You don't have to knock yourself out with this."

"But it's a wonderful cast and a wonderful play," Jackie replied stubbornly. "It's something I want to do."

No logic, no reason could shake sense into her head. Sure, the cast was outstanding. Blanche Yurka, in the title role of the Jean Giraudoux play, had once been a very fine actress. She had made her debut in *The Bohemian Girl* some seventy years earlier; now, well into her eighties, she, too, was living out an impossible fantasy of returning to the stage.

Peggy Wood was a truly great actress. The others, Lois Wilson, Frederick O'Neill, Hilda Simms, and Eric Rhodes, were extremely competent. The play was intriguing and had been a big hit in its original run on Broadway. For the young Jackie, newly arrived in New York, the role of the attorney in *Madwoman* would have been a terrific opportunity. But for Jackie, the bestselling novelist, it was nothing short of ridiculous.

She went ahead, anyway.

Rehearsals began while I was still recovering from surgery. They went badly. The show went badly. The reviews went badly. The whole project was a disaster. The only kind word was uttered by the critic of the *New York Post*, who described Jackie as "unstoppable." No argument about that. But Jackie never had any regrets about doing *Madwoman*. Somewhere, deep within her, it answered a need to act at least once more on a real stage among live actors in front of a living, breathing audience. The audience may have been breathing, but also it may have been snoring.

You've probably seen the stress charts that assign point values to major traumas—loss of a parent, change of job, divorce, your teenager runs away—and advise you not to pile up too many stress points at any one time. As if you had a choice. Well, Jackie had a choice, but she went right on piling up points.

We had been in our apartment in the Navarro for twenty-six years. That's a long, long time to be in one place in New York. Or anywhere. From year to year, we'd put off the horror of painting, but now Jackie decided to paint—or move. After the two robberies and the loss of Josephine, we were ready for a new beginning. We decided to move.

So between my polyps surgery and *Madwoman*, Jackie apartment hunted. She saw several in our neighborhood she liked and was trying to make up her mind when she mentioned to Gene Klein that she was looking for an apartment. Klein said he happened to have two he was giving up, one in the Waldorf Towers and one on Central Park South. He invited Jackie to look at them.

Momentarily, I think, she was intrigued with the idea of living at the Waldorf—it could be a grown-up version of Eloise at the Plaza, and, of course, at the Waldorf there was day and night, hot and cold room service. But she fell in love with the apartment on Central Park South. It was in the neighborhood we knew and loved, it overlooked her Wishing Hill, it had a marvelous view of the park, and it was large and spacious. Sadly, no room service.

We leased the apartment in March, took over most of the Kleins' furniture, which we had refinished and reupholstered, and before moving in in June, we had the walls painted, mirrors and a bar installed, all the decorating completed. Jackie chose for the living room the sunniest of yellows and called the new apartment her golden egg yolk. The place spilled over with sunshine—for a while.

We had hardly moved in before it was time to launch the publicity campaign for *The Love Machine* paperback, which was scheduled for publication in July. Early summer, we had learned, was the best send-off time for a paperback novel. People have a little more leisure to read, they can easily slip a paperback into a beach bag or overnight case, they're relaxed and going on vacation, and with a few extra minutes on their hands, they browse—and buy—at book counters in airports and resort lobbies.

Our first major stop in the promotional campaign was the annual American Booksellers' Association convention in Washington, D.C., in June. The ABA brings together some 4,000 publishers, bookstore owners, buyers, and authors. At this domestic version of the Frankfurt Book Fair, Jackie was the undisputed star. Crowds pressed around her booth; people followed her everywhere, whispering, shouting, "There she is," "Hey, Jackie!" "Sign my book, Jackie."

Bantam had a brilliant idea. Every book dealer who stopped at the booth to meet Jackie was photographed with her in front of a large *Love Machine* logo. Three copies of each photograph were made, and Jackie autographed two of them. One signed copy went to the dealer at home, the other signed one to the store, to be displayed in the window, and the unsigned one, with an appropriate caption, to the dealer's home-town newspaper. The response was fantastic.

When I got the schedule of the national tour for *The Love Machine*, I blinked in disbelief. Nobody could keep to that timetable and live to reap the rewards. But Jackie had no thought of shirking her job. She just had to find a better way to handle it.

Gene Klein turned out again to be our good angel. We were

dinner guests at his home in Beverly Hills one night when Gene mentioned something about his plane. It was a $7 million Grumman jet. Jackie's antennae shot up.

"How much does it cost to rent your plane?" Jackie asked.

Klein laughed and said it was like J. P. Morgan's yacht—if you have to ask, you can't afford it.

"I wasn't thinking of paying for it myself," Jackie said. "I was counting on your generosity."

Suddenly, it seemed like a wonderful idea—not generosity but plain good business. Esther Margolis worked out all the details of the two-week tour. Two pilots were assigned to the plane, and *The Love Machine* was painted on each side in letters twelve feet high—they could be read or photographed from half a mile away.

The plane tour crisscrossed the country, and every day it was the grand march from *Aida*, without the elephants. At every airport, cameramen and reporters besieged the plane. Local dignitaries came aboard. Jackie was always the gracious hostess. Books were autographed. Interviews were given in the plane's lounge or in the VIP lounge at the airport. Flashbulbs popped like heat lightning. We usually slept at a hotel. We had a ball.

In Houston, Maxine Messinger, the queen of the local press, and her husband Emil gave a party where we met Dr. John Stehlin, the great cancer expert, and Jackie asked the famous Dr. Denton Cooley if he would like to play Robin Stone in the movie.

In Dallas, she told the *Morning News* that "literary value is a lot of bunk devised by critics who never sold their own books." In San Francisco, she said, "Books are like lovers—you always think the current one is the best."

In Detroit, journalist Shirley Eder and her husband Eddie gave a marvelous party. At some stops, there were more than thirty press interviews, book signings, store visits, and TV and radio appearances in the typed schedule for a single day's activities. All along the route we provided lifts to our next stop to friends or to anyone connected with the book trade.

There was never another promotional tour like it. Who else had a private jet? Who else had a paperback book that began with a print order of 2.5 million copies and was instantly number one and selling 60,000 copies a day—faster even than *Valley of the Dolls*? When we flew into Los Angeles, there was double-header action—for both the paperback and the soon-to-be-made major motion picture. Mike Frankovich gave a dress-as-you-please party at the Friars' Club, which included: Robert Wagner, Jack Haley, Jr., and Sr., Jack Benny, Tony Newley, Jim Aubrey, George Jessel, Linda Johnson Robb, Goldie Hawn, Lola Falana, Tina Louise, and Ann Miller. People were wearing everything—jeweled headbands, micro-minis, trailing chiffons, Indian princess suedes, caftans, tutus—you name it, it was on someone's back. Jackie, I remember, wore a black silk pants suit with many gold chains draped, harem fashion, around her neck and under her arms.

Anita Louise and Henry Berger gave a *Love Machine* party at their home in Bel Air, the Slatkins gave us a party at their home, and Richard Gully, who is probably the politest man in the West, gave a series of parties for Jackie at the Bistro.

In August, we hit Washington, D.C., Baltimore, and Philadelphia, then on to San Francisco, Los Angeles, and Las Vegas. "How come everyone else is at the beach and I'm knocking myself out selling books?" Jackie asked one sweltering day.

"Say the word and you can have any beach you want," I told her. "You can buy the damned beach. Which one? Waikiki? Nice? Deauville? Caneel Bay?"

Jackie laughed. She knew and I knew she'd rather be a star on the book circuit than a mermaid on any beach in the world.

Then, on one wild day, Jackie was scheduled to appear in a fashion show at Alexander's in New York in the morning and on the Mike Douglas show in Philadelphia at noon. Which did she cancel? Neither, of course. We borrowed Francine Farkas's helicopter (her husband owned Alexander's) and called our friends Jean and Johnny Taxin, who owned the Old Original Bookbinder's restaurant at Second and Walnut Street in Philadelphia, to clear a space on their parking lot. Just minutes after the fashion show, we hopped aboard the copter at the East 61st Street heliport in New York, and only a few minutes later, after I pointed out two bridges across the Delaware and a couple of other local Philadelphia landmarks to help the New York pilots, we landed in the restaurant's parking lot. Mike Douglas's studio was right across the street.

After the program, we took the two pilots into the restaurant for coffee, said hello to the Taxins, thanked them for the use of their lot, and flew home.

In October, on the Johnny Carson show, Jackie introduced Brian Kelly as the star of *The Love Machine* film. He was to play Robin

Stone. Our old friend Maurice Chevalier was also on the show. I remember because he came over to Jackie in the green room and said, "You remind me of someone I used to know."

"I bet it was Kay Francis," Jackie said.

Chevalier looked at her in surprise. "How did you know?"

Love Machine started production in November. At first, we had very high hopes for it. The original screenplay was by Sam Taylor, who had written the wonderful *Sabrina Fair*. Later, the script was polished by Mary Anita Loos, a wonderful novelist and a niece of Anita Loos, author of *Gentlemen Prefer Blondes*. I think some other writers had their hands on it, too, and by the time everyone in Hollywood had edited a line here and fixed up a scene there, the script had died of improvements.

We were on the coast at the time, seeing the dailies, and I shared an office with Mary Anita Loos. Jackie rarely went on the set except to play her cameo role as a TV reporter. At dinner one night, we told Frankovich we thought the performance of the actor who played Gregory Austin, the network president, was too weak. Frankovich must have shared our doubts because he said, "Who would you like?"

Jackie said, "I'm thinking more of a Robert Ryan type."

Mike said, "He would be good, but I don't think he's available. Isn't he doing a play?"

I said, "Let me find out." I learned that his agent was David Begelman. I called David in New York and asked if Ryan would be available for four or five weeks to do *Love Machine*. I also wanted to know about Ryan's health. There were rumors he was not well. Begelman suggested I fly to New York, talk to Ryan, and have a look at him.

I flew in. Ryan looked perfect for the part. Ryan and Begelman were both very candid with me. In about six weeks, Ryan was going into the William Inge play *Dark at the Top of the Stairs*. But he could fit in our movie before his Broadway rehearsals started. Yes, he was eager to do the film, and he needed the money badly.

But he did have a problem. He had been operated on for lung cancer. He was okay, but there was the question of insurance. It was doubtful whether Columbia could get insurance for him, and the business side of the studios always required insurance coverage. I don't know how the details were worked out, but someone said the magic words, and we got Ryan. He was a thrilling actor and absolutely marvelous in the role.

Dyan Cannon was wonderful, too, and so were Jackie Cooper, Shecky Green, and David Hemmings. Everything seemed to be under control, so Jackie and I escaped to Philadelphia for Thanksgiving to spend a little time with Jackie's mother. On Thanksgiving Day, the phone rang. It was Mike Frankovich. "This is not a happy call," he said.

"What happened?" I asked.

"Brian Kelly ran his motorcycle into a wall."

"How bad is he?"

"Bad. We can forget about him for the film."

I hated to tell Jackie. I remembered how gorgeous and vibrant he was on the TV show with Chevalier.

Jackie was terribly upset. "Why do things like that happen?" she asked over and over.

Frankovich had to scrap three weeks of shooting and find a new leading man. George Chasin suggested George Peppard. Jackie and I both liked him. We called Frankovich. He said, "Too late, I've already signed John Philip Law?"

"What's he done?" I asked.

He was in *The Russians Are Coming, The Russians Are Coming*. He was very good in that, but he turned out not to be right for *The Love Machine*. He didn't fit the character of Robin Stone as Jackie had written it.

During the shooting, Jackie spent a lot of time around the pool at the Beverly Hills Hotel with an old pal from Philadelphia, Beverly Robinson, who looked like a slender Elizabeth Taylor. Beverly, whose children were in school in California, had married into the same Robinson family that Jackie had almost become a part of, so they had a great deal in common, and there was always much bantering and laughter during their marathon gin games.

When we finally saw the completed film in February 1971, all scored and with the theme sung by Dionne Warwick, who had also done *Valley*, Jackie hated it. Again, she thought her book had lost its depth and subtlety in translation to the screen. She loved Mike Frankovich, but she did not love the movie.

In May 1971, we went to the Cannes Film Festival with the Frankoviches, stopping in London on our way to the south of France. Mike's wife is Binnie Barnes, whom Jackie and I loved from the day we met her. Mike and Binnie had lived in London when he was head of production for Columbia in England. Binnie is English and had played with Charles Laughton in *Henry the Eighth,* among her many pictures. Between them, Mike and Binnie knew everyone in London and the surrounding countryside.

We went with them to dinner at our favorite White Elephant and made the rounds of the gambling clubs on Curzon Street. Binnie and Mike are great gamblers, and you can imagine what a marvelous time Jackie had with them.

One day, Binnie took us to lunch at the home of some friends, Mary and Gerald Lascelles. He was second son of the Princess Royal and first cousin to Queen Elizabeth. We drove out to a beautiful place in the country; the host and hostess were perfectly charming, and lunch was exquisite. It was only when Jackie walked around the house, looked at the paintings on the walls—nearly all of them portraits of royalty—and glanced at the signed photographs on the tables that she began to realize where we were.

We were in Fort Belvedere, the historic spot where our friend, the Duke of Windsor, as King Edward VIII, had made his historic abdication speech.

Several very friendly dogs played at our feet and demanded to be petted. Outside the door, Jackie noticed another dog gazing wistfully at all the fun and attention he was missing. Jackie's heart immediately went to the outside dog, and she asked, "Why isn't that cute dog playing with the other dogs?"

Our host looked outside and then said, in a tone that ruled out any further discussion, "Oh, that's the cook's dog."

Jackie, naturally, marched right out and made a big fuss over the cook's outcast dog.

After our visit to Fort Belvedere, Binnie rushed us off to meet some people she kept calling Tick and Tock. Jackie said they sounded like a television quiz show. Binnie said, no, they were marvelous interior decorators.

We went to a showroom near Ascot that was filled with incredible things—statues, pottery, English and French furniture, bronze and brass candelabra. Jackie could not take her eyes off all the wonderful stuff and wandered up and down the aisles, admiring and exclaiming. Then she saw the clock. It was very ornate with an enamel face and bronze frame. Either Tick or Tock saw Jackie staring and said, "Do you know the history of that clock?"

Jackie admitted she wasn't up on historic clocks.

Tick (or Tock) then explained that the clock was a gift to the

Duke of Wellington from Queen Charlotte, wife of King George III, after the battle of Waterloo. It was for sale and absolutely authentic.

"With a history like that," Jackie said, "the clock must cost a fortune."

"That's right," Tick said, "but there'll be some dummy from the United States who will be fascinated by its history and buy it."

To jump ahead, sometime later we were at the housewarming of the new Beverly Hills mansion of our friend Gene Klein. As Jackie took the grand tour through the magnificently furnished rooms, she looked up and saw—the clock. Gene, following her glance, asked, "Do you have any idea where that clock came from?"

Jackie said, "Why, of course."

"How would you know a thing like that?"

"You want to bet ten bucks I know?"

"I'll bet you a zillion."

"I don't want to bet a zillion. I want to bet ten bucks."

"Okay, what clock is that?"

"That's the clock the queen gave to the Duke of Wellington after the battle of Waterloo."

I thought Klein would faint. "How do you know that?" he asked.

She said, "I was at Tick and Tock's before your decorator went there, and they told me then that sooner or later some shnook from America would buy it and overpay for it."

Every time Jackie saw Gene after that, she asked him if the clock was keeping good time.

From England, we flew to Nice and drove to the Carlton Hotel where we shared with the Frankoviches a giant suite with three bedrooms and a big terrace right on the corner.

In front of the Festival Hall was a huge logo of *The Love Machine* cover. The film was not entered in the festival—it was being advertised and promoted. Of course, everyone else at the festival was ducking into one movie after another, but every night we went to the casino where Jackie and Binnie were partners in either chemin de fer or roulette.

One day we were invited by John Heyman, an important movie and TV producer and distributor in England, to a lovely luncheon in the harbor at Cannes aboard the *Kalizma*, the yacht belonging to Elizabeth Taylor and Richard Burton, which Heyman had chartered. The ship was a beauty, and Liz's bedroom was all shimmering white with reflections of the blue-green water dancing on the walls.

Jackie, always curious, checked out Liz's book shelf and was delighted to find four copies of *Josephine!* and two of *Valley*. One was the copy Jackie had autographed to Liz and given to her in the dining room of the restaurant of the Dorchester Hotel in London.

Cannes is a funny place during the film festival. It is jammed with the film elite from all over the world and also with hopefuls of all persuasions—would-be producers, actors, writers, call girls. The hopefuls show their esoteric films in tiny side-street theaters. Or they walk around with yellow or blue scripts that they try to peddle to expensively dressed producers sitting at open-air bars along the promenade. It's a tossup whether there are more deadbeats strolling the avenues or more sexy young girls dreaming of making it with a hot-shot producer who will, in an ecstatic moment, whisper the timeless promise "Honey, I'm going to make you a star."

Jackie loved watching the action at the cafés and on the promenades. Her head spun as she tried to catch each nuance of byplay and intrigue. I could see her filing away scenes and dialogue in her head.

Now I come to the hight point of that incredible summer. As I recall what happened next, my heart is heavy for I write this within days of the tragic death of Princess Grace. I think everyone felt her passing as a loss in the family; I did especially because of the close friendship shared by Jackie's and Grace's fathers and their own warm feelings for each other.

That summer, naturally, we let Her Serene Highness know that we would be in Cannes. We were not surprised to receive a gorgeously engraved invitation to a party at the Royal Palace in Monaco on Saturday evening, black tie.

Jackie called Princess Grace and explained that we were with the Frankoviches. Princess Grace understood perfectly, and in less than an hour a courier delivered an invitation to the Frankoviches. At dinner that night, Mike mentioned that he and Binnie had been invited to the Rainers on Saturday night.

Jackie said, "We're going, too."

Mike said, "That's wonderful, we'll all go together."

Mike then asked me if I had a tuxedo. I did not. I travel all over the world with a dark blue suit and a nice silk bow tie, and together they look enough like a tuxedo to satisfy me. But this arrangement did not satisfy Mike.

"I tell you what I'm going to do," he said. "I want to buy you a dinner jacket as a gift."

I said, "No, thank you. I can get by."

There was no stopping Mike, and the next morning he took me to Pierre Cardin's, where they could not get a regular tuxedo ready for me in time, but they did have a white dinner jacket. I said, "Absolutely not. That thing will make me look like Allan Jones in one of those college movies."

Mike grabbed me, peeled off my jacket, and made me put on the white jacket. It was my size, but the sleeves were too long. The salesman brought out another white jacket, but it was at least two sizes too small for me. They decided they would adjust the shoulders and sleeves of the larger jacket. Mike paid for the jacket and the tailoring, and I gave the clerk my room number at the hotel. It would be delivered on Friday.

On Friday, when the jacket was delivered, Jackie asked, "What's that?"

I said, "It's my new Pierre Cardin white tuxedo jacket."

"White jacket? Well!" She was laughing already. "The senior prom, of course."

Jackie had no problem. She was going to wear one of her beautiful Stavropoulous evening gowns, which she had just happened to bring along.

On Saturday night, while Jackie was making up her face and fixing her hair, I put on a white shirt—my regular shirt, not a tuxedo shirt—my bow tie, and my dark blue pants. Then I took the tissue paper out of the sleeves of the white jacket and tried to put it on. There was something wrong. The sleeves were up to my elbows. The front didn't come anywhere near closing. There was a seven-inch gap in front.

"I can't wear this," I told Jackie. "It doesn't fit."

"Sure it does." She tugged at the sleeves and got them halfway down my forearms. But there was nothing to do about the front.

The Frankoviches knocked on our door. Mike, of course, was all caked up in a wonderful-looking tuxedo. I started complaining about my jacket, but he wouldn't listen. "What are you talking about? It looks fine," he said.

"I'm not going like this," I said. "I can't even button the buttons. I'm putting on my suit jacket."

Mike wouldn't let me. He said, "Leave the jacket open. It's informal. You'll take it off when you get there."

[224]

I could see that Jackie and the Frankoviches were having a good time over my predicament.

We drove to the palace, which was very beautiful, with guards who looked like toy soldiers out front. Princess Grace was beautiful and charming and grabbed Jackie with both hands and kissed her. The room was full of wonderful people. Everyone was introduced, and then Princess Grace said, "I want you to meet His Majesty, the former King of Bulgaria." A tiny little man got out of his chair to shake hands with me, but his sleeves hung so far over his hands that he couldn't slide his hand out. He was wearing a white jacket.

I said to him, "Your Majesty, do you live at the Carlton Hotel?"

He said, "Yes."

I said, "Your Majesty, did you recently buy a white jacket at Pierre Cardin?"

He said, "Yes."

I said, "Please come over here with me."

We walked to the corner of the room, and we exchanged jackets. Suddenly, we both looked very good. I think the poor fellow had been sitting down earlier because he couldn't walk around with his sleeves hanging eleven inches over his hands. We were both happy, and Princess Grace came over with a twinkle in her eye and wanted to know what was going on. I told her, and soon everyone was laughing.

But wait. This story goes on. A year later, Rex Reed was at our apartment in New York interviewing Jackie and telling us that he was leaving soon for the Cannes Film Festival. Rex leads a very daring life because he goes to the festival, writes terrible pieces about some of the pictures, which really are a disgrace, and somehow gets invited back. Of course, they invite him because he's a real journalistic star and the best writer there is.

I said to him, "Rex, I have a present for you. I want to give you a white dinner jacket."

He tried to say no, but I wouldn't let him. I was about to tell him that I hadn't worn it since I'd gotten it off the King of Bulgaria, but I didn't think that was very polite, so I said that I hadn't worn it since I'd gotten it from Pierre Cardin. He finally tried it on. It looked great on him, and he took it.

At Cannes, at the final night of judging, Rex found himself sitting next to Mike Frankovich, and Mike was looking at him so intently that Rex began to feel self-conscious. Finally, Mike said to him, "Rex, that's a good-looking jacket."

Rex, who is a completely honest person, said, "You know where I got it?"

Mike said, "From Irving Mansfield."

Rex asked, "How did you know that?"

That's the famous story of the white dinner jacket.

The Love Machine opened in August 1971 to less than favorable reviews but enormous crowds.

$\mathcal{S}$uccess was absolutely splendid for Jackie. She had sought it so long and so desperately you might half expect it to go to her head, turn her bitchy and unapproachable. But it never did. She glowed and flowered in the spotlight. Fame was liberating for her. Of course, she loved all the perks and privileges of stardom: money, instant recognition wherever she went, invitations to everything (half of them from people she didn't know), limousines, chauffeurs, first-class plane tickets, flowers by the armful, champagne at her elbow, the best tables in restaurants, the best seats at theaters, bridal or royal suites in hotels.

Once her Paris publisher, Presses de la Cité, notified us that they were putting us up in some quaint, out-of-the-way hotel where Balzac once lived. I cabled them, "Jackie doesn't want to live like Balzac, she wants to live like Marie Antoinette. Please book us at the Ritz."

Jackie loved the sudden silence in a room as she entered and then the buzzing and murmuring: "It's Jackie!" "Oh, look, it's Jackie Susann!" "Jackie's here!"

She lit up a room the way a Sinatra does or a Liza Minnelli or a star of that magnitude.

One time, at Les Ambassadeurs in London, a stout man with a little brush mustache approached and said, "Aren't you Jacqueline Susann? We are in the same line of business. I'm James Clavell."

Jackie said, "Oh, Mr. Clavell, it's a pleasure to meet you. This is my husband, Irving Mansfield."

Clavell said, "Well, already I've lost fifty percent of my ambition." He was kidding and very charming. That same night, Michael Caine and Sean Connery said hello to Jackie—remarkable only because we didn't know them.

At a tribute to Rodgers and Hammerstein that Anna Sosenko was producing at the Imperial Theatre for the Museum of the City of New York in 1972, Richard Rodgers introduced Jackie to James Michener.

"You know," he said, "your name is a dirty word in my family."

"Why is that?" Jackie asked.

"Back in May 1966, your *Valley of the Dolls* replaced my book, *The Source*, as number one on the *Times* bestseller list."

He said it so charmingly that Jackie knew he was not really angry. She, in turn, charmed him by saying, "All your books are respected in my house."

I guess everyone loves meeting celebrated people. Jackie was no exception. It was important for her to move among men and women of accomplishment and fame. She had never been a total nobody—remember how impressed I was by her friends when I first went to Philadelphia. But she adored it when she herself became part of the world of headline makers. When she met Henry Kissinger and his two children at a party, she was thrilled that his children wanted her autograph. She didn't have any books with her, so she autographed a piece of paper. Then she said, "By the way, Mr. Kissinger, I'm not getting any royalties from Taiwan. Can you do anything about that?"

He said, "Jackie, I have troubles enough. Taiwan has its own printing plants and doesn't recognize our royalty arrangements."

That's when she asked him about changing her birth date on her passport, and again she struck out.

Jackie and Joan Crawford became good friends. Jackie and Joan often lunched together at "21" or the Russian Tea Room, and Jackie, Joan, Van Johnson, and I had many dinners together. Jackie admired Joan for her sense of grandeur, the way she dressed and played the total movie star. As soon as the bowing and scraping stopped whenever we walked into "21" on a Saturday night, they put a special, huge glass at Joan's place, filled with Stolichnaya vodka. She knocked it off in two seconds, and it was immediately replaced.

One Saturday night, when Jackie was out of town, I took Joan to dinner. We had decided on a Chinese restaurant just around the corner from her apartment in Imperial House. I walked over there; the doorman knew me and let me up. A few minutes later, Joan and I came down in the elevator; then she looked out the front door of the building and frowned. "Where's your car and chauffeur?" she asked.

"I didn't order the car. We're just going around the corner."

"How are we going to get there?"

"We're going to walk."

"I can't walk into a restaurant just like that."

"Yes you can—you've got two perfectly good feet."

Joan complained the entire minute and a half it took to walk from her door to the restaurant. In her mind, it was unsuitable for a star of her magnitude to arrive, even at a neighborhood Chinese restaurant, in anything less than a long, sleek limousine—unless it was a gilded coach. Jackie roared when I told her the story. "You missed your chance, doll. You should have carried her."

On one of our trips to Paris, we went to a cocktail party at Edith Piaf's apartment. Marlene Dietrich was sitting next to Jackie, and who wouldn't love the chance to chat away with the glorious Dietrich.

Later, Piaf said, "Jackie, you spent all the time talking to Marlene, and you didn't pay any attention to the woman on the other side of you. That was Colette."

"Colette?" Jackie asked. Then it struck her. "You mean *the* Colette?" Piaf nodded. "Oh, my God, why didn't you tell me." All the way home and for days afterward, Jackie berated herself. "Colette, Colette," she kept saying. "Can you imagine, I had a chance to talk to someone who is really immortal, and I blew it."

There was another wonderful writer Jackie didn't meet, and that time she was lucky. Years before, when I was producing "This Is Show Business," George S. Kaufman asked if I could give a little writing job to someone who was down on his luck. It was Dylan Thomas. I told George I didn't have an opening for his friend. But when I mentioned it to Jackie, she said, "Oh, but he's such a great poet. Can't you find a little something for him to do?"

"He's drunk all the time."

"I know—but he's a poet. Why don't you at least talk to him. And I'd like to meet him."

A few days later, Dylan Thomas arrived at my office on the fourteenth floor at the CBS building. It was like a brewery walking in. He sat down, we made small talk, he borrowed some money from me, and then he asked to borrow my portable typewriter. I said, "Okay, but be sure to bring it back."

He took the typewriter, went downstairs, and hocked it for fifteen dollars at the typewriter repair shop in my building. When I found out, I had to pay twenty-five dollars to get my own typewriter back. "Boy, what a deadbeat," I said to Jackie.

"No," she said loyally, "what a poet."

[229]

Jackie loved all the interviews and headlines and her photograph on magazine covers. The clippings came in like snow slides of paper, and everything went neatly into large albums covered in tooled leather. There are five scrapbooks just for *Valley of the Dolls* and five just for *Love Machine*—nearly two dozen altogether. The clippings from English and German newspapers often carry her name in screaming headlines all the way across the first page, and the pages have to be carefully folded to fit into the scrapbooks.

Jackie was endlessly patient about posing for photographers and knowledgeable about makeup, lights, and camera angles, usually willing to stay for "just one more shot." She did not have a bad side. She could be photographed from any angle and her nose, her cheekbones, her profile, her mouth, were always perfect. The famous photographer Philippe Halsman once said to her, "Jackie, there's no picture I can take of you that isn't a good picture. If you take a bad picture, it's the fault of the photographer."

Jackie never really had a money problem. Even in her early days in New York, her father or her grandmother had always slipped her a little something extra. When we were first married, she was very careful with our money. She never rode first-class or took a parlor car on the train to Philadelphia, and she checked with me on big expenditures—and big was anything over twenty-five dollars. After I got out of the army, through the 1950s and the first half of the 1960s, I made a very handsome living as a producer. Even after Guy's bills were paid, there was plenty to keep Jackie in room service.

But when the money from her books began pouring in, in torrents—royalty checks for $100,000, film company checks for $1 million—Jackie took to limousine living as effortlessly as if she had been born a Rockefeller. Quite literally. Every second year, she bought a new Cadillac. For a while, we had our own limo and chauffeur. We also used Manhattan Limousine, a service that sent us a stretch limousine whenever we needed one.

When Jackie drove the car herself, she wanted to get there *fast*. She was a born speeder. The cops were always stopping her on the way to the golf club. She got into the habit of carrying a stack of her paperbacks in the car, and when an officer stopped her, she'd say, "What's your name, sir. I'll write it in my book while you write in yours." You'd be surprised how often the officer put away his book and accepted hers, with a warning to slow down before she killed herself.

Gucci's is a store on Fifth Avenue famous for its high-priced Italian designer goods and its highhanded attitude toward customers. When I go there to shop—and by now they know that at Christmas I buy quantities of gorgeous ties, scarves, and belts—they look beyond and through me until I finally catch someone's eye. Then they're eager to rush me out. But Jackie had only to get a foot through the door and two members of a deposed royal family grasped her by the elbows—it was not permitted for her precious tootsies to touch the ground—and propelled her into the manager's paneled office where they offered her coffee, cognac, flowers, and "What is madame's pleasure to see today?" Merchandise appeared at the snap of a flunky's fingers. She loved it, and so did I.

She always carried at least $200 with her, sometimes a lot more. One day, she came home and said, "Guess what I did today?"

I said, "I think you met the Shah."

"No."

"You bought a Ferris wheel."

"No, you're not playing the game right. I bought a mink coat."

I said, "Beautiful."

"Aren't you going to ask me where I bought it?"

"Jackie, are you trying to make a straight man out of me?"

"Oh, come on."

"Okay, where did you buy it?"

"Bergdorf Goodman."

That was an odd place to buy a mink coat. Most people we knew had a furrier down in the fur district where they thought they saved a lot of money by going wholesale.

What happened was that Jackie walked by Bergdorf's, saw a coat in the window, a very sporty coat combining mink and leather, and went in and said, "I'd like that coat."

They got a coat from the fur vault that was exactly like the one in the window. They wouldn't give her the one in the window—it had been in the sun for a week. She put it on, liked it, and wore it out of the store. She modeled it for me in the living room. It was a great coat to wear with pants.

"It looks wonderful," I said. "How much did it cost."

"I don't know. I didn't even ask."

That was Jackie. When she wanted something, she just walked in and said, "Charge it."

But the more she got, the more eager she was to give. She

[231]

lavished gifts on friends, family, business associates, people she hardly knew. Helen Gurley Brown still cherishes a little gold ring Jackie gave her. She spent a fortune on beautiful gold watches and was always giving them away.

She was constantly writing a check for someone who was hard up. She didn't have to be asked; she *knew* when a small or a large amount would be a lifesaver. Toward the end of her life, she sent hundreds of dollars on a regular basis to Betty Bruce, a wonderful singer whom Jackie hardly knew. But Betty, like Jackie, was dying of cancer; only Betty was under financial pressure, and Jackie knew the illness was bad enough without severe money worries.

When Carol Bjorkman was in Memorial Hospital with leukemia, not only did Jackie visit her daily and deliver Carol's column to *Women's Wear Daily*, but later, when Carol was too ill to write, Jackie wrote the column for her but told no one. People couldn't get over how brave Carol was to keep up her work right to the end. Jackie loved Carol.

She worried about her friends' health. Once, Anna Sosenko wanted to borrow Jackie's car to go to Philadelphia. "When was the last time you went to the doctor?" Jackie demanded. "When did you last have a Pap test? No Pap test, no car." Anna had to have the test to get the car. The next year, when she wanted to use the car again, she had to be tested again.

One night in California, when we were having dinner with Doris Day, a man came over to Doris and asked how she felt; they had about ten minutes of casual conversation. It was obvious that Doris couldn't introduce him because she didn't remember his name, so to save her embarrassment, Jackie began talking to me in a very animated way. After the man left, Doris started to take a bite of her hamburger, then put it down and said, "Oh, my God, do you know who that was? My God, that was my first husband. That's terrible. I didn't know who he was."

Jackie told Doris to go over to where he was sitting behind us with a group of people and tell him she hadn't seen him clearly because the light was in her eyes. Doris was reluctant, but Jackie insisted. Doris was away from the table for about five minutes. When she came back, Jackie asked, "Do you feel better now?"

"No," she said. "It was terrible of me not to know him and introduce him."

Later, we went back to Doris's house where she told us stories about her band-singer days, her first picture, which was *Love on the High Seas*, how she opened at Billy Reed's Little Club in New York, and how hard she worked all the years she was Hollywood's number-one box-office attraction and then didn't wind up with any money because Marty Melcher, her third husband, mismanaged it or lost it gambling or hid it away in a Swiss bank account.

Jackie felt a sense of outrage for her friend, who had worked so hard and been so adored by the public and had nothing to show for it but her house in Beverly Hills and her heartache. "I think you have a great book," Jackie said.

"Who would be interested?" Doris asked.

The next morning, Jackie called Esther Margolis at Bantam and Sherry Arden, vice president and publicity director at Morrow. Both thought it was a terrific story but doubted anyone could get it from Doris. Jackie said, "Don't worry about it. I'll arrange everything."

People from Morrow and Bantam made the deal and got A. E. Hotchner to do the book. He was very patient with Doris and had a great way of making her talk. She really had a good time working with him. The book was a bestseller in both hard cover and paperback. Doris, who made money from it, felt better for unburdening herself. Jackie did it all for her friend with just two phone calls.

Jackie did the same thing for a woman she hardly knew, Mary Daniels, a reporter for the *Chicago Tribune* who interviewed Jackie on one of her swings through the Midwest. Mrs. Daniels had just written an amusing feature article about Morris, the disdainful cat in the cat-food commercials. Jackie and Mary talked about Morris and Josephine and Jackie's book about Josephine. Suddenly, Jackie said, "Why don't you do a book about Morris?"

Jackie called Sherry Arden, who asked, "Morris who?"

Mary wrote the book for Morrow; it was a big success but perhaps a little ahead of its time. Today, it seems as if *only* books about cats are permitted on the paperback bestseller lists.

After Jackie wrote *Josephine!*, people were constantly calling her or writing her for advice about their dogs. Later, after *Valley*, people turned to Jackie for advice about their emotional problems and their most intimate lives. They reasoned that to have written such a book, she must be truly a woman of the world, shock proof and full of wise counsel. Several times, when we got home after a party, she'd shake her head and say, "Why do they all think I'm Ann Landers? The blonde married to the producer—the one you were giving the eye—

dropped her whole life story on me two minutes after we were introduced. You couldn't print three words of it."

Once, a very famous woman, so famous she turned up regularly on national lists of most-admired women, called Jackie and asked if she could come to see her. This woman arrived in a limousine, walked into the apartment, obviously nervous and self-conscious, declined the tea Jackie offered her, and with a look of anguish on her face, got right to the point. She said, "I appreciate your giving me this time—I know how busy you are. But there's something I have to ask you." She looked at her hands, took a deep breath, and said, "How often does your husband make love to you?"

Jackie instantly understood the question behind the question and came up with a beautiful and wise answer. She said, "As often as I ask him."

It was a perfect answer—it did not add to the poor woman's sense of rejection, and it opened the possibility that perhaps she should make the first move.

The Duchess of Windsor confided in Jackie. They had first met at the party for Josephine. Then, years later, Francine Farkas invited Jackie and me to a dinner party she was giving for the Duke and Duchess. During the evening, Jackie talked to the Duke about golf, but when the discussion turned to politics, Jackie noticed that the Duchess was getting very uneasy. Jackie threw the Duchess a reassuring smile.

A few days later, the Duchess invited Jackie to lunch and explained that political discussions always upset her because they invariably seemed to lead back to Stanley Baldwin, the British prime minister who had engineered her husband's abdication. Baldwin had said the Duke was the most disgraceful king in all of English history. Which is something when you think of all those scheming scoundrels on the throne in Shakespeare's plays. The Duchess got livid just thinking about Baldwin.

Then, in that little French restaurant, over lunch, the Duchess told Jackie what a hell her life had been. Yes, she had been ambitious; she had hoped to be Queen of England. But she had really loved Edward when she married him. He had expected to be able to keep the throne. When he was forced to abdicate, then dumped onto a little island as governor during the war years, he had turned bitter. According to the Duchess, not a day, not an hour had passed since then that the Duke had not reminded her of what she had cost him, what he had given up.

Jackie came home completely drained. "What a nightmare marriage that woman has," Jackie said. "What a price she's paying for her ambition."

I don't quite know why people chose to confide in Jackie. Maybe it was the quality of attention she showed. She listened carefully. She let others have their say. She always remembered every detail. She followed up without fail. If she said she'd make a phone call for someone, she did, or called to explain why she couldn't. She remembered occasions—birthdays, anniversaries, special events. She had a lap board she used in bed. In it were tucked all kinds of stationery, cards, short sheets, long sheets, always from Tiffany, with her name beautifully engraved. Every night as we watched television, she dashed off her notes—thank yous, congratulations, greetings, bread and butter letters. Her mother had taught her well about such things. And her father had taught her to watch people, to tune herself into them.

Her enthusiasm and zest also strengthened her relationships. She was always ready for a trip, a lark, a golf game, a walk in the park, a midnight movie, a bicycle ride down to Greenwich Village for croissants at Sutter's, the bakery shop on 10th Street. When we were in Rome in 1970, we took the bus to Naples on the ancient Roman road and then a little sailboat with an auxiliary motor to Capri. We looked back on Vesuvius—what a marvelous sight! When we went to the Grotto Azura, we were with another couple—strangers we had met on the boat.

Jackie took one look at the aquamarine water, started peeling off her dress, and dove in. The other woman took off her dress and shoes and followed; the other man and I jumped in, too, in our shorts. I would never do that on the beach in Miami or in California, but when Jackie got caught up in the excitement of this beautiful place, far from home, we followed her wild lead—and had a wonderful time.

Jackie exulted at her friends' good news and cried at their bad news. But if a friend failed her, woe betide that friend. After Judith Crist, the movie critic, said some unkind things about Jackie and *Valley* on the "Today" show, Jackie used to croon, "I've got a little list. It starts with Judith Crist."

At the Palm Bay Club in Florida at Christmas time in 1972, Jackie called, "Hello, Vera," to her friend Vera Swift, who was playing in a big-money backgammon game. Vera was concentrating too hard to answer. Jackie called out the greeting again, this time louder. Again Vera ignored her. At the third "Hello, Vera," Vera said, "Hello, Jackie," but hardly looked up from the board. Jackie was sizzling.

I said, "Jackie, you shouldn't interrupt her at a time like this."

"But she's a friend. I would never ignore a friend. You know what I'm going to do? I'm going over to Worth Avenue and buy her the most expensive damn gift you ever saw and sign the card 'Guess who?' She won't sleep, wondering who sent it."

We went over to one of the very elegant shops where Jackie spotted a Chinese backgammon table inlaid with ivory, two elaborately carved chairs, and a backgammon set of solid ivory. "That's beautiful," she said to the shopkeeper. "How much is it? I think I want to send it to a friend."

"The pieces are priced separately," the proprietor explained. "The table is thirty thousand dollars, the chairs are seventeen thousand each, the backgammon set is twenty-five thousand. If you take them all, it's—"

"Never mind," Jackie interrupted. "To hell with Vera Swift."

Jackie had many good friends among the press people. She first met Rex Reed when he was doing a story on the women in *Valley* for *Cosmopolitan* magazine. We joined him for a drink at the Polo Lounge where he introduced us to Denise and Vincente Minnelli. Jackie and Denise, who is now Mrs. Prentis Hale of San Francisco and a leader of international society, became very good friends. And Jackie and Rex became best pals. They were always on the phone together. Then one day Rex did a full-page article in the *Daily News* about a woman Jackie absolutely could not stand. Jackie was so mad she called Rex and said, "We're not friends anymore."

She hung up and started to cry. "I don't think I did the right thing. It isn't that I hate this woman, it's that I love Rex more."

"Then why the hell did you call him?"

"I couldn't help it."

"Then call him back and tell him to forget about it."

"I can't do that. It would hurt my pride."

I said, "Let's figure out this thing. Either you've got pride, or you love Rex. Which is it?"

She didn't have an answer. Two months passed; we were in the south of France, and we came face to face with Rex in the Carlton

[236]

Hotel in Cannes. He looked as if he was going to say hello to her, but Jackie walked right by him. She turned the corner and started to cry.

"What the hell are you crying for?"

"Because I wanted to say hello to Rex."

"Then why didn't you?"

"I don't know."

Then Jackie discovered from Margaret Gardner, her press agent in London, that Rex had done the story at Margaret's particular request. Jackie said to Margaret, "Oh, my God. I should be mad at you, not at Rex." Soon after that, we gave a party for Margaret, Rex came, and everything was all right.

Jackie was fearless in counterattacking if she thought she was being wronged. In Detroit, at the time the newspapers were full of stories about *Beyond the Valley of the Dolls*, Shirley Eder warned Jackie that if she went on Lou Gordon's disc-jockey program, he would give her a hard time. As soon as she was on the show, Gordon said, "I want to ask you some questions about *Beyond the Valley of the Dolls*."

Jackie said, "I had nothing to do with it, and I don't want to talk about it."

When Gordon insisted and said, "This is my program, and that's what I want to talk about," Jackie took him on.

She said, "If you mention that movie once more, I'm going to leave."

He said, "If you want to leave, you can," never believing she would.

Jackie got up, unbuttoned the microphone from her jacket, looked at his bad toupee, and said, "By the way, is that a hat you're wearing or a breaded veal cutlet?" and walked out.

Jackie always had a lot of admiration for Rona Barrett. She thought it terrific that Rona had worked her way up from head of the Eddie Fisher fan club to a big shot in the entertainment business. "You've got to respect that lady," Jackie used to say. "She's okay." But when Mike Frankovich gave the announcement of his one and a half million dollar purchase of *The Love Machine* to Joyce Haber, Rona got upset and wrote several pieces Jackie was unhappy about. Jackie always regretted that she and Rona never resumed their friendship.

Jackie always got along beautifully with Liz Smith. Liz seemed to have a special compassion for writers and directors. She understood the intricacy and the competitiveness of the movie business and really loved the people in the industry.

Jackie's five closest friends in the later years were Joyce Matthews, Anna Sosenko, Muriel Slatkin, Bonnie Silberstein, and Beatrice Cole. I think she told them things she didn't tell me. They were a good sounding board for her because they were so different she could get five very different reactions.

Valley of the Dolls was all about the price you have to pay for success. Did Jackie have to pay such a price? No, she never did, not after she made it big. I think she paid her dues up front in the long years of struggle and frustration and minor-scale accomplishment. She took pills to sleep and toward the end for pain, but never to shut out the loneliness, for Jackie was never lonely. She had very little family—just her mother and me—but she was rich in friends, who became her family. She worked hard—God how she worked—writing her books, promoting them, selling them, but it was a labor of love. That's what she most *wanted* to do in all the world.

I was the one who worried for her—for her safety. Day after day, she was out there, working the crowds, in that weird era of the 1960s when fame seemed to invite violence. I watched every crowd, standing on the outskirts, my eyes scanning the men and women who pushed close around her. Once I saw a man clench his hand and shove it into his raincoat pocket in a way that spelled "gun" to me. I rushed him—he had only an invitation in his hand.

Several days after the Sharon Tate murder, when all of Los Angeles was still on the edge of hysteria, Jackie got a threatening phone call at the Beverly Hills hotel from a man and then a woman. The message was "You'll never leave here alive."

We called the police. They wanted to know if we recognized the voices. Of course, we didn't. We moved upstairs to the suite that Princess Margaret and Tony Armstrong-Jones had just vacated because it was more secure than our regular suite. The police put a watch on the phone. The man called again, and I answered. He said, "Your wife will never get out of California alive."

I said, "Why are you doing this?"

A woman took the phone and said, "He's not kidding."

Jackie was scared to death. At another time, she might have put on her Apache act, swaggered out of the room, stood in the middle of Sunset Boulevard, and shouted, "Come and get me if you have the nerve!" But Sharon's murder by the mad Charles Manson just days earlier had taught us that terror lurked everywhere.

The police traced the calls to a building at Sunset Boulevard and took pictures of everyone in the building. For the rest of our stay in California, Jay Allen and I saw that there were always at least two people with Jackie, and we wouldn't even let her go into a ladies' room alone. Fortunately, nothing came of the threat.

I've been asked many times to reveal the secret of Jackie's spectacular success. What was the magic formula that zoomed her to the top? I don't think there's any single answer. To begin with, her books were lively, exciting, easy to read, and full of glamorous characters who lived in a thrilling world of luxury, sex, and achievement. The books, in their way, dealt with contemporary problems at a time when women were seeking new answers to the challenge of sexual freedom, personal liberation, and finding a place in the world. Her readers were never disappointed. They always wanted more.

After the books were written, Jackie put as much effort into selling them as she had into creating them. Because she was as glamorous as her heroines, witty and responsive, she was a perfect guest for radio and TV. Her skills as an actress gave her an extra dimension when she went on the air or before an audience.

Working together with Jay Allen and with the very capable promotion people of her publishing houses, she and I could put on a virtual blitz for each book. Once the forward momentum was established, we rocketed ahead. At the beginning, we spent our own money for trips and ads in total faith that ultimately we would be rewarded. We were right, because later her publishers and film producers were willing to commit hundreds of thousands of dollars to publicity and advertising. Withstanding the worst that they could throw at us, we never let ourselves be cowed by high-brow critics and book reviewers. "It's funny," Jackie used to say, "but only the public loves me."

The public, of course, is always hungry for a new star. Jackie, born with the feeling she was destined to zoom across the sky like a meteor, was ready to shine and dazzle.

But at the peak of her success, something very interesting was happening to Jackie. She was beginning to move on to another level. She was growing and seeking other values. Her youthful dream, which she had held to so tenaciously, centered her under the spotlight as the music crescendoed, the crowd roared its adoration, and Jackie, the heroine of it all, sank into a graceful bow, acknowledging the adulation of multitudes.

Once she had achieved it, Jackie looked around and asked, "Is that all there is?"

It's funny to think about, but Jackie's life was imitating her books. Through Jackie's eyes, her readers entered the world of producers, stars, tycoons. They visited sensational locales, lived in the grandest hotels, traveled in the best circles, ate in the finest restaurants. Sooner or later, they said to themselves, "Wow, I'd really like to live like that."

But then Jackie told them it was not a life of milk and honey when you reached the top. There were problems, disappointments, heartbreak. And it was the woman who usually got the short end, the bad bargain. The woman always paid and paid.

Now Jackie herself was asking about success, "Is this all?" She didn't ask the question ungratefully or cynically. She asked it in true puzzlement. Anna Sosenko was the one she asked because Anna straddled the worlds of entertainment and of intellectual accomplishment. For twenty-three years, Anna had managed Hildegarde, the singer. She ranked high in ASCAP for writing "Darling, Je Vous Aime Beaucoup," "I'll Be Yours," and "J'attendrai."

Anna was aware that Jackie was finishing with tinsel and shallow values and was beginning to search for deeper meanings and for relationships based less on hero worship and more on lasting substance.

"I'm going to get rid of people who bore me," Jackie told Anna toward the end, "people who are just rich or have their names in the papers. There must be a million people out there I could relate to and learn from, people who have led fascinating lives without getting into the columns and the headlines. There's so much I have to learn, so much that is important."

But in the final serving of the vinegar with the wine, there was simply not enough time for Jackie.

*J*ackie's third major novel, *Once Is Not Enough*, was written in bits and pieces from 1969 to 1972, with a big push in the summer and early fall of '72. *Once* is again a strongly autobiographical novel. Beautiful young January Wayne is in love with her father, Mike Wayne, producer, gambler, lover, exciting man of the world. Her search for herself, for a man she can love more than her father, for her own place in the scheme of things, takes her through the worlds of show business, publishing, the very rich, and the very rich spaced out on speed—all familiar turf to Jackie.

The plot is intricate and twisting. Jackie had two blackboards going this time as she wrote. She did research on convent life in prewar Poland and Nazi bestiality to the nuns to authenticate the background of an aging film star who was a bisexual recluse. She and I both slipped into the office of a notorious "Dr. Feelgood" and had ourselves goofed up with amphetamines so she could give an accurate rendering of strung-out behavior. She created the character of Tom Colt, a writer located about midway between Ernest Hemingway and Norman Mailer, and turned him into an untrustworthy bastard, probably to get her revenge on the literary establishment.

To Mike Wayne, she gives the glamour and power of her own father, and to his daughter, January—in all her novels Jackie had an important female character with a name beginning with J—her own early longings for recognition and need for love. The conflict/affection between father and daughter is handled very tenderly.

In the seduction of January by David Milford, a worldly stock-broker, she went back to a theme she touched on in all her books—a young woman's sexual awakening, her fears and hesitations and sense of abject failure.

"Sexual revolution or no sexual revolution," Jackie used to say, "women never get over the first time. It haunts them before and after. It's always *there*." And she always wrote about it.

Once was primarily under contract to Bantam for paperback, but arrangements had to be made for publication of the hard cover. Simon and Schuster had treated us most handsomely, but there was a problem. They also published Harold Robbins and Irving Wallace, both competitors of Jackie's on the bestseller lists. Jackie admired many of these writers. She especially liked Robbins, Sidney Sheldon, and Joe Wambaugh. She used to say she found them more entertaining than Hemingway or Faulkner. But she felt she might be better off with another publisher.

Oscar Dystel arranged a lunch meeting at "21" for Jackie with Larry Hughes president of William Morrow and Company and Sherry Arden. They all got along very well. Sherry had been associate producer of the ABC-TV special about Jackie and *Valley*. Hughes told Jackie that Jim Landis would be her editor. Hughes was describing at length what his company could do for her, but in the middle of her filet of sole, Jackie interrupted him and said, "Let's cut the bull. I know Morrow's a great publisher. I'd love to work with Sherry Arden again. So I'm going to sign with you. Okay?"

Hughes rushed out, ordered flowers, and had them sent to Jackie at the restaurant.

Once the contract was signed, Jackie really had to dig in to complete the book. She wrote like a fury through that spring and summer. But it was difficult for her to give the book her undivided attention. Guy was on both our minds.

The situation at our son's school had deteriorated so severely that we knew we had to find a new place for him. Guy was twenty-six. He hated any change in routine, but it was impossible to continue where he was. Once again, we inquired, searched, visited. I can't tell you how sad it is to make the rounds of the schools and institutions for the retarded and autistic and to see the sorrow on the faces of the parents, who go through a ring of fire each time they visit their children.

In March, we flew down to Texas to look at a school that seemed better run and better administered than the others on our list. The medical staff was highly recommended. There was an atmosphere of kindness and concern.

The red tape in moving someone like Guy is endless. He finally made the change in April 1972; we went to see him later that month, several more times before summer, and on a special trip in July, on the way to Los Angeles in August. The school was well off the beaten track, and on each trip we had to change planes, rent a car, remain overnight, and do the same on the way back. But it was worth every bit of the trouble because Guy adjusted well and stayed in Texas for nearly eight years.

In 1968, Jackie had begun to keep regular appointments with her new doctor, Dr. Clifford Spingarn, an internist, who became our family physician. Jackie admired him and trusted him and tried to follow his first advice to her, which was—as you might easily guess—to stop smoking. Jackie tried—she tried over and over—but all her efforts came to nothing. She went right on smoking, and her smoker's cough hung right in there. Early in 1972, Dr. Spingarn renewed his warnings about smoking. This time she cut back, but the cough held on.

In February 1972, I got Jackie into the sun for a week in Florida, and in May she stole a week away from her typewriter when we were invited by Cindy Adams to Dorado Beach in Puerto Rico. Jackie, along with Ed Sullivan, Cleveland Amory, Rita Moreno, Walt Frazier, Halston, Joey Adams, and Connie Francis, were to be judges in the Miss U.S.A. contest. It turned out not to be a restful trip.

While the contest was being televised at the Cerromar Hotel, we heard an explosion that sounded like Pearl Harbor. We were ordered to remain in our seats until an all-clear was sounded. The damage to the hotel was only minor, but we had been bombed by a revolutionary group. The next day, Jackie and I played nine holes of golf with Ed Sullivan and Cleveland Amory, then flew in a small plane to the San Juan Airport to board a jet to New York. Later, we learned that several golfers had been badly beaten up the same afternoon we had been on the course.

"We could have stayed home and gotten mugged," Jackie said on the plane. But at least she had a good tan and looked rested.

Jackie coughed off and on all spring and summer, tried various allergy medications, drank bottles of cough syrup, fought off a sore throat. Her great triumph was getting her cigarettes down to one or two a day.

After lengthy writing sessions in July and August, on September 8, Jackie pulled the last page of *Once Is Not Enough* out of the typewriter and turned in the final copy to Morrow on September 18, 1972. Jim Landis, her editor, came to the apartment every day for a week, and at the big table in the living room he and Jackie edited the book. They ordered lunch in and worked right through the day.

After that, Jackie took it easy for the rest of that fall. It was her first real time off in years—her latest book completed, no book or film to promote, no heavy schedule of interviews, TV appearances, photography sessions, or fittings, Guy comfortably settled, her mother doing well after the stroke she had suffered in 1968.

We relaxed together, we walked Joseph in the park, we played golf, we savored the free hours with each other.

We did not know that it was the last of the good times.

That New Year's, as we saw in the year 1973, we were guests on the *Amerada*, the magnificent 120-foot yacht of Harriet and Paul Ames. Harriet was a sister of Walter Annenberg, the publisher and philanthropist who also served as our ambassador to Great Britain. The yacht was tied up at the Peruvian Dock in Palm Beach. It was a beautiful vessel that slept eight and had a crew of eight and a fine chef. Jackie's friend Bonnie Silberstein was also aboard, and Lee Guber joined us for a while.

Jackie spent a lot of time in the sun as we cruised to the Palm Bay Club, and again she got a wonderful tan, but her cough, a heavy, wheezing cough, was very bad. Harriet insisted that Jackie and I stay aboard another two days after the others left so that Jackie could rest a little longer. At least one good thing was accomplished on the trip— Jackie was finally off cigarettes.

At the end of the year, she wrote her doctor, "Dear Dr. Spingarn, My cough coughs better—more resonance and wheezing than ever. Of course I'm trying not to worry, but can one have a cough for eight months unless she's Camille?"

Early in January, when we got back to New York, Dr. Spingarn sent Jackie to Dr. Max Som, a renowned throat specialist who arranged for her to undergo bronchoscopy to see if there was anything seriously wrong in her chest or lungs.

She entered Mt. Sinai Hospital on January 11, 1973, and was in such an anxiety state that her heart rate was 120 beats a minute. Jackie was in utter terror. I've never seen such fear. There was no way I could calm her down. It wasn't a hysterical fear or a baseless fear; it was a rock-solid fear growing out of Jackie's deep intuition that the doctors would find the worst.

They did. They found an obstruction in the bronchial area,

which they biopsied. The biopsy was positive. Positive—that dread word once more!

Jackie had cancer. Again.

If you want to know about rage, I can tell you about rage. Because Jackie was in an uncontrollable fury that alternated with despair. How could this be? How could this happen to her all over again? On every checkup since her mastectomy, she had come through with flying colors. It was ten years since that surgery had been performed. Ten wonderful, fabulous years. Jackie had shot the moon and roller coastered around the sun. She had had every success she had ever dreamed of—and more.

But now it was over. All over. She was sure it was.

I tried to persuade her otherwise. This was just a small thing. A little something on a bronchial tube. Not a major problem at all. It could be taken care of with chemotherapy. The next day, we were seeing Dr. Ezra Greenspan, one of the world's leading oncologists— an expert on tumors. He would tell us that this was only a small, temporary setback.

The waiting room of Dr. Greenspan's office on Fifth Avenue was filled with sad eyes. It was hard to tell whose eyes were sadder, the eyes of the patients or the eyes of the accompanying husbands, wives, or parents. For Jackie, the doctor recommended an immediate course of cobalt, five days a week for two weeks, then alternating two weeks off, two weeks on, and daily chemotherapy injections consisting of a combination of four powerful anticancer drugs and testosterone, or male hormone. Her treatment was to begin the very next day.

We went home, and Jackie poured two shots of vodka over a rock and said, "What are we going to do?"

I said, "We're going to do exactly what we've always done before. We'll go on by loving each other."

"And how long do you think you're going to get to love me?"

"I don't know. But I know you'll have a remission. You've been lucky once. You will be lucky again. You've had a lot of luck. You were born beautiful. You have a great talent. You're a great story-teller. It's true you're a little offbeat when you sing 'Come Rain or Come Shine.' "

She started to laugh and said, "Do you remember that terrible night?"

"Of course, I do."

"How could I have been so dumb?"

[245]

By talking to her like that, I calmed her. Finally, she said, "I'm going to lie down." She went into the bedroom, took several sleeping pills, finished the vodka, and in ten minutes she was fast asleep. I sat beside her for quite a while. Then I heard the phone ring down the hall in the study. I went to answer it. While I was still talking, I heard Jackie call out, "Who was that?"

Can you imagine—in despair, knocked out by pills and vodka— she still had to know who was on the phone. Later that night, after we had walked around to the Carnegie Delicatessen and had an omelet, we sat looking out the window at the lights in the park and in the tall apartment buildings along Fifth Avenue. Jackie said, "There's only one good thing about this."

I said, "There's nothing good about this, but you'll be able to fight it. You're a great fighter."

She said, "No, there's a good thing. You won't die first." And she started crying.

After a while, I said, "Jackie, we've been through tough times, we've been through good times. We're having a rough time now. But we'll get through it. You'll feel fine. You'll get your enthusiasm back."

"I don't know," she said. "Why shouldn't I end it right now instead of going through this painful treatment. People on chemo- therapy are sick all the time. They get pneumonia. They feel rotten."

I said, "Jackie, you're the strongest woman I've ever known in my life and the toughest. You're going to beat this. We'll be back at the Beverly Hills this summer. We'll go to Europe. You'll see. It's been a happy life. And it's going to be happy again."

She let out a long sigh and said, "Well, we don't have to buy calendars anymore." Then she said, "I guess I've destroyed your day."

I said, "No, the doctors did that."

She drank two more vodkas and took two more sleeping pills. I couldn't see any reason to stop her.

"I'm not going to put you through this for too long," she said.

"Don't ever threaten me," I said, and reached for her hand.

We sat for a long time watching the moving chain of lights on the cars driving through the park. She talked and rambled a little bit. Then her tongue got very thick. She was too punch-drunk to get up.

I picked her up and carried her back to the bedroom. I undressed her as well as I could. I took her to the bathroom, carried her back to bed, tucked her in, and kissed her good night. She was out.

I lay back in bed and tried not to look into the future. But I could see this was just the beginning. It didn't take a lot of imagination to figure out what the months and years ahead would be like. But, hell, if I couldn't act like a damn good husband, what kind of a man was I? We had been married thirty-four years, all of them great. I had dedicated ten years to working with Jackie and helping her achieve the success she had always craved. The rewards for both of us had been beyond anything we had been crazy enough to hope for. Now we would go on ahead together. I would make everything as easy for her as I possibly could. That was the only way I could show my love.

In the morning, I woke up and heard voices in the kitchen. Jackie was telling Louise what she wanted for breakfast. "Hi, doll," she said, "do you feel like a corn muffin or an English muffin?"

Jackie's mood improved enormously as treatment got under way. By the second week in February, her wheeze was gone, and she was coughing less. But she became agitated and depressed. She brooded about impending death. The doctors told me to keep her occupied. We started going out, to the theater, to movies, rarely with other people, usually just the two of us. One day, when we were sitting in a restaurant, Jackie took out her lipstick and compact, and after she looked at her face, she said to me, "What is this smudge?"

There was a dark smudge on one cheek, and when she touched it, she discovered it was hair. It had never been there before. She let out a shriek. The next morning, she literally ran to the doctor. By then, her face was covered with dark hair. It was caused by the male hormone, which was part of her medication. The doctor changed the medication. Jackie went every other day for electrolysis to a wonderful woman named Reba Pommer. It took six weeks to remove every trace of hair.

During that time, Jackie's face was swollen and sore, but in the end, it was baby smooth and glowing—smoother than it had been in years.

Then one morning she awoke with a piercing scream. Half her hair was on her pillow. "I'm not going through with any more chemotherapy," Jackie raged. "I don't care if I die. They didn't tell me about this. They never said a word."

But of course they had told her. They had told her that maybe it wouldn't happen to her, but more likely than not, it would. Her hair would fall out as a side effect of the chemotherapy, which kills fast-growing hair cells along with fast-growing malignant cells. Poor Dr. Spingarn—Jackie refused to believe he had told her, but he had. This new development was too terrible to face. She didn't want to live if she was going to be bald. She didn't want me to have to wake up beside a bald woman in the morning. I had seen Jackie furious before. But never like this.

The irony was that Jackie knew all about hair loss in cancer patients. In *The Love Machine,* she had described in almost horrifying detail Amanda's shock when her hair fell out shortly before her death from leukemia.

Jackie's closetful of wigs got her through this dreadful time. She had enough for every occasion. She could dress up, put on her makeup, pin on wigs and falls, and no one would ever know anything was wrong. When her hair began to grow back in, it was fuller and curlier than it had been before. It grew in like a little curly cap.

Once again, as she had before, Jackie insisted on total secrecy about her illness. No pity. No sorrowful looks. No one was to say, "Poor Jackie," or, "Brave Jackie," or cry for her. Jackie herself would do all the crying that was necessary. We slipped in and out of doctors' offices through side doors and lobby entrances. She wore dark glasses and a scarf over her head. Doctors cooperated; their nurses cooperated. I don't think we told any of our friends at this time.

At the end of March, she was in Doctors Hospital for two weeks with lobar pneumonia. Somehow we kept that secret.

When *Once Is Not Enough* was published in April, Jackie was feeling a lot better. On May 6, less than a month after publication, the book made number one in *The New York Times.* This time, it was Frederick Forsyth's *Odessa File* that was shoved back into second place and *Jonathan Livingston Seagull* grounded to third.

Most of the reviews, as usual, were not for framing, but they were a little more respectful than in the past. Jackie had become an institution. She was not a one-book fluke. She was a phenomenon— they had to recognize that. Three successive novels in the number-one spot—nobody had ever done that before. Maybe, some of the critics admitted begrudgingly, she's doing something right.

"Jackie Susann just doesn't write a novel," the *Chicago Tribune* said. "She sends it out like a heat-seeking missile, straight for first place on the bestseller list."

"Jackie's best-written novel," Joyce Haber said in the *Los Angeles Times.*

"This is a powerful novel about the confusing drama of life and the potency of love," Helen Joseph wrote in the Associated Press.

Taylor Caldwell sent Jackie a note that she always cherished: "Greetings from a sister novelist. I have just read your latest novel and I think it is the best thing you have ever done—and you may quote me if you wish."

But now the book tour was different. Wherever we went—New York, California, England, France—Jackie had to check in daily with a doctor for her chemotherapy shots and the regular taking of blood. When you're a cancer patient, they're always after your blood to count platelets and a million other things they must keep track of. One of the drugs in the anticancer combination she was taking was called 5FU, and when Jackie was feeling well enough to be her old, joking self, she'd say, "It's FU time, doll, I'm off to the doctor's."

In California, her doctor was Dr. Henry Jaffe at Century City Hospital. He and his wife, Diana Gaines, who was a novelist, became good friends of ours. Dr. Jaffe was also treating Susan Hayward. We didn't know it at first, but Jackie saw Susan in the elevator when she went down to the underground, lead-lined radiotherapy room for cobalt.

Every second day or so, Laurence Harvey, who had been a neighbor in New York, used to drop in to see us. In the past, he had always been funny and full of life, but now he was very ill with cancer, and he would say to Jackie, "I'm going to die, and nobody cares, nobody in the world cares."

"I care," Jackie would say, "and you're not going to die. You're going to outlive us all." But after Laurence left, Jackie always cried and said, "I'm closer to the end than he is and he's getting me closer." I could not let Jackie get depressed like that, so I tactfully pointed out to Harvey that Jackie was so sensitive he was upsetting her. Harvey was a little more careful after that.

In May, when we were in New York, Doris Day called to tell Jackie that on Sunday, June 3, Actors and Others for Animals, Doris's favorite cause, was holding its annual charity drive on the Warner lot in Burbank. They needed help or the affair would be a disaster. Jackie immediately called Joan Crawford and arranged for her to supply 28,000 bottles of Pepsi Cola, huge ice buckets, and about a ton of cracked ice, plus five handlers for the drinks. Joan also donated for the raffle a beaded coat and dress that must have cost $5,000. I called

Bantam and had them send out 500 copies of *Every Night, Josephine!* in paperback.

Since we were going to be in California a little later in the month for the ABA convention, we arranged to arrive in time for Doris's benefit. On the Burbank lot, we found that Jackie's chair and table for the autographing had been set out in the scorching sun. It must have been at least 104 degrees. I managed to move the chair and table under a shady tree. People gave whatever they wanted to the animal charity in exchange for an autographed copy of *Josephine!*

Hordes of people surrounded Jackie, and I could see her getting paler and paler under her tan. But she hung in there tenaciously. She had made a promise to her friend. And when Jackie made a promise, that was it.

Several days later, when the big ABA cocktail party for *Once* was coming up, Jackie was too knocked out by her treatments to stand for hours at a time to greet the hundreds of guests. I called Doris Day and asked her to be cohostess with Jackie. Doris agreed. I asked Jay Allen to pick her up and bring her to the party.

The party was spectacular, but after about two hours, when I could see that she was wobbling on her feet, I sent her home to bed and stayed on with Doris for another hour.

No one at the convention or the party suspected anything was wrong with Jackie. She carried off every minute of it beautifully with style and courage.

Jackie had good days and bad days. The cobalt proved effective on the bronchial obstruction, and it was gone. But now there was an involvement with her right lung, and the chemotherapy had to continue on. She was on cortisone for a while, but that was discontinued when her face and neck puffed up. Some days she was horribly depressed. Other days she was agitated. Sometimes her vision blurred. There were days when she wanted to die. And days when she was all excited about the zooming sales figures of *Once* and talking about her next book.

The Love Machine was coming out in France, and Jackie had a new publisher there. A very small house owned by Pierre Belfond and his wife Franca offered a modest advance for *The Love Machine* but a first printing of 20,000 copies—a daring, large-scale launching for France. Belfond and his rights manager, Sylvie Messinger, were very aggressive book merchants. Belfond had been in New York and observed first hand the feverish American promotional activities for *Love Machine* and wanted to generate the same excitement in France. He sent us first-class tickets on Air France and reserved a suite at the Ritz.

I was torn—whether to encourage Jackie to go or persuade her to stay home. I knew she was best able to hold despair at bay when events were swirling around her. That old trouper instinct charged her up with energy. But should she exhaust herself with a fast roundtrip across the Atlantic?

I didn't have much choice in the matter. As soon as Jackie heard Paris and Ritz, she was ready. She packed very lightly, got the name and address of a French doctor, and we arrived in Paris on June 25, 1973. From then to late in the day on June 29, it was round-the-clock media madness.

One of the press conferences was held in an elegant salon at the Intercontinental Hotel with 100 journalists crowded into the room, and klieg lights reflected blindingly off the dazzling silver foil that covered the display counter. Pretty girls in T-shirts printed with the French title *Une fois ne suffit pas* handed out books and drinks.

It was fantastic, and Jackie held up to the very end.

Only once did we get a chance to slip away for a quick tour—I guess Jackie knew it was a farewell tour—of the places we loved so much in Paris. Our driver took us to Notre Dame where we walked through the nave of the cathedral, which was heavily scented with incense that day. We tilted our heads far back to catch the gorgeous blue and red light filtering through the high stained-glass windows.

We drove to the Louvre, got out of the car, strolled through the gardens, and from under the small arch there, gazed up the long, incredible vista through the Tuileries gardens and the Place de la Concorde, up the Champs Élysées, all the way to the grand arch at the Étoile. We held hands without saying a word. When Jackie could no longer hold back her tears, we got back into the car. As we drove to our hotel, we caught several glimpses of Sacre Coeur up the sloping streets leading to Montmartre. Jackie had always loved to look up the hill to the shining white dome and used to try to find the streets that Utrillo had painted.

"Why does it have to end?" she asked in the car, sobbing into my shoulder. This time, I had no answer for her. But in a few minutes, she was calm enough to stop for a drink at Fouquet's, her all-time favorite restaurant in Paris.

The eventual sale of 140,000 copies of *The Love Machine* in bookstores in France, another 130,000 through book clubs, and 130,000 in the first four months of publication in a pocket edition made publishing history. It also put Belfond on the map as a major French publisher.

The summer of 1973 passed quietly. Again Jackie had good days and bad days. *Once* held its number-one spot. Each night, Jackie played solitaire in bed, as she had for years, searching for answers in the fall of the cards. If the game played out, that meant she would get her wish—her book would stay number one for another week, or we'd get a good report about Guy, or whatever it was she wanted. But solitaire, as you know, is a frustrating game, and you rarely go out. So Jackie was always furious at the cards.

Now, of course, she was demanding that the cards tell her that she would get well. When they refused to give her the answer she needed, she angrily swept them off the bed onto the floor. "This is a rotten deck," she'd say. "Get me another deck, doll." At one point, I bought a dozen decks—I didn't want to have to go shopping for cards in the middle of the night when the stupid things thwarted Jackie.

We took long walks together. Then, when her mood darkened, she walked endlessly alone. Sometimes she took Joseph with her. Often, she went to the Wishing Hill and lingered there quite a while. She still wore her Marlon Brando outfit—black pants, black jacket, the little Dutch cap. In that get-up and with dark glasses, almost no one recognized her.

In September, Jackie's English publisher, W. H. Allen, wanted us to come over for a big publication party for *Once*. Jackie wanted to go, and I wanted her to go even if I had to carry her. Dr. Spingarn gave his consent for the trip. It turned out to be quite an expedition because Doris Day, her friend Rack Rael, and Rack's mother, Rose Gordon, were coming to New York for a few days, and then, on September 21, we were all flying to London together.

On the plane, Jackie sat with Doris. I remember Jackie was wearing an olive-colored felt hat and Doris a blue-denim cap. Both of them were belting down vodkas at a pretty fast clip. Somewhere out over the Atlantic Ocean, with her caution numbed by the altitude and the vodka, Jackie told Doris about her illness. I must say, to Doris's everlasting credit, that she respected the confidence.

On September 24, W. H. Allen gave a terrific dinner party on the Terrace Roof of the Dorchester Hotel for members of the British press. Melina Mercouri and Jules Dassin came, as did Carroll Baker,

Jack Martin, and Margaret Gardner. It was a wonderful evening, and Jackie seemed like her old lively, radiant self.

But every day she secretly visited a doctor on Harley Street for her chemotherapy. One day, he mentioned that he was surprised she was not using marijuana to reduce her nausea. That was common practice in England. He gave Jackie some marijuana cigarettes and arranged to send us some at our hotel to take back with us. "How will I get them through customs?" Jackie asked.

The doctor wrote a very impressive-looking prescription. I think Jackie, the desperado, was almost hoping she would get busted. What a wonderful scene! But the sensible Jackie knew that would blow her carefully kept secret. We were both very nervous as we approached customs at JFK Airport, but we had nothing to worry about. The agent recognized Jackie and waved her right through, saying, "Welcome home, Miss Susann."

When the British doctor first examined Jackie, he looked at her mastectomy scar and said, "You know, we don't do that anymore. We just cut away a little piece and leave the rest of the breast. We call it lumpectomy."

Well, that was all Jackie had to hear! She had already decided, quite irrationally, that her doctors were the villains in her whole unhappy situation. Ten years earlier, the doctors had cut off her breast, and now she had cancer again, anyway, so she should not have been tortured in the first place, should not have had to undergo the mutilation, she reasoned in her unreasonable way.

She was furious at her doctors. When she jotted down her appointments in her appointment book, she always had a black scowl on her face and wrote down the doctor's name and the time with such anger that her pen sometimes tore right through the page. After the English doctor mentioned that the newer cancer surgery left the breast almost intact, Jackie felt she had a bigger grievance than ever. I tried to point out that this was more than a decade after her operation, that procedures had changed, and progress had been made.

Forget it. If this was the way she wanted to discharge her anger, I couldn't change her.

I didn't know at the time of Jackie's illness—I've only found out recently in the course of writing this book—that there was a serious difference of opinion among her doctors as to the cause of her cancer recurrence.

The cancer specialists who were working with Dr. Spingarn had diagnosed her bronchial and lung cancer as secondary to her earlier breast cancer. Her present trouble, according to them, grew out of her earlier trouble.

Dr. Lesnick, the breast surgeon, did not agree. He felt the bronchial and lung lesions were completely new cancers, most likely related to her lifetime of heavy smoking.

How could experts differ so widely? And what is the significance of their varying opinions? As it has been explained to me, in part, there is a genuine difference in interpretation of biopsied tissues. Different experts can legitimately come to different conclusions after examining the same slides.

But in part there is also a philosophical difference—a difference between hope and despair.

A metastatic cancer from a primary breast malignancy will often respond well to chemotherapy. There is hope that the treatment, with all its devastating side effects, will significantly prolong life.

A primary lung cancer will not respond to chemotherapy.

So, in a sense, Jackie's doctors had chosen hope.

How Jackie would have chosen, if she had been asked, I don't know. She might have decided against chemotherapy and avoided an enormous amount of agony. On the other hand, she might have suffered even greater agony toward the end if she thought her decision had shortened her life.

I can only believe now that all the doctors did the very best they could for her.

One day, in the fall of 1973, Jackie got a phone call from Leonore Hershey, the editor of *Ladies' Home Journal*. They got together, and Leonore said, "Jackie, what do you dream about?"

Jackie said, "I dream about stopping the show. I've dreamed that since I was a little girl. I'm taking my fifteenth bow, and they're piling flowers on the stage for me. Why do you ask?"

Leonore said, "I dream about cover lines."

Cover lines are the teasing words on the cover of a magazine that make you want to snatch that issue right off the newsstand, rush home, and read it before you take your shoes off.

"At this moment," Leonore went on, "I'm dreaming of the words 'Jackie O by Jackie S.' I can see them in a headline across the top of the cover of the *Journal*. Does that appeal to you, Jackie."

"It's a great line," Jackie said, "but it's not the kind of thing I do.

You need a nonfiction journalist for that—someone who does heavy research."

"No, we can get a dozen writers to do a bio. This is something that only you can do. Please think about it."

Jackie was intrigued with the idea, but she didn't want to spend weeks in the library reading up on the life of Jackie Kennedy Onassis. On the other hand, she didn't want to let go of the project. Suddenly, she had an inspiration. She put paper in the typewriter, dashed off six pages, and sent them to Leonore.

Jackie had proposed doing the piece as fiction: Dolores Cortez Ryan, a glamorous, fictitious first lady, with a strong resemblance to the real Jackie Kennedy, widowed very young, worshipped by the public, beset by difficult personal problems, finally remarries a baron, short on looks and long on billions.

Leonore was delighted. "We'll buy it for twenty thousand dollars," she said.

"Now I have to finish it," Jackie said.

The Rupert Murdoch Organization got word of the project and wanted to buy it for *The Star*. We worked out a deal for him to get second serial rights.

Dolores ran in the *Journal* in February 1974. In a brief lead-in, Jackie wrote:

Most of my novels have been show-business oriented, but I believe the characters I invent could have the same impact with different backgrounds. To prove the point, I let my imagination play with a political background. As in many of my books, I try to show with my fictional Dolores that the everyday woman really has a better life than the women she reads about, admires and envies.

Dolores was a sensation with readers. They grabbed the magazine right off the newsstands. They didn't mind that the story was sketchy and episodic—more the outline of a novel than the novel itself. They lapped up the familiar tale, only slightly disguised, and they were stunned by the ending. All the wallop of *Dolores* was concentrated in the final paragraph.

Somewhere on the gossip circuit, Jackie and I had picked up a story that on their wedding night—after the private wedding ceremony on Onassis' private island of Skorpios, after the frantic spying by the world's press—Aristotle Onassis had abandoned Jackie, his bride, to spend the night with Maria Callas, his true love.

The final paragraph of *Dolores* reads:

And he had left her . . . untouched. He hadn't tried to deceive her. It was as cut and dried as that. She held out her hand and stared at the ring. It glowed like fire in the semi-darkness. She rubbed it against her satin nightgown . . . and stared at it as the tears ran down her cheeks . . .

The fable of the wedding-night switch was clearly not true, much as Callas wanted it to be and insisted at various times that it was. But it did contain a strong poetic truth, which Jackie recognized. It also had enormous emotional impact, and again Jackie was back to the crucial moment in a woman's life that never ceased to intrigue her—her first sexual encounter with a man, or with a particular man, or the failure of that encounter. After the success of *Dolores* in the *Journal*, Larry Hughes wanted to do the story as a book. It was published after Jackie's death by Morrow in July 1976. I went on the road to promote it and it reached ninth place on *The New York Times* bestseller chart. The following year, the Bantam paperback hit number one, thanks to the terrific work of publicist Stuart Applebaum, who has a great awareness of what has to be done to put a book across.

Going back to the fall of 1973, in mid-October, we went to Palm Beach, and when we returned to New York, Jackie was running a fever. She checked into Doctors Hospital for three days. This time it was a respiratory infection.

In November, she had pain in her right upper abdomen. Her doctor ordered a liver scan. It was done in New York in November, and the results were questionable. It was done again in California in December. We sat in the California sunshine as we waited for the results. The news was bad. The cancer had spread to her liver.

This was the worst yet, for a liver cancer is an implacable, deadly enemy.

We asked for the name of the absolute top cancer expert in the country. We were told to see Dr. James Holland, one of the world's leading tumor authorities, who was then at Harvard but is now at Mt. Sinai Hospital in New York. He was brought in as a consultant. He ordered the chemotherapy stopped, and cobalt treatment for the liver continued.

Then, in February 1974, Jackie underwent a bone scan.

The cancer had spread to her spine. It was in the sacrum area.

Jackie and I now knew there was no hope—not even a slender thread to hold on to. She was right. We no longer needed to buy a calendar.

*I*n January 1974, Rose Susan was celebrating her eightieth birthday with a big party that we were giving for her at the Yorktown Inn near Philadelphia. I had ordered an elaborate dinner and champagne for seventy people—it was my present to Rose. But when the day of the party came, Jackie was back in Doctors Hospital. I drove to Philadelphia with Bea and Anna, and we told Rose that Jackie had a very bad cold, so bad she couldn't leave the apartment.

Then I called Jackie on her private phone at the hospital, and I said to Rose, "It's Jackie on the phone. She wants to wish you a happy birthday."

"Oh, she can get on the phone, but she can't come," Rose said in a chilly voice as she took the phone.

"Happy birthday, mother," Jackie said. "I just wish I could be there."

"What daughter doesn't come to her mother's eightieth birthday?" Rose demanded angrily.

"Mother, I just can't make it. I'll explain one of these days, but trust me now. You know I'd be with you if I possibly could."

Rose was not easily placated. "Just name me one thing that is more important than my birthday. Just one thing."

Jackie was defeated. She had never told her mother about her illness, not even back at the time of the mastectomy. She had passed off her rush to get to a doctor after the around-the-world trip as another false alarm—just one of those benign cysts. She had not said a word about the recurrence or the chemotherapy or what she was going through. What point was there in worrying an eighty-year-old woman?

But now Rose was maddeningly insistent. "What's more important? Name me one thing."

"All right, mother," Jackie said. "I'll tell you. I'm in the hospital, and I have cancer."

Jackie told me later that she was shaking all over when she hung up the phone. She felt completely beaten down. "I guess I did a terrible thing in telling her," she said to me, "but I couldn't help it. I didn't mean to do it, but I couldn't help it."

"Don't worry about it," I told Jackie. "It's not so terrible. She won't fall apart."

I was right. Rose did not fall apart at all. But I can't say she enjoyed her birthday.

When Jackie got out of the hospital, she began cobalt treatment again, this time for her liver. Then as the outlook got bleaker, her instinct to fight became stronger. Alternating day by day between despair and gritted-teeth determination, she went on with her life; we went on with our lives.

The big activity was the filming of *Once Is Not Enough*.

George Chasin had made the movie deal with Howard W. Koch of Paramount Pictures. After two major films, I had become aware of what I can only call Hollywood's creative accounting. When you sell a property to a film company for a large down payment and a percentage of the net, you never know what you will really get.

Before you reach the net, untold sums are deducted for first-class jet flights all over the world, for caviar dinners, and for limousine service for several dozen people. Whoever gets the net is way down at the end of the line.

This time we were smarter. We sold *Once* for nothing down and ten percent of the gross. The gross is easy to monitor because theater receipts have to be reported accurately. Of course, we lost the glamour and the publicity value of a multimillion-dollar advance payment, but we had already had that thrill with *Love Machine*. Now we were willing to skip the glamour and take the cash. In the end, it worked out beautifully.

Paramount conducted a highly publicized competition for the role of January. The two finalists were Deborah Raffin and Jane Seymour. Jackie and I looked at the final test in a screening room in the Gulf & Western building at Columbus Circle. We loved Deborah Raffin for her quality of vulnerability and her good looks. We were very happy with that choice. George Chasin wanted Tony Quinn for the macho writer, but the director didn't. We then decided on David

Janssen. The director didn't like him, either, but Koch gave the director an hour to like Janssen, who was perfect in the role.

Kirk Douglas was cast as Mike Wayne, January's father, and was wonderful in the part. Alexis Smith played the very rich woman who marries Mike, Melina Mercouri was the movie-star recluse, George Hamilton the seducing stockbroker, and Brenda Vaccaro the editor of the women's magazine. Brenda won a Golden Globe Award for the role and was nominated for an Academy Award. It was a sensational cast, and they were all wonderful to work with.

In February, off chemotherapy and feeling a lot better, Jackie flew with me to the coast. I had work to do as executive producer of the film, and Jackie was to play the cameo role that had become her trademark in each of her films. In *Once* she played a TV newscaster. Paramount gave Jackie a beautiful office-dressing room and decorated it, to her delight, in the lemony yellow she loved. The porthole windows made her feel as if she were aboard a ship.

Frank Sinatra was to move in to do his TV special, "Old Blue Eyes Is Back," after Jackie moved out, and on the last day, she left him a welcoming note: "Make sure everyone takes his shoes off before entering, but you can leave yours on because everyone knows after you wear a new pair of shoes once, you throw them away."

During our stay in California, we developed a very warm friendship with Howard and Ruth Koch. We spent many evenings with them and went to parties with them, and I marveled at Jackie's undiminished capacity for friendship. Here she was, desperately ill and completely aware of how ill she was, but even so, able to reach out and gather new friends into that circle of vitality that she still radiated wherever she went.

In March, we were back in New York, and that's when Jackie began to get panicky about her loss of weight. Every time she stepped on the scale, another few ounces and then another half pound seemed to have slipped away. It got so that she dreaded the scale. We were both reminded of those early months with Guy when his weekly weighing became such a terrible ordeal. Now, once again, the scale was the enemy.

"This damned thing's broken," Jackie complained furiously one day. "I can't possibly have lost half a pound since Tuesday."

I rushed over to Bloomingdale's and bought a shiny new scale. It didn't behave any better than the old one. She gradually went down from 120 pounds to 110, then to 100 and then under 100. She tried to eat more, but that didn't seem to help—not even binges of her favorite butter pecan ice cream. I think the weight loss worried her more than anything else.

"It'll come back," I tried to reassure her. "It's just this stage of the treatment. Wait and see. We'll go out for a steak tonight."

The nights were the worst. Jackie had trouble sleeping. She'd sit in the living room, drinking vodka, taking sleeping pills in addition to all her other medication, and calling Anna Sosenko. Anna didn't sleep, either, so she never minded the calls. Jackie talked on and on to Porky, her affectionate name for Anna, about what was preying on her mind. Anna tried to tell her that her fears were exaggerated, that everything would work out.

"It's not fair," she would tell Anna. "It's just not fair. I struggled for thirty years to make it. Then when I did it, when I wrote books that people really want to read, it's all being taken away from me. I'm going to die. How can that be? I don't want to die. I don't want to leave Irving."

It was not easy for Anna, and I bless her for her patience. Jackie and Anna talked a lot about Betty Bruce, a delightful dancer and performer, who also had cancer. Betty's illness was somewhat more advanced than Jackie's. Jackie always had to know exactly what was happening to Betty. At one time, when Jackie was in Doctors Hospital, she insisted that Anna go to see Betty in Roosevelt Hospital. Anna didn't know Betty very well, but she had no choice—she paid the visit and then gave Jackie a full report, told her exactly what medication Betty was getting and how it affected her.

Jackie worried about me. "Irving's a wreck," she'd say to Anna. "I'm wearing him down. It's not fair to him."

"Don't worry about Irving," Anna told her. "He's well, and now you have to concentrate on getting well."

April was a very difficult month, but memorable because it was the last month we were able to live at the frenzied pace that had been our special way of life for all the thirty-five years of our marriage.

On April 1, Jackie made what turned out to be her last public appearance. We were in California again, working on the film. Jackie was invited by the Amazing Blue Ribbon 400, an organization of wealthy and charitable women in the Los Angeles area set up by Mrs. Otis Chandler, owner of the *Los Angeles Times*, to participate in a panel discussion on public taste. The other panelists were Oscar winner William Friedkin, director of *The Exorcist*, author and ranconteur Garson Kanin, the *Los Angeles Times'* entertainment editor, Charles Champlin, and Jackie's good friend, Helen Gurley Brown, editor of *Cosmopolitan*. The moderator was NBC newsman Bob Abernathy.

I didn't see how Jackie could possibly make a speech before such a large audience—they were bringing in five busloads of Los Angeles high school students to join the gathering of outstanding women at the Chandler Pavilion. But Jackie, eager to play the desperado just this one more time, accepted the invitation.

On the day of the event, she had a temperature above 101. I put her to bed at the hotel and went downstairs to tell whoever was picking her up that she wouldn't be able to go to the meeting. The car drove up with Helen Gurley Brown and Rhonda Fleming in it. I opened the door and began to offer Jackie's apologies, but while I was talking, to my astonishment, Jackie stepped out of the hotel, all set to go on.

I shook my head in disbelief. At least she let me arrange for her to be the first speaker. She gave her talk, then slipped away from the dais, and we drove straight to the airport to fly back to New York with pal George Barrie in his private plane. She didn't dare take her temperature on the plane—neither of us wanted to know.

Her fever stayed high, and a week later she was in Doctors Hospital with a cough and a sore throat. She was treated with steam aerosol and antibiotics and was home again in three days.

The next day, she put on a pants suit and a little crocheted hat, and we strolled over to Central Park to watch the filming of an important scene for *Once Is Not Enough* at the Wishing Hill, a place of so many sweet and bitter memories. Jackie's carefully applied makeup barely covered her pallor and could not disguise the heavy darkness under her eyes. One of her full, shoulder-length wigs hid her crew cut. She wore her dark glasses and her little peaked cap.

Jackie watched quietly as director Guy Green worked with Deborah Raffin and Kirk Douglas. A reporter came over and asked Jackie about the significance of the location. "It's always been my Wishing Hill," she said. "I would come to sit here with my poodle or come and pray when I was having a bad time. It was so clean twenty years ago, no beer cans or broken glass."

Then the still photographer shot a picture of Jackie and Deborah. It was the last picture ever taken of Jackie.

That same month, I found that my abdominal polyps had returned and had to be removed again. I dreaded telling Jackie. How could I add my problems to hers? As I expected, she reacted with total hysteria—not so much for herself as for Guy. Who would worry about him, arrange for him if anything happened to me?

Our good friend Dr. Spingarn came to our rescue at this very bleak moment. He told us about new laser beam surgery that literally whisked away polyps without the risks of regular surgery. I was in and out of the hospital overnight and feeling fine in days. Jackie was enormously relieved.

The next few months are a blur in my mind of quick trips to California by both of us (I had to go to work on the picture, and Jackie would not let me go without her), longer and longer stays in the hospital for Jackie, and desperate lies to keep the press at bay. Rumors were beginning to surface in the gossip columns that Jackie was seriously ill. We denied everything—it was overwork. Who wouldn't be exhausted after the schedule she had been keeping? Yes, she had had pneumonia a couple of times, but she was fine now.

In May, fluid accumulated around Jackie's heart. She went into the hospital in California to have it drained away. The laboratory found malignant cells in the fluid. She went back on a modified program of chemotherapy and continued with radiation treatments on her lower spine. In June, in California again, she was back in Century City Hospital for several days with fever and an allergic reaction to some of her medication.

Whenever Jackie went into the hospital, I had a pact with her doctors. They were never to whisper to me in a corner of her room or call me out of the room for a conference in the hall or say something in a too casual voice like "Irving, come outside with me for a minute."

That would have driven Jackie wild. I think there is nothing more demeaning than to be talked about behind your back and nothing more frightening than to suspect your doctor is sharing with your husband news that is too terrible for your ears. Several times when I was really worried about Jackie, I made an excuse about going out to get a newspaper and then tracked the doctor down and put the hard questions to him. Or I called him from the corridor phone booth or from home.

I had an agreement with Dr. Spingarn and Dr. Jaffe that they would never lie to Jackie but would present the medical facts in the most optimistic way they could. I thought it important for her to have hope at all times. But I did not want her ever to have the slightest suspicion that she was being lied to. If she did, she would lose all confidence in her doctors and probably walk away from their treatments.

That June in California, Jackie was feeling well enough to go to several parties with Ruth and Howard Koch. One was the American Film Institute tribute to James Cagney. We stayed just a little while— you could do that and get away with it because in California everyone is always rushing off to the next event.

Jackie was invited to be one of the judges in the Miss Universe contest in the Philippines. She had accepted when the invitation first arrived, but now she knew the trip would be much too strenuous. She called Cindy Adams, who was in charge of rounding up judges, and suggested that Leon Uris take her place. He went with his wife and had a very good time. On one of her better days, we had a delightful dinner with Marilyn and Mort Farber at Le Cirque, an elegant new restaurant owned by her friend Sirio. It was to be Jackie's last dinner out.

Sometimes the medication plunged Jackie into a despairing mood. The combination of depression, fear, sleeplessness, and pills ground her down. She would get out of bed in the middle of the night, prowl the length of our apartment, mix another drink, and sit alone in the living room if I was asleep, staring at the sky and the lights in Central Park. Sometimes she fell asleep on the couch. One night at about four in the morning, a thumping sound in the living room awakened me.

Jackie, in her nightgown, was lying on the floor in front of the big window overlooking the park. She was too dazed to give a coherent explanation. But it was obvious. She had managed to open the window partially, then had fallen when she tried to climb onto the sill. I carried her back to bed.

The next morning, I walked over to one of the pawn shops on Eighth Avenue and bought a pair of handcuffs. They looked like police cuffs, but they were the trick kind used on stage. That night, I handcuffed Jackie to me in bed. Amazingly, she did not protest. "What if I have to go to the bathroom?" was all she said.

"I go with you."

I had to turn over whenever she turned over. It was very uncomfortable for me, but I didn't care. Jackie was uncomfortable, too, but I think she was so frightened at what she had attempted in the befuddlement of drugs, booze, and despair that she was willing to be shackled.

"You're not going anywhere without me," I told her. "Is that clear?"

Then one night about two weeks later, she said, "Okay, officer, you can uncuff me now. I'm no longer your prisoner of Zenda."

That crisis was over.

But Jackie still wept nightly on Anna's shoulder. One late spring night, she stretched out on the yellow-velvet couch and called Anna at three in the morning. "I'm looking at the stars," she said. "It's a beautiful night. I know all the trees are in flower. The whole world is in flower. But I'm not going to see it again."

Porky listened and tried to soothe her.

In California, in June, we knew it was time to tell the people at Bantam that Jackie would not be able to go out on the extensive promotion tour that was being planned for the paperback publication of *Once* in July. "I guess I'm not the warhorse I was," she said. "And there will be a difference in the way I look on television. I don't want people to see me like this."

I phoned Oscar Dystel. He and Esther Margolis immediately flew out to California. The four of us went down to the dining room, and Jackie said, "Oscar, I hate to let you down, but I can't go on the road."

"Is it serious?" he asked.

She said, "Yes, I have cancer."

Well, that kind of broke up the dinner. It was not a very cheery meal. Then Jackie got up and said, "Now you stay here. I'm going upstairs." I knew she was leaving because she was going to cry.

"How long has this been going on?" Oscar asked.

"Since before you knew Jackie. Since Christmas 1962."

I never saw two such flabbergasted people.

They had seen her under the most adverse conditions, in rainstorms, in snowstorms, on days when she had held her own against fifty interviewers, on open platforms in 110-degree heat, at banquets of inedible food, at book autographings that went on for six hours. She was always there when she was called. She never objected to anything.

And through all of this, she had kept her secret. I asked them now to keep it for her a little longer.

On the way back to New York, Jackie and I stopped in Texas to see Guy. Jackie must have known it was her last visit. She was exhausted by the change of planes, the long car ride. But she did not complain. Guy, as always, was delighted to see us. He slapped hands with me, hugged Jackie, and showed off by putting together in about five minutes a jigsaw puzzle with what looked like a thousand tiny pieces.

Jackie just sat there watching him. Her face was thin, and there was a dark look to it that was not sun tan, and she had heavy circles under her eyes. She reached out and touched Guy's arm or shoulder every time he went by. But she hardly spoke to him. I knew she didn't trust herself; she was afraid she would break down.

How terrible not even to be able to say good-by to your own son.

To make up for Jackie's silence, I kept up a running chatter about baseball and TV and what I thought they'd be doing on "M.A.S.H." the next week.

When we left, Jackie tried to hold Guy in her arms, but he wriggled away, just as he had when he was a little boy, impatient to get back to his toys or his tricycle. He was still a little boy, a little boy of twenty-eight.

In the car and on the planes going home, Jackie was completely limp. I made no effort to cheer her up. I thought it best this time to leave her alone with her grief.

Once Is Not Enough came out in paperback in July with a printing of 2.5 million copies and immediately became number one.

But Jackie was not able to enjoy her success. For the whole first half of July, she was back in Doctors Hospital with pneumonia and her spreading cancer. She responded well to the medication for pneumonia and came home on July 17. Then, she went back to the hospital on July 27, and she remained there until August 18.

When Jackie came home that hot August day, she knew it was for the last time. But she wanted desperately to be in the apartment once more, to sleep in her own bed, to sleep in my arms.

She was home for only two nights. Then she had trouble breathing, and her pulse began racing. Dr. Spingarn told me to get her to the hospital. I called the ambulance service, and they said they'd be there in about seven or eight minutes.

While we waited, Jackie complained of having something stuck in her tooth. She was very upset about the tooth. I called Dr. Arvins, our dentist, who luckily had his office in our building, and he came right up. I lifted Jackie and held her in a chair near the window while the dentist worked away with a piece of dental floss and got the thing out.

She said, "Thank you, that's a lot better."

The ambulance drove into the garage entrance, and the attendants put Jackie on a stretcher and took her directly down to the basement and got her out of our building without creating a commotion in the lobby.

I sat next to her in the ambulance. As we pulled away, Jackie looked back and said, "You know, this is the last time I'm going to see this house."

"Of course not," I told her. "That's silly. You'll be back in two weeks, a week maybe."

She shook her head. "No, it's the last time."

We went east on Central Park South and north on Madison Avenue. Jackie was lying on her side, her eyes half open, and she was holding my hand. "I hate for you to go through all this," she said. "I've put you through it so many times, and I feel very guilty about it."

I said, "Jackie, you know something? Having you, being married to you for as long as I have, there have been more treasures than calamities. And I don't consider this a calamity. I think this is just a temporary setback."

She said, "No, I know it's not."

"Well, I'm sure it is."

We stopped for a light at about 72nd Street, and she said, "Look at that car. It's the same color as ours."

A midnight blue limousine was waiting for the light right next to us. When the light changed, the limousine pulled ahead, and Jackie exclaimed, "My God, it's *our* car."

I looked, and she was right. The dark blue Cadillac had license plate JSM 5. It was our car—probably running someone out to the airport on gas we had paid for in a little scam operated by the fellows in the garage.

Jackie went into her regular corner room at Doctors Hospital, which she seemed to occupy alternately with Lyndon Johnson's brother, who had a chronic health problem. She was admitted at 1:45 P.M. on August 21, 1974. She was listed as suffering from metastatic carcinoma of breast, hepatic (liver) carcinoma, hepatic insufficiency, and pulmonary edema.

She was heavily sedated, drowsy, and unresponsive for several days, then a little more alert for a day or two, then drowsy again, feverish, depressed, then on the upswing once more. I slept either in her room or in a nearby room or in the reception room. I went home from time to time to shave or take a bath. Anna came to see her, and Bea came before she and her husband had to leave for Europe. The only other visitor was our housekeeper Louise.

At one point, Jackie let herself wonder out loud if she had made a mistake in keeping her illness a secret. I think the isolation was getting to her. Here was one of the friendliest, most gregarious women who ever lived dying virtually alone because pride and a desire not to be pitied had sealed her lips.

"Maybe we've had too many secrets," she said with a deep sigh. "Guy, my illness earlier, my illness now. Maybe it was a mistake keeping it all to ourselves."

I still don't know whether our secrecy was right or wrong. But taking a cue from Jackie's words, on one of the days when she was feeling more alert, I called Muriel Slatkin in California and told her that Jackie was desperately ill and this might be the last chance to see her. Muriel flew to New York that same day with Doris Day and Rack Rael. I told Jackie they would be coming for a brief visit. She was a little disturbed because her voice was very thick, and she was wearing a bandanna over her short hair, but she said she would be glad to see them.

Before they went into Jackie's room, I stopped the three women in the corridor, and I said to Doris, "I know you've been in about forty or fifty movies, but this has to be your best performance. I don't want you to cry. I don't want Muriel to cry. I don't want Rack to cry. Just act as though she's going to be out in a couple of weeks."

All three promised, and they kept their word. They smiled at Jackie and joked and told her about the fun they'd all have when they got together in California. At one point, I said, "You know, Jackie has the cutest crew cut you ever saw." Jackie took off the bandanna, and they all admired her short hair. They left after about fifteen minutes.

Once they were safely out in the hall, all three broke down. They cried. I cried. We all cried together. I finally thanked them for coming. They probably cried on the plane all the way back to California.

During the seven weeks Jackie was in the hospital, I didn't know what time it was. If my watch stopped, I didn't care. I sat with her; I held her hands for as long as I could. The doctors and the nurses were always chasing me out of her room. The minute they let me, I went back in.

I guess I expected a miracle. Somehow, I always expected a miracle with Jackie. Jackie had been in tight positions all her life and had gotten out of them gracefully and with dignity. I thought somehow she would get out of this, too. Maybe she would fight her way out. Maybe a new wonder drug would be announced at the eleventh hour and she would be saved. Maybe our prayers would be answered and there would be a spontaneous remission.

But now I knew we were coming to the end of the road.

One evening, when Jackie was clearer-headed than she had been for some time, she made me sit down next to her, and she said, "Now don't interrupt. I have things I have to tell you. First, I want you to get married again. I worry about you living alone. It hasn't been easy for you this last year. You deserve a healthy wife. You need someone to eat with, someone to hold your hand in the movies, and someone you can make love to and someone to love you back."

"Look, Jackie . . ." I tried to say, but she wouldn't let me talk.

"Don't interrupt me. I don't know how often you've lied to me, but if you tell me I'm going to get better, it's the ultimate lie and insulting to my intelligence. Now hold my hand and tell me how much you love me. But if you raise my hopes about the future, I won't be able to die with dignity. So let me go. Do that for me—please let me go."

I held her hand until she slipped into sleep. And from that sleep she drifted into a coma; for the next two weeks, she floated in and out of the coma. I stayed beside her every minute I could.

One day, she surfaced into consciousness, looked around to see where she was, and said, "Hey, doll, let's get the hell out of here." Then she slid under again.

On Saturday, September 21, Dr. Spingarn said, "Irving, why don't you go out to dinner. It's going to happen, but probably not tonight. You should get out for a while."

I called my attorney and said, "Arthur, do you want to go out to dinner with me?"

He said, "No, you come here and have dinner with us."

I left his phone number with the hospital and had my driver take me to his apartment at the Alwyn Court on 58th Street. Arthur Hershkowitz and his wife, Lastone, who is the youngest sister of

Portland Hoffa, who was married to Fred Allen, have been my friends for almost all my life. Soon after I got to their apartment, the phone rang. I was hoping against hope it was not for me. Arthur answered, and I heard him say, "Yes, he's here." He handed me the phone.

It was my son's school in Texas. A voice said, "We have bad news for you, Mr. Mansfield. Someone kicked your son, and we think his jaw is fractured."

I said, "Oh, my God, how is he?"

He was as all right as he could be. He was getting the best possible care. "I'll be there as soon as I can," I said. "I'm having some problems here myself."

I started telling Arthur and Lastone about what had happened to Guy, and while I was talking, the phone rang again. I answered it this time. A woman's voice said, "Is Mr. Mansfield there?"

"This is Mr. Mansfield."

The voice said, "We have very, very bad news. Mrs. Mansfield passed away at 9:02."

It was then about 9:05.

"I'll be right there," I said.

Arthur insisted on going to the hospital with me.

Jackie was still in her room. Now, at last, she looked relaxed and peaceful. I kissed her and whispered my good-by, and for the last time I said, "I love you," remembering how long ago, before we were married, she had told me never to be afraid to say those precious words.

Dr. Spingarn had waited for me, and we talked briefly about arrangements that had to be made. I was in too much of a daze to make much sense of things, but I had help from many people. I made a few calls to California—to Muriel Slatkin, Doris Day, and Howard Koch. Someone called Joyce Haber.

Somehow I got involved in selecting a coffin, which seemed to be crazy because Jackie was to be cremated. But under the rules a coffin was required, and my lawyer had to go through the indignity of arguing about the price of a box that was about to be sent into the flames.

I called Mrs. Byron in Philadelphia, a friend of Rose Susan's. I said, "I have to tell you that Jackie has passed away."

She said, "My God!"

"I don't want you to tell Rose tonight. But tomorrow, around

[270]

nine in the morning, I want you to be at her place. I'm going to call her then, and I want you there with her."

When I called the next morning, Rose screamed. It was a blood-curdling scream. I told her a car would pick her up on Tuesday, bring her to New York for the funeral, and take her home.

By Sunday, the news was in all the papers and had been on the air. I don't know how I got through that day and the next. I went to Campbell's where they had Jackie in a closed coffin under the blanket of yellow roses. People streamed through the receiving room at Campbell's and then began coming to the apartment, and by Sunday evening the place was jammed. Lee Guber had thoughtfully ordered quantities of food from a Chinese restaurant, so there was enough to feed the crowds who came to pay their respects.

Telegrams were stacked up everywhere. The first telegram came from, of all people, George Ritz of the Ritz Hotel in Paris. We had never met him—never even known there was a Monsieur Ritz. The apartment filled up with flowers and cakes and baskets of fruit. I think everyone in New York came by at some point.

The funeral service was on Tuesday afternoon, September 24, 1974, at Campbell's. The crowd spilled out of the building onto the sidewalk and into the street. Reporters and TV cameramen buttonholed the mourners and asked for statements. It was a scene exactly like the one Jackie had already described for Jennifer's funeral in *Valley of the Dolls*.

Dr. Ronald Sobel, the rabbi from Temple Emanu-el, conducted the service, and Oscar Dystel delivered the eulogy. Oscar spoke of the shock of Jackie's friends at her death, her courage in facing cancer a dozen years earlier.

"Her decision to be silent," he said, "was a gift to the rest of us. It allowed us to face her, to know her, to challenge her, openly and honestly, as we would have any other person in our lives, and not as one whose time was marked."

He spoke of her dream, her dedication, her will power. He spoke of her special gifts as a story-teller, as an observer of people's lives and the world she lived in. He talked of her loyalty to her friends.

"She was a total professional," he said, "who achieved unparalleled success in our industry and made contributions that were pioneering and massive. She had more imitators in concept and style than any writer I know . . . but she had no equals.

"She had seen them all—the kings and queens of show business, the giants of industry, the great and the nearly great. And she left her mark. As her husband Irving would say, 'Boy, how she left her mark!'

"Jackie, we will never forget you."

After the service, Jackie was taken to the crematorium in Westchester. I was not permitted to go there, which was probably just as well. The crowd surged back to our apartment—hundreds of people came by to offer their sympathy.

Rose Susan, gracious, regal, and still beautiful, sat in her wheel chair and accepted the condolences of the famous and the unknown who had loved Jackie.

I handled the crowds as best I could. I was too dazed to know what I was feeling or saying. People we didn't even know must have joined the crush. I can't believe it was anyone we know who stole Jackie's wallet with five $100 bills in it.

Louise had handed me the wallet before the funeral, and I had tucked it under a hatbox in Jackie's dressing room. Then, later, Louise whispered to me that several women were poking around at Jackie's clothes in her closet. When I approached, they melted back into the living room—with the wallet, I suppose, because the next day it was nowhere to be found.

That's when I slammed my fist into the wall as the realization struck me like a boulder dropped on my head. Jackie was gone. Really gone. I could never tell her that she had been ripped off at her own funeral and listen to the laughter roaring up from deep within her and hear her say, "Well, doll, you can't win them all."

*J*ackie's ashes were returned to me in a bronze container the size and shape of a large desk dictionary. On the spine is the inscription:

JACQUELINE SUSANN

1921-1974

I used the birthdate Jackie had chosen for herself, and I placed the bronze box on our library shelf among the dozens of volumes of Jackie's books in hard cover and paperback, in English and in languages spoken in the far parts of the world.

My first of many tasks was to acknowledge the thousands of messages and letters of condolence. That project kept Bea and me busy for several weeks.

I had been calling my son's school almost daily since the evening of Jackie's death. Guy was recovering well and was in good spirits. I talked to the head of the school and his doctor, and they assured me he was fine. I was terribly anxious to see him, but as the lawyers and the accountants and the publishing and movie people threw urgent problems at me and demanded instant decisions, I had to put off my trip to Texas from one week to the next.

Now I had one last assignment to carry out for Jackie. For thirty years, she had kept an annual diary in which she wrote down our appointments and sometimes made brief reminder notes about people and events. In the spring of 1974, when we were going over some papers with our attorney, Jackie had said, "Artie, if anything happens to me, please be sure that Irving destroys my date books. I don't want to leave any bad feelings."

"Bad feelings about what?" I asked. How could there be bad feelings, I wondered, about all those lists of three decades of dinner parties, TV rehearsals, theater openings, and doctors' appointments?

[273]

"Oh, you know how mad I get at the doctors sometimes, and I call them some pretty nasty names when I write down my appointments. And sometimes I write 'bitch' next to the name of a reporter or a critic who gives me a terrible review. I don't want anybody to see that stuff."

I had promised Jackie that I would destroy the diaries—without reading them.

Our apartment has no fireplace, so I began by burning one of the books in the kitchen sink. To my horror, the flame flared up, and I knew that was not going to work. Then I started ripping the covers off the books and tearing the pages into a large wastebasket, and when that was filled, into a big box. I was working in the living room, and from time to time I casually glanced over to the park. It was the first week in December by then, and the weather had turned chilly.

Smoke wreathing up from a wire litter basket in the park caught my eye. Some teenage boys had lit a fire in the basket to warm their hands. That gave me an idea. I took my wastebasket of torn-up diary pages over to the park and dumped it into the fire. The boys were delighted to see the sparks dance upward. I came back for a second load and dumped the rest of the diary pages and the cut-up covers into the park fire.

Then I went home and sat at the window, watching the days and the hours of Jackie's life turn to ashes. My thoughts ranged back and forth over the years—so many memories, so much pain, so much joy. I felt anger wash over me—anger that I no longer had a wife. We had been so much a part of each other. We knew each other's moods, we knew each other's temperaments, we knew just how far we could go with each other. I could look at her from across a room and know what she was thinking. I knew when she was bored and wanted to leave, when she was vibrating with excitement over meeting one of her heroes or hearing a blues song sung the way she would have loved to sing.

Everywhere I looked there was a vision of Jackie sitting, writing, dictating, screaming at somebody on the phone, whooping with laughter, kissing Josephine, gossiping with her old friends.

At six-thirty, I involuntarily looked toward the telephone. Whenever she was traveling or I was traveling, she always called me at six-thirty, and if she didn't get me then, she tried again at midnight. Except for the army period and the time she went around the world with her mother, I don't think more than a handful of days went by when Jackie and I didn't speak to each other at least once during the twenty-four hours.

My only regret, I thought, still sitting at the window, was that I did not extend myself for her as much as I should have. I gave her 100 percent of my love and thoughts and efforts. But it should have been 110 percent. My own success had come early and easily in those years. I could have done more for her, fought harder for her career. The one thing about which I had no regrets was devoting the last ten years to her success—turning my career into her career so that together we had achieved what neither of us could have done alone.

I thought of that all-powerful drive in Jackie to be someone and all the deals she had made with God. She had believed with almost childlike simplicity that if she was a good person, if she was considerate and honorable and fair in her dealings with people, if she worked hard and never lost faith in herself, God, in His turn, would grant her wishes. Jackie practiced the golden rule with God.

After her first surgery, she had asked for a reprieve. She had asked God for only ten more years and she would prove she could make it as a writer, as the number-one writer.

God had given her those ten years. Jackie would have liked more. She would have liked more good times, more love, more laughter. But it was not to be. I remembered at a party when Jackie, Rex Reed, and I had watched as someone helped Noel Coward, ill and feeble, into an elevator. Jackie had said to Rex, "Gosh, I hope I die before I grow old."

As Rex later wrote, "Jackie always got everything in life she wanted, but this is one wish she got too soon."

It was almost dark, and the fire in the basket in the park was dying down. I had kept another promise to Jackie.

Friends wanted me to come down to Palm Beach for a rest. Howard Koch wanted me to fly out to California to finish the film of *Once Is Not Enough* that Jackie never got to see. TV programs were after me to talk and reminisce about Jackie. I did only one show, and that was for Barbara Walters whom Jackie and I both adored. The publishers wanted me to go on the road to promote *Once* in paperback. The lawyers wanted to talk to me about the lawsuit over *Beyond the Valley of the Dolls*, which at that time was still pending. There were plans that had to be made for Rose Susan, who now was my responsibility and would continue to be until her death in 1981.

But first, before I turned my attention to any of these things, I had to go see Guy. I took the plane to Texas and the local plane to the airport near his school where I was picked up and driven to the school. I spoke first to the director and explained why I had been so long in coming and got from him an encouraging report about Guy and his recovery.

Then I walked into my boy's room with my arms filled with presents. I put the gifts on the table so we could slap hands and say, "Hi." Guy looked fine; his jaw was completely healed. His face was as handsome as ever—he has that special beauty of the Susanns. Then he noticed that I was alone. He looked at me in a puzzled way, then from me to the empty space next to me, where Jackie had always stood.

Guy frowned, then ran past me and looked out the door into the corridor. Maybe Jackie was playing a new game; maybe she was hiding from him. I let him make sure I was alone before I gently drew him back into the room, put my hands on his shoulders, and said, "Guy, your mother will not be coming to see you again."

He peered searchingly into my face. Our eyes held in an intense gaze. Of course, he couldn't understand my words. But somehow he knew because he took my hand and he never looked for Jackie again.

ACKNOWLEDGMENTS

Thanks must go to the following for their help: Jay Allen, Stuart Applebaum, Sherry Arden, Noel Behn, Franca and Pierre Belfond, Penny Bigelow, Isabel Biron, Jesse Block, Nat Breen, Marilyn Cantor, Joe Cates, George Chasin, Beatrice Cole, Mary Daniels, Edward D'elia, Ervin Drake, Oscar Dystel, Shirley Eder, Larry Eisenberg, Harry Feeney, Gerold Frank, Mike Frankovich, Sid Garfield, Milton Goldman, Regina Gruss, Lee Guber, Richard Gully, Lupe and Alfred Hemlock, Dagmar Henne, Leonore Hershey, Arthur Hershkowitz, Judy Hilsinger, Mildred Hird, Nina Hoffman, Dr. Henry Jaffe, Hana Karol, Fred Klein, Howard W. Koch, Dr. Gerson Lesnick, Esther Margolis, Robert Musel, Louis Nizer, Racquel Rael, Rex Reed, Harold Robbins, Beverly Robinson, Herman Robinson, Joyce Matthews Rose, Al Rylander, Bonnie Silberstein, Joan Castle Sitwell, Muriel Slatkin, Anna Sosenko, Dr. Clifford Spingarn, Alan Susman, David Tebet, and Howard Teichman.